THE POST-RACIAL MYSTIQUE

CRITICAL CULTURAL COMMUNICATION

General Editors: Sarah Banet-Weiser and Kent A. Ono

Dangerous Curves: Latina Bodies in the Media
Isabel Molina-Guzmán

*The Net Effect: Romanticism,
Capitalism, and the Internet*
Thomas Streeter

*Our Biometric Future: Facial Recognition
Technology and the Culture of Surveillance*
Kelly A. Gates

Critical Rhetorics of Race
Edited by Michael G. Lacy and Kent A. Ono

*Circuits of Visibility: Gender and
Transnational Media Cultures*
Edited by Radha S. Hegde

*Commodity Activism: Cultural
Resistance in Neoliberal Times*
Edited by Roopali Mukherjee
and Sarah Banet-Weiser

*Arabs and Muslims in the Media:
Race and Representation after 9/11*
Evelyn Alsultany

*Visualizing Atrocity: Arendt, Evil,
and the Optics of Thoughtlessness*
Valerie Hartouni

*The Makeover: Reality Television
and Reflexive Audiences*
Katherine Sender

*Authentic™: The Politics of
Ambivalence in a Brand Culture*
Sarah Banet-Weiser

*Technomobility in China: Young
Migrant Women and Mobile Phones*
Cara Wallis

*Love and Money: Queers, Class,
and Cultural Production*
Lisa Henderson

*Cached: Decoding the Internet
in Global Popular Culture*
Stephanie Ricker Schulte

*Black Television Travels: African
American Media around the Globe*
Timothy Havens

*Citizenship Excess: Latino/
as, Media, and the Nation*
Hector Amaya

*Feeling Mediated: A History of
Communication Technology
and Emotion in America*
Brenton J. Malin

*The Post-Racial Mystique: Media and
Race in the Twenty-First Century*
Catherine R. Squires

The Post-Racial Mystique

Media and Race in the Twenty-First Century

Catherine R. Squires

NEW YORK UNIVERSITY PRESS
New York and London

NEW YORK UNIVERSITY PRESS
New York and London
www.nyupress.org
© 2014 by New York University

References to Internet websites (URLs) were accurate at the time of writing.
Neither the author nor New York University Press is responsible for URLs that
may have expired or changed since the manuscript was prepared.

LIBRARY OF CONGRESS CATALOGING-IN-PUBLICATION DATA
Squires, Catherine R., 1972–
The postracial mystique : media and race in the 21st century / Catherine R. Squires.
pages cm. — (Critical cultural communication)
Includes bibliographical references and index.
ISBN 978-0-8147-6289-9 (hardback)
ISBN 978-0-8147-7060-3 (paper)
1. Mass media and race relations—United States 2. Cultural pluralism in mass media—
United States. 3. Post-racialism—United States 4. Race and media. I. Title.
P94.65.U6S77 2014
302.230973—dc 3
2013043409

New York University Press books are printed on acid-free paper,
and their binding materials are chosen for strength and durability.
We strive to use environmentally responsible suppliers and materials
to the greatest extent possible in publishing our books.

Manufactured in the United States of America

10 9 8 7 6 5 4 3 2 1

Also available as an ebook

CONTENTS

Acknowledgments   vii

Introduction: Welcome to Post-Racial America   1

1. Post-Racial News: Covering the "Joshua Generation"   17

2. Brothers from Another Mother: Rescripting Religious   65
   Ties to Overcome the Racial Past

3. The Post-Racial Family: *Parenthood* and the Politics   97
   of Interracial Relationships on TV

4. Post-Racial Audiences: Discussions of *Parenthood*'s   133
   Interracial Couple

5. Not "Post-Racial," Race-Aware: Blogging Race in the   165
   Twenty-First Century

Conclusion: Back to the Post-Racial Future   187

Notes   207

Index   233

About the Author   235

ACKNOWLEDGMENTS

I often complain to colleagues, family, and friends that I have a bad habit of picking research topics that stress me out; nonetheless, I am quite fortunate to have people and institutions supporting me as I do the research and writing. I owe a lot of my productivity to the FOCI Writers' Group at the University of Minnesota. I am so glad we pulled it together, and that we're still going strong two years later. When I get writers' block, it's good to know folks are counting on me to set up our writing space so we can all get motivated. Many thanks and hugs to Mary Vavrus for reading early drafts of the *Parenthood* chapters, and for well-timed family dinners and venting sessions. I owe you, sister, and can't wait for your next book to drop!

I received valuable feedback on the news chapter when I visited the Rhetorical Studies Group at the University of Illinois. Conversations with Kent Ono, Cara Finnegan, and their colleagues and students were right on time for my revision cycle. Likewise, Daniel Brouwer and his colleagues at Arizona State University gave me a warm welcome and feedback that helped me work out ideas for the conclusion of the book. And although my mother, Helen, and sisters, Theresa and Leah, are excellent editors and sounding boards, any and all errors are my own. Thanks again for all the phone calls and tweeted encouragement—in addition to everything else over the years. Most of this research would not have been accomplished had I not received generous funding at two universities. Much of the work on *Justice Sunday III* was supported by a grant from the Howard R. Marsh Center at the University of Michigan. The other chapters were researched and written using funds from the Cowles Chair for Journalism, Diversity, and Equality at the University

viii << ACKNOWLEDGMENTS

of Minnesota. Without these sources of support, I would never have been able to hire such excellent research assistants: Sarah J. Jackson (now *Professor* Jackson!), Meagan Manning, Anna Popkova, and the amazing Ruth De Foster.

As always, I am extremely grateful for the continuous supply of affection and strength I get from my better mathematical half, Bryan, and our twins, Will and Helena. I am happy to now have more time to thank them for their support.

Introduction

Welcome to Post-Racial America

As my son and I walked down the street, taking our usual route with our dog, we crossed paths with a man I'd never seen in our neighborhood before. He appeared to be white and seemed to be looking for something specific, as if he needed directions. He smiled at us as we approached, looked at the dog, and asked from a few yards away, "What breed is that?" I told him she was a mix: "Australian Shepherd and Beagle, or so we were told by the dog rescue society." He petted her, smiled, and then looked me right in the face to ask his next question:

"What kind of mix are you?"

Just another day in post-racial America, I thought.

* * *

How is it that in what's termed "post-racial America," people seem to keep finding ways to keep talking about race? Race is a common topic of conversation and a predictable source of moments of confusion and comedy, as well as of desolation and violence. We are regularly told that things have changed—we are now "post-race"—but exactly how and why those changes have come about and what the changes mean are matters of continuing debate. In mundane and formal settings, citizens confront race in subtle and obvious ways every day. From celebrations of the inauguration of the first *black* president to news of a neo-Nazi attack in Norway, race and racism remain salient features of our world. In the wake of social movements for justice, generational change, cultural exchange, immigration, and other phenomena that reshape our racial realities, a new question has erupted in the last decade: Are we post-racial?

The Post-Racial Mystique explores how a variety of media outlets— the news, network television, and online independent media—define, deploy, and debate the term "post-racial" in their representations of American politics and society. Media discourses and imagery help us to map the contours of change in society's understanding of race. The book draws upon a variety of disciplines—communication studies, sociology, political science, cultural studies—in order to understand emergent strategies for framing discussions of post-racial America. Each chapter presents a case study of these strategies and explores how and whether each contends with (or ignores) remaining racial inequalities and social tensions, as well as what (if any) future for race is imagined. The diverse case studies illuminate the ways in which media texts and appeals cast U.S. history, reimagine interpersonal relationships, employ statistics, and inventively redeploy other identity categories in a quest to formulate different ways of responding to race.

The cases in this book were selected in order to sample (although not systematically) different genres and media outlets. Because the public engages in a mix of specialty and mass media consumption, it is important to survey how both broad-based and niche media wrestle with questions of race in the twenty-first century. Moving from media targeted to general audiences (mainstream news and prime-time television series) to messages targeted to particular well-defined groups (specialty Christian digital media and progressive blogs) and to audience interactions (Facebook discussion groups and focus groups), the case studies shed light on some of the emerging modes of contemporary post-racial discourse, revealing recurrent themes and problematic tensions around race, gender, family, and political allegiances. Across these varied expressions of the post-racial, I explore how communicators work to (re)create and/or re-envision a sense of community, inspire (or reject) new vehicles for multicultural inclusion, and confront the facts of persistent racial inequalities in the United States.

The Emergence of "Post-Racial"

While the term "post-racial" was not commonly used in the 1980s and 1990s, discussions of the *meaning* of race—particularly the meaning of *black* identity—were widespread. In the explosion of black media and celebrity culture of the 1980s and the culture wars, commentators from a wide variety of media, political, and scholarly venues pondered the meaning of blackness in the so-called "post–civil rights era." Nelson George, bell hooks, Toni Morrison, and Cornel West wrote about the pop culture and political spectacles of blackness from Michael Jackson's dominance of the pop charts to Clarence Thomas and Anita Hill's hearing, hip hop, OJ's ride, and Lisa Leslie's WNBA dunk.[1] Debates over the meaning of black identity and the continued existence of racism swirled around Spike Lee's films, novels such as *The Women of Brewster Place* and *The Color Purple*, and the TV juggernauts of the *Cosby Show* and *Oprah*. Vernon Reid's band, *Living Color*, NBC's *A Different World*, painter Jean Michel Basquiat, the quilters of Gee's Bend, and curator Thelma Golden introduced multiple audiences to a wide variety of black subjectivities, artistic expression, and intra-group differences.[2] In this mix were considerations of law (the war on drugs, abortion, police brutality), immigration (do Caribbean-born blacks have a superior culture of middle-class success?), religion (why are church pews still so segregated?), education (should affirmative action remedies continue in colleges?), and politics (why don't more black people vote Republican?).[3]

Although most of these high-profile media discourses about race centered on blackness, Latinas/os, Asian Americans, and whites were also implicated and specifically mentioned as well. Often this was done via comparison. For example, commentators wondered if "immigrant" populations were more culturally attuned to educational and workplace success than African Americans. Others posited that Asian Americans didn't really need affirmative action or equal cultural representation since they were "model minorities." The advent of Whiteness Studies occasioned some hand-wringing as well, with discussions of whether academia had gone too far in analyzing the dominant racial group. In the wake of the violent unrest after the Los Angeles police officers were acquitted of beating Rodney King, news media seemed surprised to find inter-group tensions between black and Asian American groups in

Figure I.1. Barack Obama and Joe Biden at the 2008 Democratic National Convention. Courtesy of the Carol M. Highsmith Archive, Library of Congress, Prints and Photographs Division.

California. And when the Human Genome Project began presenting its results and the mixed-race movement showed muscle in the 2000 Census hearings, *Time* magazine and others speculated on how the seemingly inevitable "merger" of human races would produce a new, unified beige human race. Still, it was not until the mid-2000s that "post-racial" became the go-to term for these kinds of changes in the American racial landscape.

Post-racial rhetoric surged during the historic 2008 election. Across the nation, pundits and politicians, bloggers and celebrities made tentative and dismissive statements about the (finally?) declining significance of race. But as the last few years have demonstrated (again), racism and racial inequalities persist and in some areas, such as wealth and health, have deepened. The gap between the aspirational post-racial discourse and the brutal realities of poverty, police profiling, anti-immigration vitriol, and mind-boggling incarceration rates for blacks and Latinos/as is wide. Yet the media continue to churn out films and shows that feature scores of people of color living discrimination-free lives. Advertisements showcase knowledgeable professionals of all colors happily giving advice or buying products for their middle-class homes—right next door to their white friends. When someone reports a racist incident on the news, sources scramble over each other to deny any racist intent or impact of the event in question. They point to millionaire black athletes, Asian American collegians, and, of course, our biracial president as proof of that America is post-racial. This book explores the post-racial mystique conjured by the disjuncture between the entrenched effects of institutional racism and the media texts that deny—or purport to resolve—racial inequalities.

Post-Racial Media

The use of the term "post-racial" is both widespread and ecumenical in media—commentators and partisans from the Right, Left, and center have embraced, questioned, and mocked the term over the past decade, with increasing intensity during the 2008 election. The proliferation of this word suggests hopes and fears about race, democratic progress, and multiculturalism—fears that stem from the decades' long "culture wars," struggles over the meaning and extent of the impact of civil rights era reforms, and the role of the state in mediating identity politics and redistributive justice. It emerged in popular discourse at a time when the human genome project "proved" that there aren't "different races;" that we humans are more alike than different; that race is a social construct, not a constituent element of humanity. However, as Eric K. Watts summarizes,

> Treating "race" as merely a social construction misses a crucial facet of its nature; the power of tropes of race . . . [that are] coded into the institutions we inhabit and the social relations regulated by them. . . . Saying that "race" is a "fiction" does very little to disable its vigorous affects. . . . The trope of the "postracial" enunciates the "demise" of "race"; meanwhile . . . strategists capture and redeploy the haunting and ravenous affects of "race."[4]

The way this trope operates, however, varies across media and depends in part on who's defining—or disputing—what "post-racial" is and means.

Post-Racial Discourses: Embracing Diversity through Neoliberal Logics

Hosts of media scholars have investigated how post-racial representations and discourses operate in the contemporary United States. Mainstream media suggest our society requires no further political or social activism to achieve equal opportunity for people of all races.[5] This post-racial vision of an already-achieved multicultural nation draws upon neoliberal ideologies of market individualism, whereby race/ethnicity presents us with specific choices to navigate: whether to or not to join groups founded by people of our race; whether to consume cultural products that reflect the customs or tastes of racial Others.[6] Post-racial discourses obfuscate institutional racism and blame continuing racial inequalities on individuals who make poor choices for themselves or their families. Post-racial discourses resonate with neoliberal discourses because of their shared investment in individual-level analysis and concern with individual freedoms. Remedies that draw upon group solidarity or require state or other kinds of intervention in the marketplace—a realm imagined to be neutral, organized by self-interested individual choices—are deemed suspect and anathema to values such as merit and hard work.

For example, scholars have analyzed how neoliberal post-racial logics of the reality TV show *America's Next Top Model* compel contestants of color to "embrace the particular aspects of their non-white racialization that the market deems attractive" and hide the rest.[7] Contestants with ambiguous skin tones celebrate how they can provide the modeling industry with an array of "looks" that are saleable in a time of multiracial chic. As one model gushed, "I could bring a lot of diversity, a lot of versatility, because I can pass for Latina . . . Asian . . . black."[8] This show and others reinforce the notion that racial identities are malleable, yet differently valued in the marketplace. However, nowhere is there recognition of the racist aspects of that valuation system that continues to value whiteness or near-whiteness over other "looks." When darker skinned contestants lose points, their failures are framed in terms of not making the right moves with their difference. The judges' undervaluation of their racial performances is understood as "objective" and just the way the business works, not a product of prejudice or deeply rooted white dominance of the fashion industry. The show fosters the post-racial idea that everyone has the same degrees of freedom to choose their preferred level of ethnic/racial identification, while ignoring continued stereotyping and the privileges of whiteness.

Likewise, in news reports about the subprime loan crisis, the banks were deemed "too big to fail," while the disproportionate number of people of color with mortgage woes seemed preternaturally doomed to failure by many commentators. When the massive numbers of foreclosures in black and Latina/o neighborhoods made headlines, many editorialists framed the issue in terms of the failure of black and Latina/o homebuyers to educate themselves on how to negotiate a sound mortgage. Copious evidence of fraudulent loan practices was swept aside in favor of a neoliberal, post-racial view of a marketplace that faltered due to naïve or greedy individuals.[9] Similarly, on "Judge" shows such as *Joe Brown* and others, the legal problems of the mostly African American, Latina/o, and poor litigants are contrasted with the bootstrapping life story of Judge Brown.[6] Brown and other TV judges consistently use racist and sexist stereotypes to lambast the lifestyles and decision-making of participants in the trials. Unemployment, single parenthood, lack of access to education—all are chalked up to lack of willpower.

A related way of conveying post-racial illusions in the media is through a "celebration" of differences. As with the models who "worked" their ambiguous ethnicity for the industry, here post-racial logic responds to demographic changes and globalization of media to maximize market share. As Jonathan Rutherford writes, "Paradoxically, capitalism has fallen in love with difference: advertising thrives on selling us things that will enhance our uniqueness and individuality. . . . From World Music to . . . ethnic TV dinners to Peruvian hats, cultural difference sells."[10] Advertisers fill magazine spots with carefully blended groups of attractive people of different races, inviting us to consume the mix without having to think about what social and political practices would be necessary to make our neighborhood or workplace as diverse as the ads.[11] Multiracial people in particular help facilitate a sense of safe diversity, satisfying the need to bring color into the frame without conflict. For example, media scholar Jon Kraszewski demonstrates how MTV's push to retool its liberal image to be more friendly to conservatives led it to increase multiracial cast members on *The Real World* after 2000. MTV feared that white conservatives had been offended by past seasons' representations of white rural contestants who expressed racist views—views criticized by urban black and liberal white cast members.[12] Casting and editing shaped multiracial people into "bridges" between black and white who could inspire tolerance in contrast to the show's prior dependence on interracial conflict for drama. This strategy echoes 1990s and 2000s news discourses that positioned multiracial people as conduits to a post-racial society.[13]

Another post-racial approach offers this solution to the race problem: Substitute more "legitimate" social identities for racial identities. While many on the Left have argued for decades that class, not race, should be the main identification for progressive struggles, the Right has recently amplified its use of this post-racial strategy in terms of religion and nation, arguing these categories provide more stability and possibilities for social cohesion than race. Moreover, in the wake of 9/11, attacks on multiculturalism were launched in part on the idea that "tolerance" of differences had gone too far. Therefore, a return to a national identity grounded in Judeo-Christian principles was necessary to squelch the alleged excesses of multicultural relativism. The September 11 attacks amplified concerns about "Other" enemies within, providing proponents of assimilation with a dramatic, violent example of what they saw as the endgame for multicultural tolerance: endless fragmentation amongst groups and internecine battles for ideological purity. After the attacks, many commentators insisted that the impetus was on people of color and non-Christian religions to prove their American-ness, to attend more to similarities with other Americans than to differences. In analyzing these discourses, Tariq Modood discusses how they presented multiculturalism either as a failed experiment or as a fait accompli requiring no further state or social intervention.[14] For her part, Susan Searls Giroux illustrates how the attacks were used to justify neoconservative revival of the culture wars, wherein the Right framed any attempt to discuss racial inequalities, the unjust profiling of Muslim Americans, and hate crimes against those who "looked Arab" as divisive and anti-American.[15]

But promoting national identity does not work equally for all racialized Others. For example, Evelyn Alsultany analyzed how non-profit and government agencies utilized advertising campaigns in an attempt to disrupt the association between American Muslims and terrorism and assert their patriotism. She concludes that the public service spots reinforced existing racist and Orientalist representations of Arab and Islamic peoples by highlighting the exceptionally patriotic attributes of individual Muslim Americans and families in images and texts that reinforced an Us-Them binary. The implied comparison group—Other Muslims who are essentially anti-Western—required Muslim citizens to "prove their loyalty to the nation for a chance at being imagined as part of the diverse national community."[16] Political rhetoric and press reports suggested strongly that only so much difference—and specific performances of difference—were tolerable post-9/11.[17] Here, being post-racial required people of color—in this case, people of Arab descent and/or Muslim faith—to silently accept racial profiling as a sacrifice for the nation and to tacitly agree to refrain from exercising their First Amendment rights to satisfy a barely tolerant majority.

Substitutions of more "legitimate" identity categories also have problematic implications for policy. Supporters of class-based affirmative action, for example, argue that if race is removed from the table, programs based on income disparities alone will solve the problem of the race gap in education. This thinking is flawed, however, as has been borne out in states such as Texas, where the lauded "Ten Percent Plan" has not increased the number of black and Latino/a students at flagship state universities as promised; indeed, some analyses found decreases in enrollment.[18] The class-not-race approach fails to recognize the intersections of race and class; thus, class-only policies will not remedy the subtle and not-so-subtle effects of racial discrimination and segregation that operate in K–12 educational institutions or in other facets of college admissions criteria. Although many liberals hope that class-based policies will resonate with white voters who switched party allegiances in the Reagan era, there is little proof that strategies of "New Democrats" for using class to get at race have dampened racial resentment.[19] This approach also fails to confront the issue of social responsibility for racial discrimination.

Post-Racial Representations: Comedy and
Casting—But Hold the Conflict

Another variant on post-racialism is what some have taken to calling "hipster racism" or "equal-opportunity offending" in comedy. Sitcom writers, stand-up comics, and others "ironically" spew racial epithets and stereotypes as part of their jokes, all the while winking at the audience that they're not really racist—they're making fun of racists, right? In the post-racial entertainment world, anything goes because we "all" know it's inappropriate to be racist—so the racist jokes are a hip way of pushing boundaries. Anyone who protests is uptight and humorless. As writer Liddy West puts it, hipster racism is expressed in the attitudes of "educated, middle-class white people (like me—to be clear, I am one of those) who believe that not wanting to be racist makes it okay for them to be totally racist."[20] Shows like *South Park*, *Tosh.O*, and countless stand-up routines, Twitter hashtags, and YouTube videos exhibit this hipster, shock-value post-racial humor. Moreover, the same kind of humor is often unleashed to refute criticism of the continued dominance of white actors, writers, and producers in mainstream media. Recently, critics of the all-white hit HBO show *Girls* were treated to lynching jokes and snarky comments about the movie *Precious* by the show's defenders and head writer.[21]

One web article on the *Girls* controversy linked to a 1979 piece by music journalist Lester Bang, in which he recounted how he decided to stop the habit of using "nigger" to prove he was "edgy" after he was confronted by the pain he caused an African American friend.

> Ivan Julian told me that whenever he hears the word "nigger," no matter who says it, black or white, he wants to kill. Once when I was drunk I [said] that the only reason hippies ever existed in the first place was because of niggers, and when I mentioned it to Ivan while doing this article I said, "You probably don't even remember—" "Oh yeah, I remember," he cut me off. And that was two years ago, one ostensibly harmless little slip. You take a lifetime of that, and you've got grounds for trying in any way possible, even if it's only by convincing one individual at a time, to remove those words from the face of the earth. . . . Another reason for getting rid of all those little verbal barbs is that no matter how you intend them, you can't say them without risking misinterpretation by some other bigoted asshole; your irony just might be his cup of hate.[22]

When hipsters are criticized, their reactions usually dismiss or ignore the pain people of color and other people who are objects of hipster bigot jokes. The freedoms and pleasures of whites are privileged over the desires of people of color to decrease their exposure to racist speech. As West wrote in her blog posting about why hipster racism is still racist, "It's all tied up with the deliberately obtuse people who conflate 'freedom of speech' with 'immunity from criticism.' . . . [Racist jokes] *hurt people*. Why do you want to hurt people?"[23] Likewise, Channing Kennedy of *Colorlines* wrote that defenders of hipster racism argue that "only bad people are susceptible to racism, so therefore it's okay for us good people to pretend to be racist for comedy's sake. Anyone who doesn't like it is the real racist."[24] The ironic/humorous post-racial stance misunderstands the meaning of the social construction of race. It translates social construction to mean that race isn't real and is malleable and that each individual can therefore make of it what s/he will. This misreading of social construction leaves out scholars' and activists' attention to how the changing construction of racial identity manifests within institutional and social processes that reinforce inequalities born in earlier eras. The power of race—even if it is not a proper biological or fixed category—is a measurable phenomenon.[25]

This is not to say, of course, that humor can't be anti-racist. Indeed, scholars such as Bambi Haggins and Mel Watkins have chronicled how African American comedians have used their routines and sketches to resist and undermine racism. But post-racial humorists aren't always clearly anti-racist, as humor need not indicate responsibility or directly indict people in power. For example, Haggins discusses how breakout comedy star Dave Chappelle appeals to white audiences in part because many of his racial sketches are often vague about issues of whiteness and power.[26] In contrast, Jonathan Rossing offers Stephen Colbert as a satirist who endeavors to make clear the privileges of whiteness in his post-racial spoofing of neoconservative pundits and politicians. He describes how one of Colbert's mock editorials disrupts "familiar discourses of colorblindness and offers a counter-hegemonic critique of naturalized ideologies of whiteness."[27] This leads to the next form of post-racialism: post-*racism*.

Post-Racialism as Anti-Racism

The proliferation of post-racial discourse is partly inspired by scholars of critical race theory and cultural studies who call for us to embrace notions of hybridity and intersectionality, constructs that should generate more and better ways to combat racism without using terms tied to essentialist understandings of identity. The broad circulation of post-racial discourse suggests a yearning for our communities to be healed of racism, not just to "get beyond race." This, however, is the least frequent connotation of post-racial in the media examined in this book. Now that institutionalized racist regimes have been partly dismantled, how do we deal with difference? This is the question that the post-racial begs: When we get "beyond race"—and, more importantly, the racism that structured our society for so long—how does race work? Certainly the physical characteristics we've identified as "racial" do not disappear from our field of vision or biological code. Do we create mechanisms to reform the partial assimilation strategies of the past that allowed for various European immigrants to "melt" into the American pot such that "visible" racial minorities also have equal access to becoming recognized as legitimate American citizens? Or is there a way for difference to matter in a more transformative way? How do we reshape society when we have few models for pluralism that don't rest on hierarchies based on racial and gender and sexual orientation differences? Post-racial media touch on these questions in varying ways.

Not all post-racial media are "bad." We should be happy, for example, that we live in a time when networks feel pressure to integrate television show casts. Moreover, we are now able to confront people who express hurtful racial beliefs, even as we acknowledge their freedom of expression. And, following Edward Schiappa's caution that it is impossible to create representations that will elicit from all audiences the "right" responses in terms of attitudes or stereotyping behavior,[28] I recognize that we cannot hold any particular media text to some standard of representational perfection to satisfy all peoples of all racial backgrounds. That being said, however, surveying the types of narratives that are widely available to audiences about what "post-racial" means show that there is a surplus of individualistic approaches and ahistorical frameworks, at the same time that there remains a deficit of representations of a post-racial society authored by people of color—the very people who would benefit most from the end of racism and racist assumptions. The most widely available approaches to the post-racial are troubling because they inherit a lot of the same elements of past articulations of how to solve the color line in ways that are seemingly oblivious to the critiques and contributions of people of color and their allies to rethinking race and racism. This book explores some of these post-racial media phenomena.

The Plan of the Book

The first chapter, "Post-Racial News: Covering the 'Joshua Generation,'" explores how the term "post-racial" became widespread in dominant news discussions of politics and culture. Drawing on an exhaustive analysis of news items collected in the Lexis-Nexis news database, this chapter illustrates how the term went from obscurity in the 1990s to a widely used framing device in the mid-2000s. Although "post-racial" is now a commonplace adjective used by journalists and pundits, what the term means remains controversial and in flux. After delineating its different uses, the chapter argues that while the debate over the term is healthy and necessary, the effect of applying "post-racial" can be to close down many productive avenues for public discussion.

Chapter 2 explores the strategy of replacing race with an ostensibly more legitimate collective identity, religion. "Brothers from Another Mother: Rescripting Religious Ties to Overcome the Racial Past" examines specialty conservative Christian media created to reach out to African Americans. These media appeals to black voters often attempt to rewrite black Civil Rights movements as primarily spiritual and Christian-oriented, thereby suggesting an impetus for Christian fellowship with whites in the present. Displacing the political and racial elements of these movements is suspect, however, and requires significant forgetting and forgiveness on the part of African Americans, who are encouraged to overlook the racially divisive strategies employed in the recent past by the same organizations and individuals authoring these media appeals. After analyzing one such appeal, the 2006 broadcast program *Justice Sunday III,* the chapter shifts to a study of African American Christians who watched segments of the program. Participants in the focus groups were generally skeptical of the motives of white speakers featured in the program—particularly those identified with the Republican Party. However, many of the participants also said they appreciated and enjoyed the speeches given by African Americans.

Chapter 3, "The Post-Racial Family: *Parenthood* and the Politics of Interracial Relationships on Network TV," features an analysis of NBC's prime-time drama *Parenthood*, a remake of the popular movie of the late 1980s. From its casting and inclusion of more people of African descent, *Parenthood* is clearly a different text racially than its movie ancestor. However, the portrayal of those African American characters is not necessarily an unambiguous step forward. While well-meaning in its attempt to engage with social issues and portray the multicultural realities of California, the intergenerational drama continues to draw upon some of the oldest tropes of black/white romantic relationships and sexual interaction.

Chapter 4, "Post-Racial Audiences: Discussions of *Parenthood*'s Interracial Couple" provides an analysis of fan responses to the show on its official Facebook site. Fans have constructed specific discussion topics and threads about the romantic pairings of black and white characters, and often remark upon what they see as fair or unfair characterizations of the couple, their behaviors, and their problems. These conversations—which often get heated—demonstrate not only that the show is problematic in its portrayals of the interracial family, but also that viewers of different racial and ethnic backgrounds are invested in talking through their different interpretations. They see the show as an important potential site for learning—or unlearning—old-style representations of interracial couples and children.

Chapter 5, "Not 'Post-Racial,' Race-Aware: Blogging Race in the Twenty-First Century," examines a handful of blogs and websites that have gained circulation within traditional media as well as the Internet. Three websites in particular—Racialicious, the Black Snob, and Color-Lines—exemplify a diverse, complex set of concerns and approaches to rethinking race in the twenty-first century. These sites provide readers with information and perspectives that were rare in the news media analyzed in chapter 1. Moving fluidly between identity groups, pop culture, and politics, these sites suggest that post-racialism requires us to be actively anti-racist in our everyday lives, and remind us that any post-racial era will be the product of much more discussion and reform.

In conclusion, the book presents a meditation on race, media, and memory and suggests that a vigorous re-examination of how we tell the stories of our racial past is necessary both to demystify post-racialism and to learn strategies for promoting racial justice.

I deliberately chose the title *The Post-Racial Mystique* not only for its resonance with Betty Friedan's classic text, but also because I believe there are parallels between my subject and Friedan's insights about the unnamed malaise felt by women of a certain age and class in the 1950s and 1960s even as the media and countless experts told them that married mothers were living the dream. While desires to think about activities outside managing a household were dismissed as folly, or even regarded as a road to psychological and familial ruin, magazines, television shows, and advertisements portrayed the American housewife as "freed by science and labor-saving appliances from . . . the drudgery [of housework]. . . . She was free to choose automobiles, clothes, appliances, supermarkets; she had everything that women ever dreamed of."[29] Likewise, members of Generation Millennial—also known as Gen M, the most multiracial generation in American history—are described as free to interact with a smorgasbord of cultures, races, ethnicities, and religions without any further need for political activism.[30] They can allegedly pick and choose how racial identity matters to them, as well as take their pick of colleges, workplaces, neighborhoods, and consumer goods in ways their forebears who fought for racial equality only dreamed.

But as with the dream concocted by the feminine mystique, the post-racial mystique is faulty in its reduction of social and political aspirations to consumer and individual choice. It narrowly interprets prior generations' struggle as one for market-oriented freedoms rather than a transformation of the society and common understandings of our humanity, our relations with each other, our responsibilities to each other, regardless of race, color, or creed. Hence, though the voices that declare or represent a post-racial utopia in America are loud and hopeful, when we are reminded by ugly incidents in the news or unkind interactions on the job that race still matters, we feel unease, and wonder what's wrong with us. The gap between many of our daily experiences of race and the shiny, happy multiracial faces that smile at us from billboards and TV screens reveals that the road to post-racial America remains very long. This book doesn't provide a single definition of "post-racial" or a solution to "the race problem." What it endeavors to do is help describe how post-racial media have further complicated, and in some ways frustrated, national conversations about race and democratic progress.

* * *

Returning to my walk with my son: When I was asked about my "mix" on the heels of giving information about my dog's breeding, it was clear to me that the man had identified me not as a canine, but as a so-called "mixed-race" human. This was confirmed when (after taking a moment to choose between a snappy comeback and a calm, honest response) I decided to provide a brief account of my parents' identities: "My mother is German American, my father is African American." He smiled again, pointing at us as he replied, "I thought so—I can see that North African in you and him. I'm a mix too—Irish, German, Lithuanian, and Jew. Most of us white folks got Jew in us, but most are afraid to admit it." He went on to say he was looking for a car he was repossessing and had to "get on with that business." After we exchanged a wave, he went up the hill toward a deserted Jeep, which he proceeded to drive away.

My new acquaintance's mode of conceptualizing identity, which mixed categories of race, ethnicity, geography, and religion, is indicative of the fluid, shifting ways most people naturalize and articulate racial identities today. It also reveals how supposedly old frameworks for race—such as the idea that "Jew" is deemed by some as "separate" from and inferior to "white" and that race is "in you" (is "North African" a race or a region?) via blood—continue to have purchase in the twenty-first century. This strange amalgamation of acknowledging racial "mixing" with ease, while still depending on biological constructions of race and culture, is also indicative of the problem with the use of "post" with "racial." As Thomas Holt notes, "post signals its ambiguity: different from what preceded it, but not yet fully formed or knowable."[31] The problem with post-racial media is that acknowledgements that we are still grafting our "new" racial understandings onto those of the past are rare. We pretend to our peril that racism is safely in our past. We must recognize that we haven't fully grappled with the legacy of *de jure* let alone *de facto* racism, and cannot allow post-racial optimism to blind us to the corrosive, continuing effects of race in the contemporary world.

1

Post-Racial News

Covering the "Joshua Generation"

The earliest reference to "post-racial" I could find in the news appeared in a 1976 *Newsweek* article about then-presidential candidate Jimmy Carter. The reporter described the Georgia Democrat as one of a small handful of white politicians who were willing to "gamble his future on a new post-racial Southern politics" in the years prior to the major legal victories of the civil rights movement.[1] In this context, post-racial politics meant a politics that would emerge when the institutional apparatus of white supremacy was dismantled. The article compared Carter to the character of Atticus Finch in *To Kill a Mockingbird*: clear in expressing his disdain for racism, but also clear-eyed about the limits of his ability to help black people in his community. After this profile of Carter, the term vanished from the news. Perhaps it didn't catch on then because violent white resistance to segregation was still fresh in the minds of journalists. In 1976, school busing and affirmative action fights were raging in the courts and in neighborhoods throughout the country. It was hard to imagine the South or any other portion of the nation being "post-" anything having to do with race. Indeed, the term didn't capture journalists' interest until the nation was on the cusp of electing the first president of African descent. Why and how the term went from a one-time use in a story about a southern white Democratic candidate in 1976 to becoming a regular feature of election year news discourse in 2008 sheds light on the factors that continue to stymie the media's "national conversations" on race—conversations that usually leave participants and observers frustrated and wanting something more.

As I discussed in the introduction, the emergence of "post-racial" as a buzzword in the media was a result of multiple factors. This chapter focuses on the ways in which news discourses of race in American politics and society adopted the term "post-racial" to describe shifts in demographics and culture which seemed to require a different set of terms than "diversity" or "multicultural" or "colorblind." When news producers seized upon "post-racial" en masse in the 2000s, it was as if they'd discovered the word they'd been searching for to temper—or end—the contentious debates of the culture wars, when talk about race, pursued in distrustful fits and starts, seemed doomed to fail. This chapter presents a content analysis of post-racial news discourses. First, I tracked the usage of the term from 1990 to 2010 to discern which uses of "post-racial" dominated discussions of race and racially inflected events. While finding that the term was used only minimally in the 1990s, compared to the 2000s, the analysis shows that similar themes accumulated around the term throughout both decades.

The second part of the chapter examines significant surges in use that occurred in the early 2000s, most often in stories about particular individuals and issues linked to African American identities and politics. Specifically, close readings of the articles show that the usage of "post-racial" accumulated around the continued debate over affirmative action, the significance of the civil rights movement in contemporary life, the style and appeal of black politicians as well as multiracial celebrities of African descent, and the fascination with rapidly shifting racial/ethnic demographic data. The term also accompanied discussions of whether pop culture consumption and racial intermarriage are clear markers of an imminent post-racial era, as commentators debated whether "Generation Millennial" would achieve "Dr. King's Dream" of a society where skin color is of no consequence. The final sections of the chapter draw from a mix of close reading and quantitative analysis of the exponential increase in appearances of "post-racial," finding that Barack Obama's candidacy and early presidency drove most of the post-racial talk, usually drawing from the same repertoire of issues and frames as in the earlier periods.

The Rise of "Post-Racial": The Numbers

The term "post-racial" is multifaceted and reflects hopes and fears, political calculations and demographic changes. Given the lack of progress in mediated public discourses of race in the 1990s, the appearance and popularity of "post-racial" in the mid- to late 2000s suggests that journalists and their sources found the term an intriguing and useful tool for reframing racial discussions in the twenty-first century. Why did this occur, and why so quickly? First, I conducted a basic content analysis to find out whether use of the term really had increased significantly over the past two decades.[2] I was intrigued—and a bit surprised—at how sharp the increase in usage actually was after the 1990s. As Table 1.1 demonstrates, "post-racial" was barely mentioned on television, radio, or in print in the 1990s. By 2008, each of these media—as well as online news—contained hundreds of uses of the term.

Importantly, usage of "post-racial" increased in frequency not just in sound bites from interviewees. Rather, as Table 1.2 illustrates, journalists and editors themselves increased their use of the term in headlines and lead paragraphs of stories in a way that suggests that by 2008, writers and editorial staff were fairly confident that audiences would recognize or be intrigued by the term "post-racial." The numbers in Table 1.2 tell a clear, if incomplete, story: "Post-racial" became a highly salient term for journalists and commentators across a host of news media outlets by the end of the 2000s. But the larger question remains: How was it being used throughout the period, and why the sharp jump in 2008?

The 1990s: Post-Racial People and Politics— In the Not-So-Near Future

"Post-racial" wasn't a major buzzword in the 1990s news media; only thirteen pieces used the word, and none in a headline. My close readings of these news items found that all of them employed the term to describe a time in the *distant* future when racial discrimination will truly be a thing of the past. As journalists looked far ahead to the

Table 1.1. News Items with "Post-Racial" in Text or Transcript

News Source/Medium	1990–2000	2001–2004	2005–2007	2008	2009	2010
Newspapers	11	55	72	767	821	575
TV/Radio transcripts	1	4	8	215	205	147
Magazines	1	9	23	130	84	75
Blogs & Web publications*	N/A	N/A	13	363	562	457
Total	13	68	116	1475	1642	1254

* Lexis/Nexis did not begin cataloging blogs, stand-alone web news sites like Politico, or web-only articles until 2005.

Table 1.2. "Post-Racial" in Headline and/or Lead-In of News Items

	1990–2000	2001–2004	2005–2007	2008	2009	2010
Headline and leading paragraph	0	4	8	226	371	257
Headline only	0	0	0	64	105	91

post-racial dawn, they consistently invoked two interrelated factors that would encourage the development of a post-racial America. First, they proposed that the demographic changes brought about by multiracial people, cultural mixing, and immigration provided a preview of a post-racial society. Second, they posited that at some point, a post-racial politics would displace race-based alliances or strategies.

Post-Racial People: Tiger Woods and Multiracial Families

As golfer Tiger Woods began his meteoric rise in the sports world, many writers argued that his success was proof that golf had overcome its racist, classist country-club history to become colorblind—or post-racial. Others surmised that his success was proof that the United States as a whole had overcome race.[3] But Cox News Service columnist Tom Teepen chastised pundits for proclaiming that Woods's expression of multiracial identity and historic win at the Masters' tournament signaled that the 1990s were already post-racial. Teepen cited continued racial antagonisms and individuals with less-than-sterling racial records to counter the hype:

> Color isn't the liability it once was, but jeopardies still attach, despite the remarkable number if lifelong racial-justice laggards who are now insisting we're post-racial. Decry if you will chip-on-the-shoulder multiculturalism, but ethnic jockeying for place is hardly surprising in a nation founded in racial inequality, only a generation past legal segregation, and now trying to fend off Hispanic and Asian immigrants. We're a ways yet from just enjoying our diversity.[4]

Other articles pointed to the greater visibility of multiracial individuals and families as a source of post-racial hope. In these pieces, though, multiracial people were portrayed as annoyed and/or oppressed by institutional requirements to articulate to the state their racial identity. The practice of recording and keeping track of racial identity, then, was portrayed as an impediment to a post-racial society, and reinforced colorblind discourse. One columnist remarked on the increase of multiracial and white college applicants who declined to indicate their racial identity. He reported that one college official believed that "the surge in Declined-to-state-ians may be because the race category on the new, post-racial preferences university application form is harder to find and fill out." Then he joked, "Wait a minute. Is she saying Declined-to-state-ians are lazy and stupid?"[5] The attempt at humor gestures toward racial stereotypes of black and Latina/o students that can get into college only via affirmative action—that is, race-conscious policy—not on "colorblind" merit alone. Thus, "racial" thinking was implied to be an outgrowth of keeping official records of racial identity, a practice considered suspect by the writer. These pieces framed the validation of group racial identities or political organizing around the shared identities as anathema to a post-racial future. This theme also surfaced in reports on the possible emergence of a post-racial politics.

Post-Racial Politics

As writers toyed with the idea of a post-racial politics, they did not provide many examples of political practices or policies that would encourage further progress toward a post-*racist* America. Rather, "post-racial"

politics meant black candidates would be able to count on white voters to support them at the ballot box. For example, in a discussion of a
1999 Supreme Court ruling that struck down a race-conscious congressional districting policy, an interviewee on National Public Radio cited
data that showed white Democrats were still likely to cross party lines
to *avoid* voting for black candidates. The guest, political scientist Ron
Walters, concluded, "We're not living in some post-racial age in the ballot box yet."[6] He and other guests noted that the (misnamed) "Bradley
Effect"—that actual white voting rates for black candidates are lower
than pre-election polls suggest—was still a considerable hurdle. But
fickle white voters weren't the only impediment to post-racial politics
in 1990s news: The motives and strategies of black politicians were also
roadblocks.

A feature on city council candidates in Dallas described the work-
ings of an old-guard black political machine, led by council representatives like Roy Williams, who was described by reporter Dan Schutze as
someone who can "intone some of the time-honored maxims of racial
politics as though he were playing a cathedral pipe organ." Then, he
contrasted Williams's style with up-and-coming candidates who hailed
from a variety of racial/ethnic backgrounds.[7] As the reporter followed
the challengers and the incumbents to public appearances, he framed
the voters' choices as follows: between black politicians who fought a
good fight against (now insignificant) white discrimination, but now
merely rest on their laurels and black voter support, on the one hand,
and new politicians who garner support based on their willingness to
solve substantial urban issues and not just talk about race, on the other.

> People here this evening pay respect to [Roy] Williams. . . . But it's his-
> tory. Everybody has seen African American council members on TV
> giving white folks hell down there for decades. But how about some new
> curbs? How about something we can see, something for which there are
> no excuses? Welcome to the era of post-racial city council politics.[8]

This description of dysfunctional black urban politics neatly illustrates
what became a dominant theme in the 2000s: "Racial politics" are practiced by (mostly black) corrupt leaders who play on white racial guilt

and stir up racial anger to keep people of color loyal. Indeed, this racial strategy is so effective, the argument goes, that voters look the other way when elected officials fail to deliver better outcomes. Thus, "racial politics" are a destructive game, pitting insiders versus outsiders in a game that benefits only the politicians. In this and other articles, little is said about instances of interracial cooperation, let alone decades of white racial political practices that deprived black people of voting rights. Thus, "race" is attached to the political practices of people of color, and white racial politics are absent.

Although the reports I've described so far refer to Democratic politicians, Republicans also began to craft their own version of "post-racial" politics. Two issues framed conservatives' approach. First was the need to change the GOP's image as a mean-spirited, anti-diversity party. This image was heightened during the conventions of 1992 and 1996, where, despite the presence of Condoleezza Rice and Colin Powell, the lasting afterimage was that of speakers such as Pat Buchanan, who called for the end of affirmative action, exclusion of gays, draconian treatment of undocumented immigrants, and so forth. After losing yet another presidential election to Bill Clinton in 1996, Republicans were advised by conservative writer Noamie Emery to reframe their policy proposals and tone down their rhetoric to better appeal to conservative black and Hispanic voters. In a special issue of the *New Republic* devoted to strategizing how to gain conservative majorities again in the United States and the United Kingdom, she suggested that Colin Powell was the perfect symbol to attract a center-Right group of non-white voters. She also optimistically predicted that the GOP could both narrow the gender gap and grab "20–40 percent of the blacks." But to do so, she said,

> conservatives should learn to reframe their issues. . . . They should take the lead in the country to a trans- and post-racial future, now that the liberals have formally endorsed the ideas of identity, grievance, and victimhood that have made the West Bank, Bosnia, and Northern Ireland such wonderful places to live. . . . They should urge that the country drop all racial classifications from the national Census, a sign that the country relates to its people as citizens, not interchangeable members of blocs.[9]

Here, Emery outlines how the Republicans should use post-racial people (Powell) and policy prescriptions (end collection of racial data) to persuade black and Latino voters to choose GOP candidates. She construes race consciousness as a direct route to civic division.

Unsurprisingly, her instruction to eliminate racial categorization on the Census echoes one of the dominant frames in news coverage of multiracial identity in the 1990s: The state is "forcing" bi- and multiracial people to "choose one race"—that is, forcing people into making a choice that allegedly devalues their individuality and judges them by the color of their skin and not the content of their character.[10] In the process, Emery sketches out the second component of the strategy to reframe the party as post-racial: present policy measures aimed to dismantle civil rights legislation as means to promote individual equality. She draws upon the same logic used by anti-affirmative action activist Ward Connerly and his allies: Using racial classifications to identify anyone for any reason is actually racist—and anti-individualistic. Thus, whereas in the past, conservative attacks that counseled colorblindness often depicted people of color as deficient, the newer strategy involves depicting race-aware policies as debilitating and divisive.

Bradley Jones and Roopali Mukherjee have traced the ways neoconservative anti–affirmative action rhetoric moved from blaming and demonizing minorities to blaming big government for incapacitating individuals' ability to make their own choices.[11] Conservatives amplified this rhetoric and leavened it with inflammatory phrases. Thus, politicians and pundits accused the NAACP, the Democrats, and activists like Jesse Jackson, Jr., of wanting to "keep black people on the plantation" of government dependency rather than liberate them. Insisting that the Republicans will deliver real freedom to people of color in the marketplace, these spokespeople encouraged voters to support neoliberal policies that take government out of education, social welfare, labor rights, and other arenas.[12] In the 1990s, then, discussions of "post-racial" were most often framed within two areas of civic life: demographic change and electoral politics. As the next section demonstrates, after 2000, journalists and commentators continued to employ the term "post-racial" within these issue domains, as well as increasing their use of the term to describe people and politics in the next decade.

The Rise of "Post-Racial": Demographic Change and a New Generation of Black Politicians, 2002–2007

In the first two years of the new century, there was no marked increase in the use of "post-racial." But in 2002, the press and political elites identified a "new generation" capable of changing the racial terrain, and the prominence of members of this generation provided more impetus for post-racial talk. The cohort included: Tennessee Congressman Harold Ford, Jr.; Massachusetts Governor Deval Patrick; Philadelphia Mayor Michael Nutter; and then-Senatorial candidate, Barack Obama. Cory Booker's 2002 run for mayor of Newark, New Jersey, jump-started the press with a story that articulated the narratives of generational and demographic change with political transformation of identities and policies.

These young African Americans—whom Barack Obama later dubbed the "Joshua Generation" (meaning they were taking over from the prior "Moses Generation" of black politicians whose careers were forged in the civil rights movement)—were suitable for the post-racial bill for several reasons.[13] First, their biographies fit neatly into a ready-made American narrative of inevitable forward progress and generational renewal. The majority of them were Ivy-League educated sons who benefitted from the civil rights struggles of their parents' generation. As such, they were heralded as proof of racial progress since the 1960s. Second, their rise to prominence resonated with the "Great Leader" narrative that has structured dominant media narratives of civil rights movements as well as foundational myths of American innovation. As many historians and memory studies scholars have cautioned, however, the emphasis on black male leadership not only under-represents the contributions of women and scores of unnamed people who fought and died for racial equality, but also suggests that once the right leader is chosen, victories will accrue.[14] This obfuscates the need for long-term planning, diligent hard work, and fortitude through times of backlash. Furthermore, another danger of the "Great Leader" framework is that it suggests we must first find a leader to define an agenda, and sets up the leader for a fall should he fail—this narrative nearly always presents a "he"—to deliver the goods.

Third, the demographic data attached to these emerging political figures—Generation Millennial, white-voter friendly, and, in some cases, of multiracial parentage—hit on the nascent post-racial themes that first showed up in the 1990s. The fresh-faced, light-skinned, Ivy League–educated black men formed a kind of post-racial "talented tenth" whose profiles were fit to a frame for "getting beyond race." And, importantly, the ways that these men talked about race to multiple constituencies facilitated post-racial labeling. Whereas a candidate like Al Sharpton ran a (brief) issue-focused presidential primary campaign to put issues of racial injustice on the table, post-racial candidates would not make such topics central to their message of change. This opened up more space for pundits to insist that the practices, issues, and figures of the civil rights era—the Moses Generation—had worn out their welcome.

Joshua versus Moses: Booker versus Sharpe and Beyond

My close readings of the news items from 2002 found that Cory Booker's run for mayor in Newark, New Jersey, provided the first full test of the post-racial politician frame. The contest generated more than twice as many uses of "post-racial" in news media than had occurred in the previous year. In the thirteen articles that used the term in 2002, six were about Booker and the meaning of his candidacy.

In these news items, journalists and sources continued to suggest that most black politics could be characterized as appeals to a misguided sense of shared identity or racial loyalty rather than as a product of struggles, strategies, and shared experiences among people of color. This caricature of the "Moses" generation infused the articles written about Booker's mayoral campaign against the four-term black incumbent, Sharpe James. News writers and pundits solidified their definition of "post-racial" politicians: They were "beneficiaries of the civil rights movement," but not beholden to its political strategies or the alleged racial chauvinism of figures like the Reverend Al Sharpton or Jesse Jackson, Jr.[15] The crucial difference between the old guard and the young turks was that the latter were described as *attractive to white voters*: This became a linchpin of post-racial politics that augured an end to uncomfortable tensions within the Democratic Party over whether issues that disproportionately affect people of color—redlining, public

Table 1.3. Comparison of News Items with References to "Post-Racial" and Cory Booker

	2001	2002
News items with "post-racial" used anywhere	5	13
News items with Booker and "post-racial"	0	6

education, poverty, police harassment, the death penalty—should be front and center in the party's agenda.

For reporters and editorial commentators, the Newark mayoral race quickly became a symbol of an imminent change in black politics. With headlines such as "In Newark Race, Black Political Visions Collide"[16] and multiple descriptions of Booker as a "vegetarian post-racial, postpartisan" candidate,[17] reporters quickly decided this election was a harbinger of a post-racial era. [18] One front page headline declared the mayoral contest was a sign of a "New Game in Urban Politics," and contrasted the candidates as follows: "Mayor James—a stalwart of the civil rights movement and part of the first generation of black municipal leaders—is pitted against an equally fervent but young Ivy League—educated reformer."[19] In another piece, this contrast was drawn in greater detail:

> [James] has been mayor for 16 years, and he was a city councilman before that, elected in the wake of riots that rocked Newark and then one major city after another in the late 1960s. Everyone elected with him in the city's black ascendancy has since retired, died or been indicted. . . . His main opponent, Cory Booker, is a black freshman city councilman half his age who moved here six years ago with degrees from Yale, Stanford and Oxford to organize poor tenants against slumlords. He has attracted glowing media coverage and a record $3 million in campaign contributions, much of it from wealthy, white donors outside Newark.[20]

Many other articles dedicated significant space to listing the various and sundry race-baiting rumors James's supporters spread, such as Booker wasn't really black, or that he was a pawn of white Jewish Wall

Street executives. *Newsweek*'s Ellis Cose depicted the intergenerational struggle and its identity politics as follows:

> Booker makes it abundantly clear that he considers himself a different breed—a post-racial man for an increasingly diverse Newark who believes in multiracial, multiethnic coalitions and non-doctrinaire thought. A child of privilege raised by corporate executives, Booker could not have existed before the civil-rights revolution. . . . James understandably views Booker's challenge as something akin to betrayal. So he has denounced the younger man, in terms not only extreme but bizarre, suggesting, among other things, that Booker is not black—oblivious, apparently, to the irony in defining blackness in terms of the very lack of privilege that James himself struggled so valiantly against.[21]

Only one article contained the suggestion that this narrative of a generational divide and/or of the corruption of the older generation might not be the most accurate depiction of black politics. Thus, towards the end of his lengthy *New Yorker* feature on the Newark race, Jonathan Tepperman included this passage about Booker's relationship to black political tradition:

> [H]e bristles when I suggest he is running a race-less campaign. "Look," Booker says frowning, "I am a black man who takes a lot of pride in my heritage and my people. I'm out there talking about race. . . . I haven't divorced myself from the tradition of African American politics, which has always involved innovation and using new tactics for new situations." He pauses. "But I don't want to be a great black politician. I want to be a great politician."[22]

Unfortunately, Tepperman failed to pursue or elaborate on Booker's statement about the innovations of black politics. Rather, he immediately provided another sound-bite condemnation of Sharpe James from an African American professor, Orlando Patterson, who characterized the mayor's tactics as playing "the black chauvinist card." Apparently, Tepperman was either uninterested in querying Dr. Patterson about other black political traditions, or felt no need to include any remarks the professor (or Booker) may have provided on the subject.

Figure 1.1. Harold Washington for Mayor campaign button.
Personal collection of the author.

In the end, readers could find nothing here or in the other news items on the Newark race to back Booker's claim about the richness and vitality of black political traditions. Surprisingly, no one mentioned a trailblazer like Chicago's first black mayor, Harold Washington, who won despite an incredibly racist campaign run against him by fellow Democrats and Republicans. Against these racially skewed odds, a coalition of liberal whites, Latinas/os, and African Americans elected Washington in 1983. But unless a reader has knowledge of Washington or other black coalition-builders, there is little evidence that anyone of James's generation has the capacity or desire to do so. Readers are left with the hope that Booker and his generation will forge interracial coalitions once the old guard has faded.

The characterization of James and other older politicians of color as racially suspect anachronisms continued to gain traction. Although associations between post-racialism and Booker were numerous— fifty-five stories between 2000 and 2007 linked him to the term "post-racial"—Booker's candidacy was by no means the only one that sparked discussions of a post-racial turn in local and national politics. This theme appeared in reports on other electoral battles, such as a 2006 race for a congressional seat in New York, where a white Jewish candidate, David Yansky, ran against three black candidates. The writer juxtaposed images of "old-school," aging black politicians with the professionalism of the opposition in an article titled "Brooklyn Bantustan." After noting how the outgoing black congressman called Yansky a "colonizer," the writer depicted the black candidates as members of a fading, perhaps dying, breed:

> Even though the contest has been cast as black versus white, when Owens, Vann, and the others stand . . . onstage and invoke icons of the sixties civil rights movement, another color is blatantly apparent: gray, the dominant hair color. . . What power this group of black leaders had is quickly ebbing.[23]

In this and other articles, the main theme was that people of color were about to shift away from voting based mostly on racial identifications to considering the actual qualifications of candidates.

Wherefore Black Leadership? The Implications of Joshua versus Moses

The articles discussed above suggest that race still matters, but we don't know really what that means other than that the candidates who avoid talk of racism or ways in which the racial past informs our present may be more successful now than those who allegedly stir the racial pot. The expectations for post-racial politicians set them up for the difficult challenge of attempting to relieve racial tensions without actually identifying or addressing the roots of those tensions. The problem is that post-racial news frames don't provide a full picture of the scope of political organizations and practices that blacks and other people of color engage in across a host of institutions, cities, and regions. If the ascendance of the Joshua Generation is the key to post-racial political change, is it also necessary that post-racial discourse simultaneously discount the older generation or demonize any form of race-conscious politics?

Few observers would argue that people should vote based on racial identity alone or that a politician shouldn't to reach out to all groups in his or her city. However, when the post-racial ideal is contrasted with a caricature of a monolithic black politics—symbolized by a mayor caught in scandals—the deck is unfairly stacked against the so-called "civil rights generation." The distortion of black politics and politicians that emerges from these articles also fits into what Houston Baker, Jr., calls the "conservative nostalgia" narrative of the rise and demise of the civil rights era.[24] This narrative—exemplified in conservative misappropriation of Martin Luther King's "Dream" speech[25]—posits that in the early days of the civil rights movement, a harmonious relationship among non-violent black protesters, benevolent, patient black leaders, and exceptional white individuals drove positive change. What stopped the tide of change? The rise of black power politics, often depicted as a violent, radical politics of self-segregation practiced by the likes of Malcolm X and the Black Panthers. This caused a rift in the movement and pushed away well-meaning white allies, thus ending the promise of King's "Dream." This story is incorporated in many popular—and scholarly—narratives.[26]

A disturbing corollary to the depiction of black power as the downfall of civil rights progress is the idea that *black* leaders are primarily responsible for getting things back on track towards a post-racial America. If they broke it, they must fix it. This not only ignores the role of white-dominated state and cultural backlash against racial justice movements, but also extends and sustains the inaccurate, and problematic, "Great Black Male Leader" narrative. This retelling of civil rights activism not only subsumes the presence and contributions of women to anti-racist politics; it also reinforces the notion that black people—black male leaders in particular—are responsible for solving the "race problem." Thus, in the sphere of electoral politics, in which the race problem of the Democratic Party has been framed, for good or ill, as "losing the white South" and white "Reagan Democrats" in the North after President Lyndon B. Johnson signed the Civil Rights Act of 1965,[27] this "Great Black Leader" narrative lets Republican operatives and white citizens who respond to race-baiting politics off the hook: The onus is on black and brown people to mute their concerns so as to not scare away the white "moderates" and "independents" who left the Democratic coalition in the 1970s and 1980s. In this scenario, black and brown people need to stop "following" the lead of "divisive figures" like Jesse Jackson, Al Sharpton, or Louis Farrakhan (or gangsta rappers or _____: fill in the blank) and find the right kind of leader (Colin Powell? Herman Cain?) who would move them in a better direction. Accordingly, this narrative bifurcates black politics into two camps: the "good" leaders like MLK and post-racial figures like Booker and the "bad" leaders like Huey P. Newton and modern-day race-men like Sharpton. On the Right, commentators tried to argue that the alleged lapse in black and liberal leadership should convince black voters to try the post-racial GOP.

Conservative Post-Racialism

Post-racial discourses on the Right emerged as Republicans tried to distance themselves from their race-baiting reputation, hoping to reintroduce themselves as "post-racial" to Latina/o and African American voters. One pitfall of this practice is that the racially suspect strategies of past—and present—GOP strategists and policy positions are the salient "pre-" that is contrasted with the "post-" moment. The racist past that the post- has supposedly overcome remains the foil to the alleged contemporary post-racial Republican Party. Moreover, the continued prominence of certain present-day Republican officials whose rhetoric and policy preferences are hard to classify as "post-racial" makes it difficult for the GOP to repair its image with voters of color.[28] It is no surprise, then, that the accompanying strategy of painting the Left and Democrats as the true players of the race card is central to conservative post-racial discourse: It is easier to paint liberals as reverse racists than to explain away decades of race-baiting politics. Thus, in the early 2000s, Republican usage of "post-racial" crystallized around two main ideas: first, that liberal Democrats and prominent black political figures use race to manipulate voters; second, that the GOP is the post-racial vanguard in politics due to its rejection of race-aware policies and appreciation of individuals of color based on merit. At the same time, though, most writers had to acknowledge that some wings of the party weren't yet riding the post-racial wave.

Republican Post-Racial Reform: Recuperating the Party's Image, 2000–2007

Proximity to post-racial politics was demonstrated by George W. Bush's "compassionate conservatism" and appointment of blacks and Latinos to his cabinet. Andrew Sullivan praised President Bush for appointing Condoleeza Rice as Secretary of State in the face of Democrats' opposition. He declared that reactions to Rice revealed "much of the Left's diversity mania is about upholding a certain political ideology, rather than ethnic or gender variety itself."[29] Bush's "management style is clearly post-racial," Sullivan decided. Though President Bush was credited with taking a "post-racial approach" to assembling his cabinet, writers were still split on whether the Republican Party as a whole was capable of post-racial politics. This uncertainty was evident in reactions to Georgia Governor Zell Miller's confrontational keynote speech at the 2004 Republican National Convention. The *New York Sun*'s Luiza Savage opined that Miller's keynote gave viewers "the scowl of a white Southern septuagenarian . . . perhaps not the most desirable face for the Republicans to project" in contrast to the optimistic, "post-racial" Democratic keynote speaker, Barack Obama.[30] Jonah Goldberg of the *National Review* agreed: There was a stark contrast between "Obama—'a post-racial, smiling, expansive young American'—[and] Zell Miller, his face rigid with anger. . . . Remember who [Miller] is: once a proud supporter of racial segregation."[31] Commentators cringed at the visibility of the GOP's continued ties to icons of Southern racism and argued that the party was missing out on the post-racial future. In their criticisms, the "racial" that is attached to "post-" is associated with old-school, racist southern politics, a politics that has been soundly discredited and, allegedly, has no impact on the seemingly post-racial present—except to scare off prospective voters. The question therefore becomes whether the GOP will reform its style and put out to pasture those politicians who refuse to get up to post-racial speed to compete with the likes of Obama.[32]

There was also significant disappointment from conservative writers who felt that the GOP's initial response to Obama's 2004 senate race fell short of the new post-racial expectations. When the party chose Alan Keyes, a well-known black conservative, to replace the disgraced white candidate, Jack Ryan, many felt their party was mimicking the worst type of identity politics. An editorial in the *Economist* declared that Keyes's candidacy "smacks of tokenism. . . . [W]hat other than racial discrimination can explain the Illinois Republican Party's decision to shortlist two blacks for the Illinois seat—and eventually choose Mr. Keyes? He brings no powerful backers . . . and was thrashed in two runs for the Senate in Maryland."[33] The editors went on to say that the GOP had neither listened to Obama's speech nor realized that he "is a post-racial candidate. . . . He appeals just as strongly to white suburban voters as he does to blacks," whereas Mr. Keyes was telling voters Obama wasn't a real African American because of his biracial, Kenyan heritage.[34] So the Right's caricature of identity politics on the Left was ironically playing out with the Republican black candidate, who questioned the authenticity of Obama's blackness.

Conservative commentators had a slightly easier time framing Ken Blackwell, a Republican conservative, as a post-racial candidate in 2006. One columnist dubbed Blackwell "Reagan's unlikely heir" for his steadfastness against gay marriage and abortion.[35] Blackwell briefly became yet another black male political star linked to the term "post-racial" when he announced his intention to run for governor of Ohio. But the post-racial case was still harder to make for Blackwell than for Obama's cohort in the Democratic Party. Young black Democrats, such as Booker and Obama, were (correctly) described as "beneficiaries of the civil rights movement"—but not beholden to the leaders of that movement. Blackwell, however, was never described as "a beneficiary" of civil rights. That clashed too much with his Republican bona fides, which required him to deny having accrued any benefits from black Americans' collective actions. Older than Booker and Obama, Blackwell was in fact involved with black student movements on his college campus in the 1960s.[36] While his supporters described him as "post-racial, post-civil rights," they did not emphasize that he was a civil rights activist in college. Instead, conservative commentators (as well as Blackwell himself) distanced him from the movement by calling him "Jesse Jackson's greatest nightmare."[37] Like the Joshua Generation Democrats, then, Blackwell was distinguished from the civil rights generation.

Conservative celebration of Blackwell's "post-racial" candidacy resonated with the argument crafted by Noemie Emery a decade earlier and deployed (as chapter 2 illustrates) in *Justice Sunday III*: Republicans should acknowledge that their divisive strategies were scaring off scores of potential conservative voters of color. In theory, any candidate should be able to leave the "old" Republican racial tactics behind and court voters of color based on shared conservative beliefs. But Blackwell's campaign in particular was seen as a test run for those post-racial political aspirations: Writers assumed that he could (finally) deliver those black conservative voters. *National Review* columnist Kathryn Jean Lopez opined that although GOP National Committee Chairman Ken Mehlman was correct to reach out to black conservatives, he "doesn't have the power that Ken Blackwell does to pull it off. In one electoral triumph, Blackwell could achieve what no task force, outreach program, or powerful speech ever will—making it 'safe' for blacks to routinely vote Republican instead of being looked at as anomalies."[38]

Lopez's assertion is problematic. First, she assumed that most black voters fear being harshly judged by other black people when they exit the ballot box. There's no recognition that voting Democratic might be a rational, self-interested choice based on the party's support for civil rights policies or progressive tax policies. The idea that liberals have bamboozled generations of black voters rests on the disturbing stereotype that black people lack the political sophistication to understand their true interests—which, according to Republicans is to reject race-conscious policies. Second, Lopez states that a white Republican will not get the same reception from black listeners because they don't share his racial identity. Paradoxically, then, she wants black voters to do what conservative writers usually condemn: listen to and vote for a candidate because he is black. Thus, the GOP post-racial strategy, when it involves black candidates, assumes that people of color will be more likely to warm to Republican ideas if conservatives of color deliver the message.[39] In other words, their "post-racial" strategy is still dependent upon color-conscious configurations of candidates and public representatives. Republican operatives understand the value in leveraging shared racial identity and essentialist notions of intraracial trust in an ostensibly post-racial era of politics, if only to overcome a sorry civil rights record.

Post-Racial Policy: Colorblindness Remixed

At the same time that Republicans and allies tried to find candidates of color to carry their banner into black and Latina/o communities, they continued to try to reframe colorblind policy as post-racial. A column by George F. Will, a writer for *Newsweek* and the *Washington Post*, encapsulates this approach. Will's column appeared in the wake of the U.S. Supreme Court's decision to uphold affirmative action in college admissions. Famously, the majority decision included a section authored by Sandra Day O'Connor predicting that within twenty-five years, affirmative action would no longer be necessary.[40] Still, Will was outraged by the decision and stated that "The Supreme Court made no sense here. It has given us black-and-white law in a post-race U.S." According to him, a key element for implementing affirmative action—namely, the state's ability to identify people by race to assess any racial harms—was itself racist. The emergence of mixed-race people, new immigrant groups, and scientific declarations that "race and ethnicity are . . . dubious scientific categories,"[41] Will argued, meant that any race-conscious policies or lawsuits are irrelevant and suspect. In other words, if racial categories themselves are not stable or scientifically valid, then no solutions based on racial or ethnic difference can be legal. He concluded: "Demographics, not constitutional litigation, are determining the destiny of a post-racial America." Thus, once racial categories become "fluid," multiply, or complicate the black-white divide, we have become post-racial, and need no race-conscious remedies to address lingering inequalities. This approach—which echoes Ward Connerly's ballot initiative drives—offers a concrete policy objective (eliminate racial categorization protocols) and resonates with well-known, easily accessed arguments about race, merit, and individualism.

Refuting Conservative Post-Racialism

Although there was an increase in discussions of an emergent post-racial politics or a "Generation Mixed," a handful of commentators still emphasized that getting past race would take time and effort. These discussions of post-racialism, like their predecessors in the 1990s, combined data illustrating racial inequalities and dismay at the premature diagnosis of a post-racial society. For example, in contrast to the George Will column just discussed, Colbert King's op-ed about the Supreme Court's decision to uphold affirmative action presents a very different view of race in America. King's column was inspired by Justice Ruth Ginsberg's reaction to the companion case against the University of Michigan's undergraduate admissions policy, which the court struck down. Quoting from Ginsberg's dissent, King agrees with the Justice that racism is not in the past, even though "affirmative action foes would deny . . . that we're not in a post-racial America in which bigotry is a thing of the past."[42] After sharing passages of the dissent, wherein Ginsberg cites continued segregation, economic disparities, and evidence of ongoing "'[i]rrational prejudice . . . encountered in real estate markets and consumer transactions,'" King lauds her for documenting this proof in "lengthy footnotes." Unlike Will, who did not even take a moment to consider the evidence of racial inequalities in education, wealth, health, and other domains, King counseled readers to continue to recognize and fight against such disparities, thereby also implying that the post-racial era will not emerge without such efforts to eliminate the remnants of bigotry.

These two *Washington Post* columnists, Will and King, present their audiences (King's smaller than Will's, since King's column was not reprinted elsewhere) with two very different visions of what post-racialism means. For Will, it is an end of an era of government interference in racial categorization and policy; for King, it is a time when bigotry and residues of racial hierarchy no longer influence the life chances of Americans of any color. Will sees a post-racial era emerging from changing demographics and dismissal of race as a biological category; King sees post-racial America coming into being only after defeating racism and racial inequality via legal and other means. Unfortunately, King's take on post-racialism was almost drowned out in the deluge of post-racial excitement that accompanied Barack Obama's candidacy.

The Obama Effect: Exponential Growth of Post-Racial Expectations, 2008–2009

As Table 1.4 illustrates, the popularity of the term "post-racial" grew exponentially with Obama's presidential campaign. This growth, in

Table 1.4. Change in Use of "Post-Racial" in News Items (All Source Types), 2005–2010

	2005	2006	2007	2008	2009	2010
"Post-racial" mentioned	11	20	75	1475	1642	1254
"Post-racial" in headline	0	0	0	64	105	91

turn, required a different methodological approach for analysis of post-racial discourse in news media. Whereas in previous years, the number of stories using the term "post-racial" was small enough that performing a close reading of all items was reasonable, between 2008 and 2010, when the number of stories increased to the thousands, I turned to a mixture of quantitative coding and close reading to make the analysis manageable.

As Susan Herbst notes, even with a seemingly infinite stream of news and opinion available through digital media, "we can still dip into the news systematically, keeping in mind that news outlets cannot be represented as neatly as they were twenty years ago."[43] My research assistants and I gathered all the news items that included the term "post-racial" and then created a random sample of 205 stories (after eliminating repeats and errors). These stories were then coded for the types of people, arguments, and definitions of "post-racial" used.[44] Data analysis from this sample is represented in Tables 1.5 and 1.6. In addition to creating the random sample, we also separated out from the entire set of stories all of those in which "post-racial" appeared in the headline (260 stories), and coded each headline in terms of whether it seemed to have an optimistic or pessimistic take on post-racial politics or society (Table 1.7). In addition, I also closely read all the stories in the random sample, as well as half of the stories that used "post-racial" in the headline, some of which overlapped with the sample. Overall, I read over 300 stories, taking careful notes of the questions, themes, and issues in each one. What I hope emerges from the combination of qualitative and quantitative analysis is a broad, yet textured, picture of post-racial discourse in the news.

As the previous chapter illustrated, reporters had already constructed frames for post-racial politics before the election. But once

Obama began having success in the presidential contest, there was a sharp increase in use of the term. In 2008, "post-racial" appeared in over 1,400 news items, compared to only 116 between 2005 and 2007. From his biracial heritage (post-racial to some people) to white voter enthusiasm (for a post-racial black politician) to his own rhetoric that, as Stephanie Li describes, "signifies without specifying" about race,[45] news media framed Obama as the perfect (or suspect) post-racial figure. In other words, the elements of Obama's persona and the historic import of his candidacy generated the perfect post-racial storm.

Other researchers who have examined news and specialty media coverage of the 2008 presidential election have concluded, as I do, that despite the diversity of candidates in this historic election and its eventual winner, mainstream media did not push beyond the usual limited frames for race and race relations, let alone include the influence of class, gender, or sexuality.[46] As Enid Logan summarized, election coverage of Obama adhered to a "triumphal narrative . . . that the 'old' politics of race, focusing on black grievance, victimhood, and protest, were vanquished" and that "newer, more effective" politics would replace the old due to Obama's victory.[47] Even when journalists and editors had space for longer-form explorations of the meaning of the campaign—such as in the multiple commemorative books and DVDs produced and sold in the wake of Obama's 2009 inauguration—mainstream media turned to familiar frames, placing "Obama's 'historic moment' within a grander discourse of immigration and freedom [and] suggest[ing] little change" in how reporters respond to racial issues or events.[48] Moreover, even as many of these commemorative narratives and news reports declared the election proof of post-racial society, they continued to emphasize black/white relations and failed to take a more nuanced look at demographic change and political realities.

While this section reaffirms the previous analyses of election-year news coverage and imagery, it also focuses on the ways in which questions about and hopes for a post-racial society built upon and solidified the themes that emerged earlier in the decade. First, multiracial people and families continued to be cited as "proof" of an emerging post-racial society. Second, optimism about Barack Obama's candidacy was framed within the boundaries of black politics drawn in previous discussions of Cory Booker. These frames strongly suggested that a presidential

Figure 1.2. President Obama and First Lady Michelle Obama at Inaugural Parade, 2009. Courtesy of the Carol M. Highsmith Archive, Library of Congress, Prints and Photographs Division.

victory for a black man would in itself signal the beginning of a post-racial era for the nation, without paying much attention to how a single electoral contest would facilitate such radical change.

Generation M: Multiracial "Millenials" and the Post-Racial Future

Discussions of a post-racial America were driven largely by Barack Obama's presence in the campaign. Running second were articles mentioning multiracial families and persons, as well as demographic changes happening within the nation. The idea that demography and the election were pushing post-racial change in 2008 lent a positive vibe to the majority of articles. Whether journalists described the

Table 1.5. Types of Post-Racial People or Political Actors Mentioned,
2008–2010

Post-racial people	2008 (N=56)	2009 (N=90)	2010 (N= 59)
Barack Obama	76.80% (43)	66% (60)	66% (39)
Celebrities, multi-racial families, "new" demographics	49.90% (28)	49.6% (45)	26% (16)
Black politicians/civil rights generation	26.80% (15)	13.30% (12)	18% (11)

multicolored mix of people that had transformed the streets of their hometowns, reflected on the increase in biracial children, or opined about the popularity of celebrity people of color, the idea that a post-racial society would emerge out of a new "mixed" generation appeared in almost half of the sample of news items.

Many commentators who described Barack Obama as a post-racial person felt he cemented that title in the wake of his famous speech on race in Philadelphia during the campaign. Although Obama had largely avoided references to racism in the early campaign, release of an edited video of his pastor, the Reverend Jeremiah Wright, exclaiming, "God Damn America!" for its racism and imperialism, pushed the candidate to make a statement about race relations. After Obama gave this March 2008 speech, National Public Radio's Daniel Schorr opined that the candidate's "post-racial" response to the furor over the Reverend Wright was promising, and surmised that "Young voters born since the excesses of the last century have generally embraced the Obama thesis" that it was past time to stir up old racial wounds.[49] Similarly, a *USA Today* columnist hoped that the next generation would move us steadily towards a post-racial future and recounted an incident in which his son replied to the query of whether he supported Obama because of his heritage by saying: "'Dad, you need to wake up to the new thinking about race in America. . . . It is not about being racial; it is not about being biracial; it is about being post-racial.'"[50] And, though scholar Richard Rodriguez was frustrated with mainstream media's continued focus on black/white, he nonetheless wrote in *Newsweek* that the United States had already experienced a significant demographic and cultural shift that foretold post-racial changes, exemplified by Obama's heritage:

Sure, there are separate cafeteria tables. But there is also flirting and unlikely friendships being formed. *A young woman from Kansas falls in love with a visiting student from Kenya.* In any American family I can name, there are cousins and in-laws of several races. There are grandchildren who do not look exactly like any of their grandparents. And many families have adopted a child from China or Guatemala. Or Bangladesh.

In this world, the political necessity is for someone who might help us imagine lives larger than racial designations. A politician might win the day, if he or she were able to speak of the ways our lives are mixed.[51]

In a related vein, historian John McWhorter told a reporter that in the next few decades, the United States "will be so hybrid a nation that any idea of black-white relations as a major problem in need of address will seem archaic."[52] Thus, through interracial mixing and generational change, society would inevitably follow Obama's post-racial lead.

Moreover, the younger generation was poised to make a historical break with the racist past by electing its first president of African descent. Indeed, in a story about the demographic breakdown of voters, journalist James Bacon wrote:

A CNN election exit poll showed a strong correlation between the age of the voter and his or her likelihood to vote for Obama. The GenY (millennial) generation voted lopsidedly for Obama, by 66 percent to 32 percent, while GenX favored him by a solid margin (52 percent to 46 percent). Baby boomers split their votes evenly between Obama and John McCain (50 percent to 49 percent), while only the Silent Generation [born in the Depression Era] tilted toward McCain (53 percent McCain, 45 percent Obama).[53]

But Bacon tempered the usual progress narrative of multiracial generational change with the following fact: "If we narrow the focus to white voters over 30, the generational shift disappears. A consistent percentage of that group—between 56 percent and 58 percent—selected McCain across the age spectrum."[54] The fact that significant white majorities across key voting age groups did not go post-racial at the ballot box went largely unremarked once the media decided this election was an historic marker of post-racial transition.

History and Hope

Excitement about the historical importance of an Obama win overwhelmed discussion of the practical and necessary measures to remedy racial inequality, let alone change the hearts and minds of people who still practice racism. An Associated Press story exemplifies the way the history-making element may have inflated hopes for post-racial transformation. In a report about how the University of Mississippi would host one of the presidential debates, the writer gushed about the way "Ole Miss" had changed from the time that the campus and state violently resisted integration. After noting that "bullets flew and tear gas canisters exploded" as whites tried to keep James Meredith off campus, "Now, Ole Miss is a diverse university where racial conflict is a topic for history classes."[55] Incredibly, there is not a single quotation from any student that suggests Ole Miss or the state itself has any vestiges of racism, any scars. Racism is over, it seems, and a state that was a citadel of white racist resistance and segregation is now ready for Obama.

In the same vein, Michael Crowley, a writer for the New Republic, declared in the first paragraph of a feature titled "Post-Racial" that "Even white supremacists don't hate Obama." Crowley surveyed white supremacy websites, like the Conservative Citizens' Council (CCC) page, that still "promote the view of white superiority over blacks." Indeed, the CCC alleged an Obama victory would "embolden blacks to be more aggressive toward whites." But he noted that he didn't see any specific racial stereotypes applied to Obama as an individual. The writer interpreted this as a sign of how post-racial Obama had "confused" the supremacists because he didn't match their stereotypes of blackness. With his biracial background and Ivy League "mild tone," Obama was "hilariously confounding the world view of white supremacists" because he "lacks certain cultural signifiers . . . that would viscerally threaten racist whites obsessed with maintaining 'white rights,' ending affirmative action, and cutting off nearly all non-European immigration."[56]

Somehow, he (and many others) overlooked the fact that Obama and his family were under Secret Service protection earlier than any other candidate in history due to death threats from white supremacists, and that his offices had been vandalized with racist graffiti. Moreover, the comments seem to contradict evidence in his own piece: How is it that the Conservative Citizens' Council was not "viscerally" threatened by Obama when they linked his victory to emboldening "black aggression" towards whites? This writer seems to have wholly embraced the idea that Obama and the Joshua Generation are so different from other black politicians that they cannot be linked to the "scary" kinds of blackness, whether it take the form of fantasies of black revenge on whites or caricatures of black leaders who demand racial justice. Presenting Obama as an exception to the rule for white supremacists, on the one hand, and as exceptional, on the other, employs the same stereotypes of racial identity and politics that delegitimize calls for direct action on racial disparities. This approach recalls Dana Cloud's discussion of how even "positive" stereotypes of racialized Others operate through a binary logic that requires the presence of negative referents in order to work.[57] In the West, stereotypes are constructed within understandings of race and nation that position people on either side of a negative/positive binary (e.g. black/white, Oriental/Occidental). As such, even the "positive" representation of a "post-racial black" candidate is dependent upon understanding the other side of the binary—the angry Black politician who plays "the race card" and ultimately wants to punish whites.

As summarized earlier, coverage of election night and the inauguration was overwhelmingly congratulatory of the nation for "overcoming" the "last barrier" of racial politics and electing a black president. Numerous journalists and commentators sighed over the coincidence that the inauguration would take place on the Martin Luther King holiday weekend, and that King's "Dream" had been fulfilled, or was on the verge of fulfillment, in our exceptional, ever-progressing nation. Take, for example, this editorial:

> Obama campaigned to be president of all Americans, not one faction, and on that basis he won. Nothing else explains the long lines of voters of all races and backgrounds. . . . But Obama's election sends an especially powerful message to African Americans. They have suffered most, and on Tuesday, they gained the most. This country became their country as never before.

When Obama says, as he often does, that "in no other country on Earth" was his story "even possible," African Americans know what story he's talking about—their story—even if his mother was white and his father was African. His victory was the culmination of two centuries of hardship and struggle.[58]

This and other editorials suggested that the struggles were either over, or were on the verge of completion now that Obama was president. If the latter were the case, how were citizens to make it into the home stretch? Beyond celebrating the first black First Family in the White House, there was no agenda for any final policy tasks or new social practices that would get us over the finish line. The ebullience fostered the unrealistic expectations that enough people were (1) invested in that symbolism; and (2) knew how to act accordingly afterwards to finish what was started by thousands of civil rights workers in the 1950s. As the 2008 news narratives articulated the "Dream" with Obama's victory, journalists and pundits made the move of assuming symbolic politics of representation were sufficient for a politics of racial justice to take hold. Only a few news items about Obama's victory hinted that it might not be so easy to achieve the post-racial dream state. One rare piece contained a cautionary quotation: Kevin Alexander Gray, a civil rights organizer who had worked on Jesse Jackson's 1988 campaign, said, "People are so focused on celebrating the history of [the election], they haven't figured out how to move beyond that, and that kind of worries me a bit. He's in; it's historic; now it's time to press him."[59] But press him on what? On the Right, it was clear: press Obama to disavow liberals and particular black leaders and to end affirmative action to prove that he is "truly" post-racial.

Barack Obama became "the" post-racial leader for the press because he seemed to emerge at the nexus of overlapping narratives of race, progress, politics, and generational change. He was literally dubbed the heir apparent to John F. Kennedy by the Kennedy clan, thereby further strengthening the notion that liberals and Democrats had gone astray when they lost the Great Liberal Leaders of the 1960s: JFK, MLK, and RFK.[60] The bright star of a new generation of black male leaders, Obama gained not only the blessing of the Kennedys,[61] but then also the support of the black males of the "civil rights generation," who, it was imagined, were finally ready to "step aside" now that the inheritor of King's "Dream" had arrived. This narrative of regeneration and renewal simplifies what happened in the intervening four decades. It is as if Obama would pick up right where the "good guys" had left off, returning us to a (mythical) national, bipartisan consensus on race and civil rights issues.

A huge problem with the Great Leader scenario—regardless of race—is that once the "right" leader emerges, people can sit back and let him (not her, of course) do the work. Elect Cory Booker, and he will transform Newark to attract corporations, white suburbanites, and hipsters back into the city they abandoned en masse decades before, decimating the tax base and school system along the way.[62] Elect Barack Obama, and he will somehow make it easier to talk about race and to figure out what to do about the entrenched inequalities and injustices in our education, judicial, and economic systems. Obama's "natural" affinities with multiple imagined publics—black, Asian, white, Christian, Muslim—will somehow release the right kind of energy to bring balance to Washington, D.C., and end the culture wars as well as the wars in the Middle East. Parallel narratives from the Right that questioned whether Obama was a post-racial savior were less visible, but regular.

The Right and the "Real" Obama: Stealth Race-Man

From the beginning of the 2008 electoral cycle, Right-leaning blogs, articles, and broadcasts questioned how far Obama's politics were from the tactics of Jackson and Sharpton. The kerfuffle over Rev. Wright provided the best opening for these attacks. To explain why he suspected Obama's motives, a blogger on *California Yankee* borrowed an English theorist's dual characterization of black leaders as being either like Marcus Garvey, who wielded "power by making whites feel guilty about [slavery] and only allowing the guilt to be relieved in return for concessions," or like Martin Luther King Jr., Oprah, and Bill Cosby, who are "bargainers," who tell whites "'I will not use America's horrible story of racism against my you if you will promise not to use my race against me.'" He then surmised that, once in office, Obama would exploit the racial guilt card, just like Garvey.[63]

In traditional news outlets, such as the *Chicago Daily Herald*, the scandal over Rev. Wright provided an opportunity for letter writers to suggest Obama was a black radical in more genteel terms.

> It took 20 years and a media spotlight on Rev. Wright for Sen. Obama to acknowledge that sermons Rev. Wright gave were "rough." What Sen. Obama lacked was moral courage to confront Rev. Wright about his sermons at any time. My guess is either Obama saw nothing wrong with Rev. Wright's sermons or was afraid that his views would make him unpopular in Rev. Wright's church and hence lose local voter support among parishioners.[64]

Why couldn't more of America see through the post-racial veil covering the rabid race-man beneath? *Atlas Shrugs* blogger Pamela Gellar reasoned that it was because the liberal media had decided to "tar and feather anyone pro-McCain as a racist. . . . The ugly secret is the real racism our state-run media refuses to cover. It is a violent racism Obama encourages and incited." She then alleged that black Obama supporters had been assaulting white McCain supporters.[65] This distorted picture of violence-inciting, guilt-inducing black leaders not only misrepresents the variety and complexities of African American political struggles; it also assumes the total innocence of white people in contemporary racial disputes and inequities. Accordingly, these caricatures made the further case that Obama was not really different from all the other black political leaders.

These conspiracy theories and the expectations of imminent post-racial change were bound for a collision. Thus, it is not surprising that after he was inaugurated, Obama's first few comments and actions related to race, power, and injustice lit off a powder keg of public reactions. When Obama criticized the arrest of Professor Henry Louis Gates, Jr., which seemed to be a case of racial profiling and abuse of authority, and when once he nominated the first Latina to the United States Supreme Court to shape binding decisions on civil rights law, the "Dream" of post-racial politics began to crumble. Obama's victory was achieved, in part, by avoiding talk about race as much as possible—a tactic that the press and pundits praised as savvy, post-racial politics. So when race talk flared early in his administration, the backlash was vicious, and the White House had few, if any, strategies for responding. This reality hit home swiftly and brutally in the first year of Obama's administration, when a handful of ugly feeding frenzies involving race erupted, and the country witnessed the level of contempt and racist invective aimed at the President and his family rising precipitously after the inauguration. The incivility and racism expressed at rallies for the McCain-Palin ticket continued amongst the ranks of the Tea Party—including its GOP-affiliates in the House and Senate. Racist images and accusations circulated widely on the Internet, and showed up in startling statistics about rising participation in white supremacist organizations.[66]

Once the dream of the great post-racial leader "completing" King's "Dream" was dashed, the lack of historical and political complexity in the media's understanding of race in America became painfully clear. Columnists engaged in hand-wringing, teeth-gnashing, and finger-pointing, trying to figure out how the seemingly widespread optimism of 2008 transformed so quickly into the ugly conspiracy theories and angry shouts heard during Obama's first year in office. On the Right, an "I-told-you-so" narrative patted Republican voters and officials on the back for not trusting Obama to be post-racial, and further energized calls to halt all race-based initiatives. On the Left, frustration, desperation, and resignation characterized explanations of Obama's fall from grace.

The Post-Racial Dream in Decline: Racial Realities and Media Spectacles, 2009–2010

Although "post-racial" appeared in the news more often in 2009 than in 2008, the term was associated more often with pessimistic ideas about politics and society after Obama's inauguration. Table 1.6 displays data from the sample of news items we coded for post-racial themes. Whereas in 2008 nearly half of the stories argued that post-racial politics were in effect or imminent, only a fifth of stories in 2009 and 2010 exhibited that optimism, while pessimism about post-racial politics doubled.

As early as January 26, 2009, *Philadelphia Inquirer* columnist Annette John-Hall warned her readers with the headline: "Race Still

Table 1.6. Dominant Themes Expressed in Post-Racial News, 2008–2010

Post-racial themes	2008	2009	2010
Conservatives are post-racial	19.60% (11)	28.88% (26)	10% (6)
Post-racial politics won't emerge soon	28.60% (16)	55.55% (50)	57% (34)
Post-racial U.S. will emerge in an egalitarian future	23.20% (13)	23.33% (21)	38% (23)
Post-racial politics are imminent	46.40% (26)	23.33% (21)	22% (13)

Matters in Obama's Post-Racial America."[67] She criticized actor Will Smith—himself often lauded as a symbol of Hollywood's "post-racial" change of heart—for saying that Obama's inauguration meant that "'all of our excuses have been removed. . . . There's no white man keeping you down, because if he really were trying to keep you down he would have done everything to keep Obama down.'" She countered Smith's assertion with a sobering description of institutional racism:

> Fact is, before we skip into post-racial wonderland together, we still have some institutional dismantling to do. Disproportionate red-lining, lack of equality in pay and lending. Inferior education. One black senator in Congress, a dearth of professionals of color in every segment, from boardrooms to newsrooms.[68]

John-Hall's words of wisdom were affirmed in other cautionary columns, such as one in *USA Today* titled: "Post-Racial Era? Go Tell Victims of Police Shootings."[69] In opinion pieces like these, writers and interviewees listed examples of systemic racism in education, law enforcement, death sentencing, employment, and housing. They tried to temper the excitement over the symbolism of Obama's rise with clear-eyed assessments of how much would have to change for our nation to merit the adjective "post-racial." In the *Albany Times-Union*, writer Ryan McAuliff Straus stated that the election didn't "prove that racism is finally dead." He then urged readers to stop thinking about racism as built on "the explicit, in-your-face violence of yesteryear . . . but on segregated, underfunded schools. It is built on different access to health care and different life expectancies."[70]

But these assessments were not matched with many ideas for how to undo the damage of racism other than restarting the "national conversation" on race. On the eve of the anniversary of the inauguration, when NPR's *Talk of the Nation* aired a segment titled "The Post-Racial Conversation, One Year In," scholar Mark Anthony Neal observed that many people hoped that Obama's "post-racial" triumph would mean "that conversations about race would disappear." But, he argued, the conversation was not even progressing; it was also shallow due in part to citizens' lack of a "sense of historical memory."[71] Predictably, discussion in the press didn't follow his advice to consider history, and instead focused on damage control and spin when the Sotomayor nomination and arrest of Gates sparked talk of race.

Obama the Race Card Shark

Even before the Supreme Court nomination, conservative commentators were priming the pump to accuse Obama of reverse racism and playing the race card—a very un-post-racial kind of politics. One important theme was that Republicans should expect to be accused of racism anytime they disagreed with the president. For example, Pete Riehm predicted in Alabama's *Mobile Register* in February of 2009, that even though everyone wants to "strive to solidify the post-racial society of Dr. Martin Luther King's dream," anyone who challenged the president would be "summarily dismissed as a petty partisan, if not a downright racist." Although the president didn't actually call any of his opponents racist, somehow conservatives assumed he and his surrogates would use this as a weapon.

This theme of liberals' cynical use of race ramped up once Sotomayor was nominated in May 2009 and her "wise Latina" comments were taken out of context and widely circulated in a media frenzy. Andrew Breitbart opined that the Sotomayor nomination was the final nail in the coffin for post-racial politics on the Democratic side. "With Barack Obama, many Americans had hoped to get a post-racial president . . . it looks less and less like they got one." He and others accused Obama of hypocrisy for not being angry about Sotomayor's "wise Latina" remark.

"It is the onerous double standard that ensures the Left wins every argument about race. And that is far too useful a weapon for the president and his Democratic Party to give up."[72]

Before the dust could settle on the Sotomayor soundbite, Harvard Professor Henry Louis Gates, Jr., was arrested in July. A white police officer charged him with disorderly conduct after he had trouble opening his door and a neighbor called police, even though Gates provided proof of his ownership of the home. When Obama was asked about the incident in a press conference, he remarked that he "didn't know . . . what role race played in that, but I think it's fair to say, number one, any of us would be pretty angry; number two, that the Cambridge police acted stupidly in arresting somebody when there was already proof that they were in their own home." Despite the fact that the charges were dropped—and were suspect at best, since disorderly conduct in Massachusetts is a violation that occurs in the public arena not inside one's own home—and despite the reams of data and documented experiences of racial profiling, Obama was quickly tagged as a reverse racist by pundits on the Right.[73] Here is one choice quotations from a 2009 post from the "Weapons of Mass Discussion" blog:

> Did you see the race baiting, anti-police garbage spewed by the Thug in Chief? Yes, he called police officers stupid. I thought this @$$clown was supposed to be the post-racial President? More like MOST RACIST President.[74]

Former Bush administration Justice Department official, John Yoo, used more polite language to insinuate that the president wasn't really post-racial. After applauding a recent court decision "against the use of racial quotas" in hiring, he wrote in the *Wall Street Journal* that the decision would challenge "the nation's first minority president . . . to help lead us to a post-racial America."[75] Yoo implied that Obama could not actually be able to be post-racial because of his support for affirmative action. Again, for conservatives, any use of race is "racial" or even racist, and thus one cannot get past race if it is used in any way, even to remedy inequalities caused by structural racism.

In their commentaries about the president's failure to follow their prescriptions for being post-racial these conservatives personalized

race and racism, focusing on Obama's alleged persona, political motivations, and "true" nature. Personalization works well with the overarch-
ing endorsement of colorblind individualism on the Right, as well as
the more foul white supremacist invectives and conspiracy theories that
Obama and other people of color are subversive, dangerous individuals
who must be stopped lest they defile the "real" America. These news
items suggest that Obama's "real" racial nature was unleashed after
the election, after he had hoodwinked enough (white) Americans into
believing he was post-racial.

The Silver Lining in the Post-Racial Cloud: Time to Talk about Institutional Racism

On the Left, commentators chided Obama for *how* he stepped into
the racial fray, even when they endorsed his decisions and agreed that
post-racialism was a pipe dream. They argued that people shouldn't
have been surprised at the reaction to Obama's nomination of Sotomayor, or his statement about Gates's arrest. In his column on Politico.
com, Roger Simon shrugged, "So much for post-racial America." He
then asked the rhetorical question, how "did things turn around so
fast?" The answer:

> They didn't. They may never have turned in the first place. Largely over-
> looked in the understandably good feelings generated by the election of
> our first black president was the simple fact that . . . most white Ameri-
> cans voted for John McCain. In fact, Barack Obama lost the white vote
> in 2008 by a landslide. While Obama won the overall vote by 53 percent
> to 46 percent, he lost among white voters by 55 percent to 43 percent.[76]

Here, Simon and a few others went back to the data that was barely
mentioned in the wake of the election: A majority of white voters did
NOT vote for Obama. At the same time, other commentators used the
feeding frenzy over Gates as an opportunity to discuss institutional racism. Professor Glenn Loury wrote in *The New York Times*, "I seriously
doubt that calling the police stupid is something the president's poll-
sters encourage." For him, it was

Figure 1.3. Madison, Wisconsin, Tea Party Rally.
Photo by Jesse Russell. Used with permission. CC BY-ND.

depressing in the extreme that the president, when it came time for him
to expend political capital on the issue of race and the police, did so on
behalf of his "friend" rather than stressing policy reforms that might
keep the poorly educated, infrequently employed, troubled but still
human young black men in America out of prison. . . . [I]f Mr. Obama
were going to lose some working-class white votes to the charge of "elit-
ism," I'd much rather it have been on countering the proliferation of
"three strikes" laws, . . . or inveighing against the racial disproportion in
the administration of the death penalty.[77]

In a television discussion that went beyond the he-said/she-said
recounting of the arrest and White House damage control efforts (like
the "beer summit"), scholars and journalists interviewed by CNN's
Soledad O'Brien urged audience members to go beyond the tip of
the iceberg of racial profiling. Unlike some in the media who saw the

meeting as a significant step forward in resolving the issue of racial pro-filing and the underlying prejudice, many on the panel thought it was a mostly empty gesture. "It is a significant brouhaha [but] I'm not sure it gets to what 'ales' (ails) us," commented panelist and Georgetown University professor Michael Eric Dyson. "The real problem is still on the streets where disproportionate numbers of Black and Latino men and women are subjected to arbitrary forms of police power."[78]

Thus, one promising development of rejecting the notion that "post-racial" was an accurate descriptor of politics is that critics had more space to discuss continuing racial disparities and injustices in the United States. In the process, they drew on both personal stories and empirical data. On NPR, a guest commentator ended a segment on racial pro-filing and police brutality by recounting how policemen accosted him and a friend without cause, and then beat him when he asked for their badge numbers. This commentator reminded listeners that his story was not unique, though it was rarely heard: "If there's any silver lin-ing to the arrest of [Professor] Gates, it's that public awareness of this problem had increased, and the country gets closer to realizing . . . ain't nothing post-racial about the United States of America."[79] While crit-ics on both sides agreed that the Gates and Sotomayor episodes proved that U.S. politics aren't "post-racial," only some used these cases to refo-cus attention on the realities of institutional racism. Moreover, even as the dream of post-racial politics was fading, post-racial people and cul-tural artifacts—multiracial families, celebrities, and movies with inter-racial casts—remained popular in the news as symbols of progress.

Post-Racial People Redux: Cross-Racial Consumption and Courtship

Some commentators continued to insist a post-racial *cultural* change had been generated by the Millennials, even if political change had not occurred. In her piece for the *Sunday Oregonian*, for example, Lillian Mongeau wrote, "While our society is certainly not yet successfully 'post-racial' my generation's concept of race, especially when it comes to black and white, really has changed." She cited growing up with a black family, "the Huxtables" of the *Cosby Show* on TV, and stated that Michelle Obama, "resembling nobody more than Clair Huxtable, rep-resents the new reality we are living in."[80] Writer Lenox Magee agreed that youth were leading the way with their multiracial tastes: "Just as . . . Will Smith changed stereotypes about the ideal Hollywood leading man, the youth market is following the same pattern. . . . There's no doubt that mainstream America is being redefined."[81] Writers continued to make links between celebrities of color and post-racial change, none more emphatically than *New York Newsday* columnist Glenn Gamboa in his response to the death of Michael Jackson. Gamboa declared that the King of Pop had "moonwalked his way through mammoth racial barriers in the "80s by barely discussing it . . . which many say paved the way for the age of Obama, Oprah, of what many call 'post-racial America.'"[82] Others also argued that Jackson's unprecedented crossover success with white audiences made him a "post-race superstar."[83] Here, music and movie choices, facilitated by stars' willingness to *avoid* talking about race, made way for post-racial culture. No mention was made of the disjuncture between the immense popularity of Jackson or Smith and the plight of other black men who are racially profiled by employers or police, for example, or of the racial undertones of the tabloid obsessions with Jackson's life. This silence is indicative of the post-racial mystique in that race is noteworthy in the realm of personal choices (media consumption, individual performances of racial identity) but deemed toxic in discussions of social and political inequality. Though post-racial people and cultural consumption still provided a ray of hope for some in the news, political commentators sounded the final bell for post-racial politics in 2010.

2010: The Dream Is Over

The change from optimism during the election year to pessimism in Obama's first years as president was also reflected in a shift in the tenor of headlines that used the term "post-racial." We coded each headline as follows: pessimistic about the state of racial politics; optimistic that post-racial society was immanent; gestures toward policies or approaches to make society post-racial; or ambiguous.

Headlines published in 2008, such as "A New Post-Racial Political Era in America"[84] were replaced and outnumbered by 2010 headlines that declared, "The President Is No Redeemer, Post-Racial or Otherwise."[85] As Table 1.7 illustrates, pessimistic headlines nearly doubled

Table 1.7. Tone of Post-Racial Headlines, 2008 and 2010

	2008 (64 headlines)	2010 (91 headlines)
Optimistic	30% (19)	4.3% (4)
Pessimistic	36% (23)	67% (62)
Policy	6% (4)	4.3% (4)
Ambiguous	28% (18)	30% (21)

between 2008 and 2010. When we coded for the prevailing opinions expressed in the body of the sampled articles, we found a similar distribution. In 2008, only 14 percent of stories were dominated by the opinion that it was premature to use "post-racial" to describe U.S. society or politics; in 2010, 48 percent of stories delivered that verdict. There was also a drop in optimism: In 2008, 15 percent of items were optimistic that society was becoming post-racial; in 2010, the number decreased to 9 percent.

The decrease in optimism was often expressed through bitter humor and irony. A blogger posted a January 2010 entry with the title, "Ring in the Post-Racial New Year: Obama Effigy in Plains, GA."[86] Shortly thereafter, the AP Wire sent one story under the headline "Hope for Post-Racial U.S. Fades after Remarks." By July 2010, the *Chattanooga Times* declared the "Post-Racial Presidency Over," and in September, *New York Times* columnist Bob Hebert' scoffed, "Post-Racial America? No Way." While a handful of headlines asked for patience ("A Little Less 'Post-Racial,' a Little More Listening")[87] and counseled cautious optimism for the impact of generational change ("A Child Will Lead Us: Post-Racial Attitudes"),[88] the overwhelming majority of 2010 headlines concluded that the election of the first black president had not ushered in a post-racial political era. At the same time, the pessimism was still expressed through many of the themes that dominated the optimistic news items in 2008. Thus, in stories that focused on President Obama's role in racial controversies, voices on the Right dominated, reasserting that the Republicans and Tea Party activists were the true vanguard of post-racial politics in the United States. In their view, Obama had proven he was a creature of leftist identity politics run amok. But as in 2009, the overall disappointment about post-racial politics did generate a little space for arguments about institutional racism, arguments that been shoved to the wayside during the euphoria of 2008.

The Blame Game: The Right and the "Real" Barack Obama, 2010

Attacks on Obama were relentless and brutal in the blogosphere and the traditional press. Writers accused the president of either deliberately stirring up racial tensions or making tactical racial blunders in response to others' provocations. Many of these attacks were laced with bitter humor and incivility toward the president, his allies, and people of color. For example, in a 2010 post on *Wonkette*, a blogger joked that she was reporting to readers "live from Thugtown USA, i.e. Obama's backyard or Chicagotown, where there are no races or post-racial relations at the polls to watch today."[89] Di Hall argued in a letter to the *Fresno Bee* that in saying in a speech that the Republican Party wanted to "turn the clock back," Obama was playing the race card for black supporters: "Could it really be that this post-racial president is saying to the black community that if they do not rally and keep Democrats in office, to the back of the bus you go? Yes! That is exactly what he is saying. Shame on President Obama! He has done more to set race relations back in America than anyone in recent history."[90] This hyperbole was not unique to Ms. Hall; it was clear from other writers that the inordinately high hopes set for Obama and fanned by media enthusiasm for the post-racial meme had crashed right at his feet. Another writer presented a litany of hopes deliberately dashed:

> [Obama] ran on being post-racial. . . . He ran loftily challenging us to leave a better world for our children. He ran on hope. The plain fact is: He has not governed as he ran. Americans, including many who did not vote for him, had hoped he could help harness the inner angels of we the people. Instead, he has unleashed the outer demons of his circle of hand-maidens and henchmen . . . [91]

Likewise, in the aftermath of Andrew Breitbart's smear of Department of Agriculture official Shirley Sherrod, media outlets gave the conservative blogger plenty of space to allege a White House, liberal media conspiracy to use racial division as a tool. Breitbart released a heavily edited video that had made it seem that Sherrod advocated discriminating against white farmers. He told the media this was proof of Obama's real racial agenda.

> "It is my belief that President Obama promised, tacitly, to be a post-racial candidate, and it is sad to say that he hasn't," Andrew Breitbart said at a news conference before his appearance at a "Uni-Tea: United Tea Party For All Communities."
>
> Breitbart accused the president of engaging in a "proxy warfare plan" using the media, Hollywood and lawmakers. . . . Breitbart accused [all of them] of [making] false charges of racism during the health care debate as well as the NAACP's recent call on tea party groups to disavow "racist elements."[92]

One would expect Breitbart to defend himself against a seemingly large conspiracy of race-card-playing liberals. But other commentators leveraged similar arguments about Democrats and allied groups. For example, many journalists and editorials equated Breitbart's premeditated attack on Sherrod—framing her and her NAACP listeners as advocates of racial revenge on whites—with the NAACP's request for the Tea Party to denounce racist propaganda materials visible at their rallies. A *Los Angeles Times* editorial (reprinted in the *Monterey County Herald*), alleged that the Sherrod incident wouldn't have happened had it not been for the NAACP's action:

> The whole sorry spectacle was set in motion last week at the annual convention of the National Association for the Advancement of Colored People, which approved a resolution accusing the "tea party" movement of harboring racists. Breitbart, a conservative Internet entrepreneur who has built a career out of taking umbrage, responded Monday by posting a short, edited video on his BigGovernment.com website that he presented as evidence of racism in the NAACP. It showed Sherrod, an official with the U.S. Department of Agriculture, making a speech at an NAACP meeting in which she confessed to giving less than "the full force of what I could do" for a white farmer who came to her for help 24 years previously.[93]

The editorial then explained how Breitbart deliberately left out the section where Sherrod explained how she changed her mind and became a friend and ally of the white farmer. However, despite this acknowledgment of deceitful editing, the editorial insisted that "the blame doesn't lie solely with conservatives. Attacks by the NAACP on the tea party movement serve only to fuel white resentment. To collectively tar one's opponents as 'racist' is the lowest form of political attack."

This is a disturbing example of how easily and quickly accusations of white racism are discredited in the news, and how little work is done even to gauge whether the accusation holds any validity. None of the pieces that condemned the NAACP's vote bothered to mention why the members might have believed there were racist subgroups within the Tea Party. Instead, they assumed that both Breitbart and the NAACP were acting on bad faith and misrepresenting the facts. Although the Tea Party has many factions, there is plenty of documentary evidence of use of blatantly racist symbols at Tea Party events.[94] Some factions of the Tea Party were amongst the loudest supporters of the "birther" conspiracy theories that Obama is not a U.S. citizen but a secret African Muslim bent on bringing Islamic law to the United States.

So, with this in mind, we might ask, why is it the "lowest form of political attack" to say that it is racist to hold up a sign at a rally depicting the first black president as a Sambo or a pimp or alleging he is a "Kenyan-Muslim" or a "Lyin' African?"[95] Why is it "low" to ask a political organization to denounce racism within its ranks? When a critique of the use of such clearly visible, visceral, and ugly racial symbols in public spaces is equated with the mendacious, unethical manipulation of a public speech to defame a black government official, the press is engaging in the worst sort of "balance" by insisting that people of color always be equally to blame for racial incidents as whites.

Other commentators didn't use false equivalencies to make their case that Obama would not usher in the post-racial nirvana foretold in 2008. Rather, they blamed media frenzies, partisan politics-as-usual, and moneyed interests for stalling progress on race relations and racial inequality. Here, writers critiqued the notion of post-racial politics by emphasizing how naïve it was to assume one election could change the deep cultural currents of race in America, and argued for a renewed commitment to fighting racism. This set of observers offered lessons from the past and specific examples of how to work through the murky and uncomfortable intersections of personal and social phenomena that reinforce racism and racial inequalities. Indeed, after 2008, writers and interviewees contributed evidence and experiences that rejected the post-racial premise in greater numbers, which rose above 50 percent in both 2009 and 2010. Those who debunked post-racial mythology in order to broaden the conversation did so in two main ways. First, they looked at the uproar around Shirley Sherrod and other frenzies as more evidence that the conversation on race was not improving; it had perhaps become more frustrating due to the use of "post-racial" to reframe race. Second, they discussed the reasons why U.S. society isn't post-racial, weaving in arguments and evidence about structural racial inequality as well as heinous acts of bigoted violence.

Critics of the term "post-racial" found in the Sherrod incident perfect proof of the lack of sophistication and fairness in debates over racial controversy. Here, they argued that reactions to the now-discredited Breitbart video were not only unfounded, but unacceptable given the background of the "reporter" and his history of racial animus. Mary Sanchez of the *Modesto Bee* declared, "Whoever came up with the insipid term 'post-racial' ought to be forced to sit down and read aloud the vile commentary that pours into any newsroom after it publishes or airs a story on race." She then noted how fearful the USDA, the White House, and the NAACP had been over the reverse racist accusations brought against Sherrod, and she wondered why no one had "suspended judgment until they had done a little research. They would have discovered that Sherrod was actually telling a much longer tale, one of redemption. She had helped the white farmer save his farm, realizing that poor black and poor white have more, not less in common."[96] Finally, Sanchez underscored that the topsy-turvy world of conservative racial "gotchas" had directed people's attention away from the real racism in agricultural policy:

> There is another racially charged dimension to this drama, one that most commentators and reporters don't mention: The Department of Agriculture is still trying to settle lawsuits with black farmers who for decades were systematically denied loans, causing financial ruin for many in lost crops and land. . . .

The Obama administration is backing legislation enabling a $1.25 billion grant to settle the outstanding claims, a plan that conservatives have attacked vigorously. That legislation was supposed to be voted on the very week Breitbart chose to release his edited video. Coincidence?[97]

Using the racial debacle to get back to a fact-based discussion of race and USDA policy, Sanchez reveals what is at stake when a supposedly post-racial administration doesn't stand up to race-baiting games.

In a similar vein, Politico.com writer David Dante Troutt lamented that the Sherrod case showed society and the media's "lack of racial bearings."[98] How, he asked, could a "career civil servant with solid credentials" be unjustly railroaded by "deeply motivated bloggers with a track record for racial antipathy?" Troutt suggested that post-racialism means "nobody has to honor a principle except [out of] the fear of immediate public backlash against any hint of racial consciousness." This, he argued, was the fruit of allowing conservatives to spin Martin Luther King's "I Have A Dream" speech to mean that we must "shut down further talk of race, racial identity, and racism." Moreover, while conservatives accuse Obama of favoring black people, "the administration's tacit acceptance of post-racialism has disfavored blacks," as seen in the rush to judgment in the Sherrod incident. These writers and others illustrate that the true cost of post-racial discourse is not just a lack of clarity on race and racism, but also the possibility that progressive people and solutions can be too easily undermined by partisan post-racial tactics.

Interpersonal Animus and Structural Racism: Connecting the Racial Dots

Many commentators who declared the notion of the post-racial a sham lined up multiple examples of where and how society still exhibited racist ideologies and practices. Importantly, some of these examples made links between the personal and the political aspects of racism, undermining the notion that racism lives in the hearts and minds of misguided individuals, not within social, economic, and political institutions. For example, on the blog *Pam's House Blend*, Pam mused about the validity of libertarian reasoning with respect to how desegregation can come about with only "market forces" in play:

If access and membership to a private club is one of the ways people "do business" with the movers and shakers in the community, the ability to bar people for spurious reasons of their choice means by default, those without access cannot rub shoulders and make deals that affect the very "market forces" that determine the out-group's economic destiny. Is this ok in communities where there is no alternative? The libertarian view doesn't provide for a lack of equivalent competition to force change. How does change occur in this world view? [99]

Those who argue the government can't "legislate hearts and minds" are thus saying that people of color need to be content to "remain on the short end of the stick until there are enough benevolent patrons ready to let you in the door."[100] She then pivoted to the recent cases finding that Alabama prosecutors improperly barred blacks from juries. The spurious personal judgments—"The district attorney, Robert Broussard, said one had seemed 'arrogant' and 'pretty vocal.' In another woman, he said he 'detected hostility'"—lead to very real life-and-death decisions made by all-white juries in capital cases, as well as others. If the Justice Department and other entities don't check the "hearts and minds" of these individuals, the inaction reinforces the structural inequities in the economy and the criminal justice system.

Elsewhere, spates of campus hate speech incidents and hate crimes were aggregated as proof that America was not post-racial. Moreover, writer Tim Barker of the *Salt Lake Tribune* challenged the idealized image of universities as bias-free intellectual zones inhabited by Millennials:

It's tempting to think of college campuses as islands of enlightenment, places where students embrace new ideas, people and cultures without the specter of hate hanging overhead.

Tempting. But it's not always the case, as demonstrated by events on campuses across the nation in recent months. . . .

There have been racial slurs and a threat of lynching at Saint Louis University. There was a swastika scrawled on a bathroom wall near a Jewish studies center at the University of Miami. There were death threats against black students left on a bathroom wall at Hocking College in Nelsonville, Ohio. And a white fraternity sparked an uproar at the University of California San Diego when it sponsored a ghetto-themed "Compton Cookout" to mock Black History Month.

To be sure, such events have always been part of the American landscape. But campus and diversity experts say they've seen a surge in the past year, poking yet another hole in what increasingly appears to be the myth of a post-racial America.[101]

Listing these incidents together, Barker pushed back against the usual characterization of hate speech as isolated acts of "bad apples." There are so many bad apples spread across so many of our higher educational institutions that it is hard to argue that the problem will disappear once the culprits are rooted out. He then included Justice Department data that estimates "12 percent of hate crimes occur on either college or school campuses." The statistic nationalizes the issue, and illuminates how educational institutions are broadly implicated in racism.

Another article illustrated the faults of post-racialism by declaring in its headline, "We Need a Post-Racial and Post-Poverty America." Writer Brian Gilmore opened his piece, which reflected on the Martin Luther King, Jr., holiday, with historical references to lynching woven together with present-day racist violence:

[F]or part of his first year in office, Obama was receiving 30 death threats a day, a 400 percent increase over the number of threats President George W. Bush was receiving. The Secret Service has attributed some of this to the fact that Obama is our first black president. [It] harkens back to the country's ugly past where thousands of black people were lynched all across the country.[102]

Gilmore then reminded the audience to remember King's words about poverty *and* race:

"Like life," King wrote in "Where Do We Go From Here," "racial understanding is not something we find but something we must create." But racial understanding is not the only issue the nation faces that could benefit from King's vision.

"Poverty is one of the most urgent items on the agenda of modern life," King said in his Nobel Peace Prize address in 1964. It's more urgent than ever right now, since poverty has worsened in the last 10 years.[103]

Unlike the post-racial appropriations on the Right that reframe King's life and work as an appeal for race-blind, Christian-oriented public policy, Gilmore's meditation reaffirms the multiple facets of the fight for equality, asserting that racism *and* economic injustices are problems that require us to create solutions, not wait for the market or hearts and minds to gradually rectify centuries of oppression.

However important these counters to conservative post-racial discourse are, they still leave audiences with few ideas for how to remedy the continued racial inequalities and injustices listed. Conservatives offer a short, easy to understand explanation: Racial inequalities are best addressed not by government, but by individuals who take it upon themselves to improve their lives and/or charitably intervene in the lives of others. The real problem is that the government and liberals continue to use race in any capacity in public life. Others who count on interracial marriage or the next generation's diversity to naturally solve the problem leave little hope for those who won't live to see the Millennials mature into post-racial citizens. While it is necessary to provide evidence of institutional racism, it is not sufficient. In the fifth chapter, I examine how some alternative online news media provide discussions that go beyond debunking the post-racial mystique to articulating possibilities for anti-racist action. Before looking at alternative online news and commentary, the next chapter takes a detour from the news and editorials to examine how many of the themes found in the news resonate in media produced for spiritual edification and entertainment.

2

Brothers from Another Mother

Rescripting Religious Ties to Overcome the Racial Past

One type of post-racial discourse suggests that other sources of com-
munal identities—nation, gender, or class—are more legitimate means
for classifying groups and organizing political action. Race, in these discussions, is often characterized as a distraction from these more valid
or "real" identities. On the Left, this is expressed most often by a concern that commitments to multiculturalism have derailed activists' and
scholars' class-based analysis and action.[1] On the Right, post-racial discourse elevates the role of the individual, but also charges that emphasis on racial identities erodes our sense of national unity and amplifies
difference at the expense of similarities. And, in particular, the Right
argues that multiculturalism promotes a kind of relativism that will dis-
able sound judgment when citizens consider Western ideological values
alongside other "non-Western" systems of thought, particularly Islam.

   What these discourses have in common is an anxiety about the ability of the nation's citizens to find common ground upon which to base
deliberations and political actions. Whereas critics on the Left are not
always specific about the types of identity that should form the glue that
holds us together (although class often rises to the top), the Right has
been clear that Enlightenment and/or "Judeo Christian" values should
remain hegemonic to facilitate democracy.[2] Our national identity,

based in these traditions, should take precedence over all other affinities to race or gender. In addition to suggesting national identity should overcome racial differences, another collective identity figured as more legitimate than race (and thus, post-racially correct) is religious identity. Arguing that the alleged excesses of multiculturalism have allowed too many groups to create enclaves for themselves and refuse to assimilate "American" values or that Judeo-Christian tradition forms the true foundation of the Constitution, conservative pundits and scholars suggest assimilation is key to overcoming remaining racial divisions and tensions.[3] In this chapter, I look at a nationally broadcast and webcast event, *Justice Sunday III* (*JSIII*), as an example of a post-racial media event that encourages African Americans to reimagine civil rights struggles and political affinities in primarily religious terms.

As the title suggests, this event was the third in a *Justice Sunday* (*JS*) series sponsored by the Family Research Council (FRC), a well-known and powerful conservative organization with many ties to Republican lawmakers, lobbyists, think tanks, and Christian faith groups. FRC's motto, proudly displayed on its website, is "Defending family, faith, and freedom." The *JS* series—which was co-sponsored by other major religious Right groups—was organized by the FRC to garner public support for then-President Bush's Supreme Court nominees as well as for pet policies of conservative Republicans and the Christian Right. In particular, the series underscored the media reach of the Christian Right. A huge network of Christian television and radio broadcasters, bloggers, and podcasters disseminated the event via live simulcast and retransmitted it on TV, radio, and the Internet for weeks afterwards. DVDs of any of the three *Justice Sundays* were for sale for at least a year after the original events. The organizers boasted on the FRC website that, with their media partners, the event could potentially reach 80 million households in all fifty states. But for the *JSIII* event, the goal was to continue rescripting the Right as a post-racial, welcoming political space for black people who share Christian Conservative values.

JSIII was held on January 8, 2006. The event was staged in a majority black church, providing an opportunity for white Republicans and Christian Right leaders to advance their argument that race is less salient and valid than religion. By performing their outreach within a black institution, the *JSIII* organizers signaled that they understood black people may still hold suspicions about the legacy of racism in the Christian Right and contemporary GOP.

In the next sections of this chapter, I place *JSIII* in the context of increasing media appeals from the GOP and its Christian allies to conservative black voters. Then, I analyze the *JSIII* broadcast, with particular attention to the presence and performances of featured white and black speakers, as well as a video that suggested a different way for defining liberty and the legacy of Martin Luther King, Jr. The final section of the chapter presents results of a focus group study done with African Americans who viewed a portion of the *JSIII* webcast. This study provides an interesting glimpse of the ways black viewers interpret appeals like these, as well as suggesting whether the articulation of religion over race as an identity for political organization has the desired effect: garnering trust and votes.

Religion, Race, and Media

Melissa Harris-Lacewell urges scholars to examine "the spaces of everyday black life where African Americans cull meaning from daily interactions."[4] Church services and media consumption are important parts of everyday life. Indeed, some black political scientists suggest that given its historical and contemporary importance as a social and political institution, the black church has had more impact on African American political beliefs than other sources of ideological influence. If black churches are spaces where many African Americans "come into contact with *ideas* that shape the direction of their political thinking,"[5] then we should take a close look when white-dominated Christian organizations provide media products for black congregants.

The rise of the Christian Right and debates over the nature of the September 11 attacks have led scholars and political activists to revisit how religious organizations and individuals use media resources. While earlier observers of religion and media assumed that religion would decline as a social force in the late twentieth century, religion thrives at present and is, perhaps, increasingly relevant to everyday life.[6] Christian Right organizations, often loud critics of contemporary "liberal media" content, have long used mass media resources from church magazines to radio broadcasts of sermons to expand the reach of the pulpit. By the turn of the twentieth-first century, their outreach became even more sophisticated with new media tools at their disposal. Religious organizations publicize "their message through sounds and image, and instigate alternative politics of belonging, often in competition with the modern nation-state"[7] and, perhaps, in competition with racial and ethnic group identities as well. With this in mind, we can view recent conservative, white-dominated Christian media appeals to black conservative Christians as an attempt to persuade black people that, in concert with a post-racial era, politics based on religious identities are more authentic, moral, or politically fruitful than a politics based on racial identity.

These appeals were highly visible in the 2004 election, when black clergymen and congregations were invited to support George W. Bush as a "man of faith" who believed in heterosexual marriage and government funding for churches. But interracial religious outreach campaigns are neither new nor newly controversial. Indeed, blacks who converted to Catholicism or who worked with the Catholic Interracial Councils (CIC) were sometimes singled out for criticism,[8] just as today black evangelicals who break bread with Ralph Reed have been accused of selling out black interests to the Republicans. In both cases, critics point to past and present practices of racial discrimination within white-dominated churches and by their Republican Party allies, questioning the sincerity and motives of white Christian outreach. While these suspicions have roots in valid concerns—given the poor track record of many denominations in civil rights—they also subtly reinscribe an essentialist view of the relationship between racial identity and political interests. That is, critics who accuse black conservative Christians of acting against their true(r) interests operate on the assumption that racial identity is (or should be) more central, or politically meaningful, than religious identity. Conversely, when the Christian Right argues that race no longer matters such that shared religious beliefs can bridge divides, they assume that religion is more essential to community than racial groups' history, shared experiences, and modes of cultural expression. Neither recognizes that race and religion are intersecting identities that cannot be so easily separated and ranked.

Recent scholarship, however, emphasizes how religion is interwoven into both racial and national identities in the Americas, and how each

inflects discourses produced about the other.[9] Thus, 'white evangelical appeals for post-racial cooperation may not succeed if they try to
erase the racial past or gloss over other matters related to racial identity. Yet such appeals are made, and so we need to ask, how do those
appeals for "post-racial" cooperation in politics based on religious values rework or reframe assumptions about party identification as well as
racial and national identity? And, importantly, how (if at all) do white
Christian media texts try to explain their own histories of racial exclusion and racist practices to black audiences? Examining the Christian
Right's interest in using mass media resources as a tool to negotiate and
repair relationships with black Christian publics, we can also see how
they reframe histories of racist exclusion and/or domination of those
publics.

In so doing, we can conceptualize white Christian media appeals
to Black publics as "racial projects." Racial projects "connect what
race means in a particular discursive practice and the ways in which
both social structures and everyday experiences are racially organized,
based upon that meaning."[10] Such racial projects are not unique to the
turn of the century; at least as far back as white Christian abolitionist
William Lloyd Garrison's insistence that his paper, the *Liberator*, was
a *black* newspaper,[11] some white Christians have created media messages seeking spiritual and political union with African Americans. I
argue that, while they weave their messages in a post-racial manner, the
white Christian institutions and Republican allies that courted African
Americans via *JSIII* were engaged in a racial project that sought to de-
emphasize the role of racial dynamics in contemporary politics through
an elevation of religious identity. Through discourses that combine
politics, race, and religion, *JSIII* attempted to reinterpret contemporary black political interests and histories of black collective struggles
through the lens of religion. The program hailed blacks as brothers and
sisters in Christ, all joined in a continuing struggle for a more righteous
and just nation.

Republicans and their Christian Right allies continue to showcase
the support of a few outspoken conservative black clergy in elections
and policy debates. Particularly at the local level—in anti-gay ballot initiatives, for example—appeals to religious belonging rather than racial
identity have been rampant, and are successful with some, but not all,

black Christian voters. Since the 2008 passage of California's Proposition 8 (which outlawed gay marriage), there have been many reports
and discussions of homophobic attitudes in African Americans communities. In particular, many point to "the black church"—a monolithic
grouping that already problematically belies the diversity of black religious experiences—as a major source of anti-gay sentiment in black
communities.

The seeming mismatch between an institution often viewed as a civil
rights stalwart and the anti-gay proclamations of camera-ready black
pastors has been raked over in the press and on the Internet many
times. But African American GLBT activists, scholars, and artists were
challenging homophobia in black denominations well before these controversies. Moreover, as historians such as Charles Payne have documented, leaders in certain Baptist churches were less supportive of 1950s
civil rights activism than pastors of other denominations.[12] Despite the
diversity of thought and theology in black churches, though, many still
tend to refer to "the black Church" as a singular entity with conservative
leanings. Even so, resistance to the narrative of a monolithic, homophobic black church has emerged in some quarters. Specifically in the
wake of President Obama's endorsement of same-sex marriage, activists point to polls and statements by leaders and celebrities that demonstrate black communities aren't "more" homophobic than whites, and
that support for gay and lesbian African Americans is more widespread
than once assumed.[13]

As progressive black clergy and organizations with strong ties to
black churches—such as the NAACP—formally endorse gay marriage and full civil rights for LGBT people, the notion that Republicans
will splinter the black vote by playing on conservative religious beliefs
seems unrealistic. Moreover, Republican candidates who take a hard
party line on conservative social policy to court black voters based on
religious and moral similarity haven't gotten very far in terms of electoral success. Black and white Republican candidates, including religious conservative favorites like *JSIII* speaker (and then-Pennsylvania
Senator) Rick Santorum, did not do well with black voters. Likewise,
appeals to conservative Christian Blacks by surrogates of the McCain
campaign did not detract from Obama's commanding lead. Regardless of its impact on voting, however, this strain of post-racial rhetoric

has emerged over the past two decades as a strategic part of the Right's media program.

Re-Engaging the "Party of Lincoln": The GOP,
the Christian Right, and Black Voters

Since the mid-1990s, conservative appeals to black Christians have become bolder. These appeals present Christian values and common-alities as more legitimate means than race for binding communities, forming political beliefs and informing voting choices. In a brilliant, clever, inspired, or cynical move (depending on your viewpoint), Christian Right groups who form a large portion of the Republican Party's support base have appropriated the rhetoric of black freedom movements (which, of course, do have affinities with religious dis-courses stretching back to the anti-slavery movement) to try to bring black voters back into the fold. For example, Christian Right organiza-tions have sponsored anti-abortion billboards that specifically charge abortion providers with black genocide, appropriating charges from black organizations that the U.S. health system has historically abused Black populations through forced sterilization and other violations.[14] In other advertisements and speeches, the appropriation and mis-representation of narrow portions of Martin Luther King's writings remain widespread. What these communications have in common is they ignore the role of white supremacy as well as tenets of black self-determination that informed original criticisms and protests against injustices inflicted on black people.[15]

Some stalwart Republican-allied religious and conservative organiza-tions have sporadically employed targeted messages to black radio sta-tions to drum up support for Republican candidates and anti-gay mar-riage amendments. These attempts have not gone unnoticed. In 2006, multiple news outlets reported on the controversy over radio commer-cials that featured (ostensibly) black women discussing politics. During the ad, one woman tells her friend, "Dr. King was a real man. You know he was a Republican," before launching into a critique of Democrats' support of same-sex marriage and abortion.[16] The ads were targeted to voters in Ohio and Maryland, where prominent black Republicans were running for governor or U.S. Senate seats.

Certainly, Frederick Douglass, Booker T. Washington, and other prominent blacks were Republicans—until a majority of black organizations, newspapers, and an overwhelming number of voters voted for Franklin Delano Roosevelt to support his efforts to end the Great Depression and defeat Nazism. The shift was further cemented during the civil rights movement when black citizens overwhelmingly voted for Kennedy, Johnson, and every Democratic presidential candidate since. As Congressman John Lewis said to a reporter, "I knew Martin Luther King Jr. . . . and I know he voted for John F. Kennedy . . . and if he had lived, he would have voted for Hubert Humphrey in 1968 and not the Republican candidate Richard Nixon."[17] Others chimed in that these ads were disingenuous, distorting not only King's political affinities, but also the Republicans' contemporary record of voting against policies that would alleviate poverty, discrimination, and other residual ills of the era of legal racial segregation which were anathema to King's life and work.

At the same time that they have strategically appropriated black civil rights rhetoric and leaders, Christian Right organizations have made some attempts to allay the suspicions many blacks harbor towards modern-day Republicans, whose electoral strategies and policy platforms have, not infrequently, used racist cues and racist logic to gain white votes.[18] For example, in one press conference, then-Christian Coalition leader Ralph Reed admitted that "For too long, our movement has been a predominantly—frankly, almost exclusively—white, evangelical Republican movement with a political center of gravity centered in the safety of the suburbs."[19] In his 1996 book, *Active Faith*, Reed wrote, "The white evangelical church carries a shameful legacy of racism and the historical baggage of indifference to the most central struggle for social justice in this country, a legacy that is only now being wiped clean by the sanctifying work of repentance and racial reconciliation."[20]

While many critics lambasted Reed's and others' "reconciliation" initiatives as cynical smoke screens meant to split the black vote, the urge to confront and atone for past racism has taken on different guises in different white-dominated churches, with legacies including the slave trade, colonialism, and imperialism. Thus, for example, best-selling author and celebrity pastor Rick Warren has gained notoriety for pushing evangelicals to contribute to the cause of fighting AIDS/ HIV in Africa and to see African debt as a moral issue.[21] Some ministries within the Baptist church have sponsored meetings between black and white congregations whose churches are within a few miles—if not blocks—from each other, recognizing the legacy of racism and segregation in the founding of duplicate churches. Others have merged, bringing black and white worshippers under the same roof for the first time ever.[22] Thus, there are many responses to multiple calls to deal with race in the church.[23]

As explained in chapter 1, Republican strategists have been arguing within the party about how (if at all) to attract black voters. The "compassionate conservatism" framework for Republican outreach during the Bush administration is one way this has been articulated. Simultaneously with Karl Rove's race-baiting tactics in South Carolina, Bush and his advisers continued outreach to black evangelicals and Catholics,[24] in ways meant to signal a departure from the party's race-baiting reputation and anti–civil rights policy positions, which included using racial cues, opposing affirmative action, weakening the Voting Rights Act, and attacking other state- and court-organized efforts to level the racial playing field. Moreover, speeches at recent GOP conventions expressed a harsh anti-immigration line and a pervasive use of code language about "special rights" and the like. Intended to counter these prevailing trends, compassionate conservatism proposed market- and faith-based programs to craft policies to improve educational and job opportunities for people of color. Support for policies such as school vouchers, which use market-based theories of competition to displace government-led initiatives, is one hallmark of compassionate conservatives' attempts to make kinder, gentler neoconservative appeals to people of color. As Steven Teles summarized, since the Nixon era, Republican strategists have used issues like welfare, states' rights, and school integration via busing to paint Democrats as elitists who sold out working class whites.[25] But, in the late 1990s,

compassionate conservatism encouraged Republicans to present themselves as allies of the poor and minorities, and to insist that "liberal elites" in the Democratic party were the defenders of ineffective bureaucracies and a morally debased culture. Instead of embracing [white] racial resentment . . . Republicans should rebrand themselves as the party of racial solidarity—*the allies of the moralizing agents of the inner cities.*[26]

Bush's compassionate conservative policies were pitched to black clergy—the "moralizing agents" identified in black communities. This approach was encouraged in part by moderates in the party, who cringed at the excesses of some of the far right wing of the GOP. It was also a prudent strategy in the face of demographic change: As the white majority began shrinking, any savvy political party hoping for a future would need to recruit more voters of color. In the early 1990s, some Republican strategists theorized that with 20 percent of the black vote, they could gain a nearly air-tight governing majority.[27] The Clinton years derailed that plan temporarily, but when George W. Bush planned his move into the White House, he and his strategists made it clear that they were bidding for black voters, and they viewed evangelical churches as a perfect vehicle to spread the word that Republicans were ready to be more welcoming and diverse. The press picked up on Bush's attempts, as mentioned in the previous chapter, and featured comments from black voters who saw some promise in his compassionate conservative stance. But most remained wary of replacing all government efforts with private sector interventions. As journalist Tracy Van Slyke observed,

> Many blacks agree that it would be good for the federal government to help churches and other community institutions play a bigger role in tackling unemployment, child pregnancy, gang violence and other social ills. But opinion polls suggest that most think such community activism should come on top of, not instead of, existing and expanded government programs.[28]

In 2001, J. C. Watts—at the time the lone black Republican congressman—was enlisted to spearhead a strategy for minority outreach. The money available from the faith-based initiative was also predicted to be a way to open the doors of Black churches to Republicans. Again, the press was intrigued, and captured the opinions of some black clergy who had accepted Bush's outreach on the basis of shared faith and

moral judgments. A *New York Times* piece described the motivations of
a few of these pastors in a 2004 feature article.

> William Turner, an African-American pastor from Pasadena who
> voted for Mr. Gore in 2000 . . . is now volunteering for the Bush cam-
> paign. . . . Others said Mr. Bush's faith, and in particular his opposition
> to same-sex marriage, had at least made their decision about the elec-
> tion a closer call. . . . Republicans strategists say they are also planting
> seeds that they hope will yield greater results in future elections, even if
> it does not make much difference this year. And both sides acknowledge
> that the endorsement of African-American clergy has a symbolic value
> among nonblack voters, in part because their status in the broader cul-
> ture as the legacy of the civil rights movement.[29]

Bush's faith-based policies provided a perfect home for compassionate
conservative outreach, and more blacks voted for him in 2004 than in
2000.[30] Moreover, as the quotation indicates, the value of visible support from black pastors lies not only in shaving off a few black voters
from the Democrats' side, but also in assuring *white* voters that the
GOP is no longer as racially hostile as it was in the 1990s. *Justice Sunday
III*, then, is but one of many recent attempts to reshape the reputation of
the Republican Party amongst black voters. In contrast to twenty-sec-
ond radio ads or billboards, the broadcast provided an extended reintroduction of the GOP and its conservative Christian allies.

Justice Sunday III

In the context of the ideology of the *Justice Sunday* series, the word
"justice" refers to the oft-made charge that "liberal activist" judges
have used their power to deliver warped interpretations of the Constitution—such as the *Roe v. Wade* decision—to serve "special interests"
and a "liberal elite" that are abhorrent to Christian beliefs. According
to speakers at *JSI* and *JSII*, damage done to the U.S. moral fiber by liberal "judicial activism" requires people of faith (led by then-President
Bush and a Republican-dominated Congress) to curtail the power of
the third branch of government. The *Justice Sunday* series thus served
as a clarion call, as well as a dare to Democrats to question or block

President Bush's controversial conservative nominees to the Supreme Court. Judge Samuel Alito was the specific nominee under scrutiny at the time of *Justice Sunday III*, and the producers sought to garner support for him amongst African Americans as well as white evangelicals.

High-ranking Republicans, including former Senate Majority Leader Bill Frist and former House Majority Leader Tom DeLay, spoke live or via video at each of the first two *JS* events. They were joined by well-known conservative preachers and activists, like the late Jerry Falwell, Phyllis Schafly, and Rev. Ted Haggard—who later lost his leadership position in the movement after a scandal involving a gay male prostitute. Held at majority White churches in the mid-South, the bedrock of Christian Right and Republican support, the first two events were attended by few people of color. Only one Black speaker, Bishop Harry Jackson, addressed the crowd during *JSII*. In contrast, *JSIII* was held in a black majority church in the midst of an urban Democratic stronghold: Philadelphia, Pennsylvania.

The Reverend Herbert H. Lusk II, described in the *New York Times* as a "maverick black minister" for his entrepreneurial drive and close connections to the Bush White House, hosted *Justice Sunday III* at his Greater Exodus Baptist Church in Philadelphia.[31] Rev. Lusk had spoken at the 2004 Republican National Convention and considered himself a good friend of George W. Bush. Many Black politicians and clergy criticized Lusk as an opportunistic sell-out, and pointed to the fact that Lusk's church was one of a very small number of black churches to receive any money from Bush's Faith Based Initiatives office. That the sum was rather large: Lusk's church received over $1million by some estimates.[32] For his part, though, Lusk told reporters that he decided to host the event because "this is what Jesus would have me to do as a pastor. I'm not following the dictates of Bush, Falwell, or Tony (Perkins). . . . I'm following the dictates of my Lord."[33] He justified his association the event by explaining that he believed the Bible spoke directly to issues of "same-sex marriage, abortion, you can go down the line," and that as a pastor, he had an obligation to address these issues.[34]

Again, the press was intrigued by the latest Republican outreach to black churches, and covered other black clergymen's responses to the controversial event. Thus, for example, Rev. Robert P. Shine, Sr., told reporters that he feared that viewers of *JSIII* would come away believing that black

Figure 2.1. Photo of President George W. Bush and Rev. Herbert Lusk.
© TIM SHAFFER/Reuters/Corbis. Courtesy of Corbis Images.

clergy in general were backing Judge Alito's nomination, even though "nothing could be further from the truth."[35] Rather, Shine said, Lusk was only "hosting this Justice Sunday by virtues of a personal relationship with the president and some financial support of his organization by the administration under the guise of faith-based initiatives."[36] As this quotation and many others from secular and religious black leaders indicate, many feared that Republican strategists were using Lusk's church to confuse and divide black voters.

Like the first two *Justice Sundays*, the third showcased well-known white leaders of the Christian Right and Republican Party, including some with dubious records in terms of race and civil rights. Amongst the featured speakers were the late Jerry Falwell (who once preached against desegregation in his ministry); Edwin Meese (who led the charge against affirmative action as Attorney General during the Reagan Administration); and FRC President Tony Perkins (who bought white supremacist David Duke's phone list of supporters for a U.S. Senate campaign). However, unlike the other two mega-church events, *JSIII* featured three black speakers: Dr. Alveda King, niece of Martin Luther King, Jr., and an ardent supporter of anti-abortion ministries; the Reverend Lusk; and Bishop Wellington Boone, a scion of the Promise Keepers (a men's ministry that urges its followers to reassert patriarchal leadership in the home) and the man who famously wrote, "I believe that slavery, and the understanding of it when you see it God's way, was redemptive" for African Americans.[37]

*Religion over Race: Post-Racial Repositioning
of Valid Politicized Identity*

The Reverend Herbert Lusk welcomed *JSIII* television viewers and radio listeners of all colors into his church on January 8, 2006, as the Bush administration fueled up for a fight over Supreme Court nominee Samuel Alito. At the beginning of the broadcast, the camera swept over the crowd at his church, revealing that most seats were occupied by African Americans, along with a sprinkling of white people. Then, Tony Perkins of the FRC took the microphone to address the media audience, noting that Christian broadcasters and Internet sites such as Sky Angel and the Christian Television Network were bringing the program to people across the country. The list of media outlets suggested that hundreds of thousands were listening on the radio or watching via cable or satellite.

Lusk's welcome to the media crowd indicated that not only had media vastly multiplied the congregants in attendance, but also that this was a rare *interracial* gathering of Christian conservatives. Lusk explicitly thematized race as he welcomed the audiences within and outside of the church:

Welcome to you all . . . those of you who are watching from far and distant places, those of you down South, the Midlands, all over the world. I
want you to know, I am your brother. [Applause from audience] . . .

Some of you, perhaps this is the first time you've had a chance to
enter into an African American congregation. I want you to know we
have many things in common. We love Jesus. We love the Lord. We love
life! We love liberty! I am your brother—I'm just from another mother.
[More applause and some laughter][38]

In effect, Lusk both emphasized the perceived racial differences
between the in-church audience (black), the usual audiences courted
by the groups who organized the *Justice Sunday* series (white), and the
media audience (multiracial), and asserted Christianity facilitates a
bond (even if one is "from another mother") that can supervene over
racial difference and the racial past. Noting that shared religious and
moral values make these different audiences fundamentally the same
(We love life! We love Jesus!). Lusk performed their post-racial broth-
erhood in Christ by physically embracing each of the white speakers
he introduced as they stepped up to the podium. Thus, he assured the
audience that they, too, would be able to embrace each together to pro-
tect their shared Christian values from liberal excesses. Lusk's invitation
to the audience to enter a black-majority church suggests that the moral
imperatives of Christian teaching allow us to transcend and aban-
don racial politics and racial identity. This idea was further reinforced
through another portion of the broadcast, a videotaped meditation on
the Liberty Bell that rewrote black freedom movements as being primarily concerned with religious liberty rather than with civil rights.

In the rhetoric favored by many politically active right-wing evangelicals, including then-President Bush, democracy is the most perfect
form of liberty, and thus God wants us to all be living in democracies—
so long as they are democracies guided by Christian theology.[39] Tony
Perkins's narration encouraged viewers to reinterpret the symbol as
follows:

Behind me is a building that houses the Liberty Bell. . . . It has become an
important symbol of our freedom. In the 1840s, the Liberty Bell became
a symbol of the anti-slavery movement [because of the inscription from]

Leviticus 25:10. Today, to quote scripture is not politically correct but it is historically correct. Atheist groups have made great progress in their efforts to eradicate all public displays of our religious history.

Perkins's framing of the biblical inscription on the Liberty Bell and its link to the anti-slavery movement asserts that our nation is based primarily on Christian principles, and that black freedom fighters, such as Frederick Douglass and Martin Luther King—both of whom were pictured in the video as Perkins spoke—were really working towards making our union more perfect in religious or spiritual terms, not in terms of racial justice. Like the commercials and billboards discussed earlier, these appeals to religion make a spurious connection between the philosophies and practices of anti-racist activists like Douglass and King and the contemporary conservative Christian movement. Their appropriation of the history and symbolism of black civil rights leaders is based on a retelling of history full of gaping holes and omissions. Not only is the Republican embrace of segregationist Democrats who switched parties (the "Southern Strategy") completely omitted, so too are the words and deeds of Reagan-era officials, such as former Attorney General Edwin Meese (a *Justice Sunday I* participant), whose goals were to end affirmative action and eviscerate the Voting Rights Act. The ugly race-baiting political ads, defenses of police brutality, promotion of unequal sentencing laws and racial profiling, as well as a regular spate of racial gaffes—all were left out of this glowing story of steadfast Christian fellowship with African Americans.

This post-racial selective memory was embodied in the presence and words of the next African American speaker who came to the podium, Alveda King. The announcer reminded the audience that she is a niece of Dr. Martin Luther King, Jr. Her family ties to the nation's most famous civil rights icon and her down-home preachy rhetorical style made her a perfect fit for *JSIII*'s attempt to articulate black religious culture with conservative politics. She began her time by singing what she referred to as "an old Negro spiritual" about freedom. Afterwards, she told the congregation:

Today in our nation we enjoy the expression of religious freedom. We also celebrate the 50th anniversary of Mrs. Rosa parks and the civil rights exodus. Liberty is a precious light we must preserve. When truth cannot be absolutely proclaimed, the lives of all people including the lives of the unborn are caught up in the battle of religious freedom before us . . .

She then invited the gathering "to share in the faith of my uncle, Dr. Martin Luther King, Jr." This faith, she said, convinced him that

> "If we are to go forward, we must go back and rediscover these precious values that all reality hinges on moral foundations." That's Dr. Martin Luther King's words, but we can affirm those words here in America right now. I want to close with one of the prayers of my father. He prayed this prayer during his lifetime. Almighty God, who is the light, the truth, the way, we come at this hour. . . . Have mercy we pray and bless our lives and this nation in which we live. Bless our rulers tonight. Make them mindful of the responsibility they have this night. Bless our nation, Lord, in Jesus' name we pray, amen!

In her speech, Ms. King excerpted selectively from her uncle's words to argue that Martin Luther King would have agreed that Christian values are under siege by the liberal judiciary (and liberal media) in the twenty-first century. Her words garnered thunderous applause from the crowd as she accused liberals of pushing God—and by extension, trying to push all good Christians—out of the public sphere. As Bill Donohue of the Catholic League told a nearly all-white, Southern Baptist audience a few months earlier at *Justice Sunday II*, "Now we're in the back of the bus."[40] The idea that contemporary evangelical Christians face a level of oppression similar to that of African Americans in the 1950s was further reinforced when Alveda King led the congregation in singing "We Shall Overcome." As she encouraged the other featured speakers to join her, the camera showed the white and black men stand up, awkwardly holding hands as they mouthed the words to the song.

When Reverend Lusk returned to the stage, he again took the opportunity make explicit references to racial differences; but here he lashed out the African Americans who had criticized him for hosting the event, further asserting Christian identity as a more legitimate foundation for political ideology and action.

I've been called a sellout. I've been called an Uncle Tom, and the *New York Times* called me a maverick to the black church. Well my friends, I just want the *Times* to note that, if a maverick can be defined as one who is pro-life, then I'm a maverick. [Applause] . . .

Fifty-five of the original signers of our Constitution were all men of God. But the foundation is being tampered with. . . . From the time in 1963 until 1999, over 18 million African American babies alone have been aborted. They say I don't speak for black people. Well, I may not speak for all black people, but there are some black folk that I speak for! [Applause] . . . We are against the redefinition of marriage, we are against partial abortion and we are against Christian bashing! . . . There is discrimination against the people of God . . .

In this rousing speech, Lusk used recognizable cadences of black spirituals. He also conveyed the main talking points in the conservative playbook: Liberal whites and Democratic-affiliated blacks have become rigid, politically correct arbiters of racial loyalty and demand lock-step agreement with the party line. By insisting on the separation of church and state, he argues, liberals are not following the Founding Fathers' prescription for religious freedom. And, of course, by supporting a woman's right to choose, they are not protecting women. Rather, liberals are oppressing all Christians—including black Christians. Indeed, with his references to abortions, he implies what is made explicit in anti-choice billboards plastered in inner cities today: Pro-choice advocates are enacting genocide on black people. As anti-abortion activists cast themselves as saviors of the black nation, they also take a page out of the playbook of conservative black nationalists who argue that white feminists are racists who seek to neuter black men and convert black women into traitors.[41] Later, Rev. Boone followed suit, racializing women's reproductive rights to describe why black Christians should reject liberals and Democrats:

You can't tell me that abortion and this matter is a white man's issue. It is an issue of black people aborting at a rate like nobody else. Black people have to stand up and pray. . . .

Judge Alito will turn back the hand of civil rights 100 years? Don't spit in my face and call it rain! That's the same old stuff they've been saying for years.

Like Lusk and Alveda King, Boon, spoke in the oft-imitated cadences of black preachers. He also alluded to intraracial debates over Republican policies and judicial appointments, and decried Democrats' opposition to Alito as insulting nonsense. However, none of these black speakers, let alone the white speakers, mentioned any major civil rights accomplishments or efforts. Other than references to anti-slavery movements, none of the speakers spoke to the substance of the rights Alveda King's uncle fought and died for in the 1960s. Nor did any of the speakers address issues that are central to contemporary black politics: voting rights, equal opportunity employment, equal education, freedom to live in any neighborhood, freedom to avoid police harassment. Rather, the only freedom described is the freedom to impose conservative Christian morality on the rest of the public.

In various ways, some of these "freedoms" do, of course, impinge on—or deny—the freedoms of others. Thus, for example, while gay marriage was a consistent talking point for *Justice Sunday* and was presented as an attack on Christianity, as many progressive activists have pointed out, restricting marital rights to heterosexuals on the basis of religious principles is discrimination, and sets up unequal status for gay and lesbian couples. Rather than defending liberty, then, many of the freedoms speakers articulated can just as easily be described as intolerance and bigotry.

Viewer Responses to *Justice Sunday III*

Whether *JSIII* or other attempts to synchronize black Christian traditions and conservative policy imperatives is successful with black audiences is a key question. Black Christians harbor a diverse set of political and theological views, and many are well aware and wary of the fact that many white churches endorsed slavery and Jim Crow segregation and that they continue to shun congregants of color.[42] Hence, it is logical to assume that many blacks would be skeptical of media overtures emanating from white Christian institutions that have historically excluded them not only from houses of worship, but also from definitions of humanity. Simultaneously, however, we must recognize that past and present black congregations share significant areas of belief with white congregations; even if they are met initially with wariness, the media appeals created by whites for black Christians may resonate with some subset of shared theology and worship practices.

This section of this chapter presents a focus-group study of religious African Americans who watched portions of the *JSIII* program. I assembled three focus groups in the late fall and early winter of 2006 at a large Midwestern university. Participants were recruited in three ways: (1) through an undergraduate research participant pool; (2) email invitations sent to African American–interest listservs, available to the public on campus; and (3) referrals from participants. Students who participated in the first group were asked to refer their African American friends to the study. Focus group size ranged from three to five participants. In all, eleven of the participants were women, four were men. Participants met in a conference room, and were provided with a light meal before and during the viewing of *JSIII*. Before the interview process began, I asked them to fill out and sign consent forms and to complete a voluntary demographic questionnaire. All participants gave consent to be audio recorded, and all of them agreed to fill out the demographic forms.

Participants ranged in age from eighteen to twenty-four. Most participants were undergraduates aged nineteen, and only three graduate students were part of the groups. Family income estimates for the participants ranged from below $29,000 and up to $99,000. Two of the graduate students reported being financially independent of their family, but the majority of participants reported family incomes of either $30,000–49,000 or $70,000–79,000. All of the participants identified as either black or African American. The majority of the participants practiced or came from a Christian faith household. Half (seven) of the participants identified as either Baptist or Pentecostal; one participant was Catholic; and two referred to themselves as "Christian" with no denominational specification. Three others considered themselves "non-denominational Christians," and one participant identified as Muslim. One student identified as atheist, and one as agnostic, but both wrote on the information forms that they had grown up attending Christian churches with their families, and still attended services when they returned home for family affairs. Both of these students also characterized themselves as "spiritual" people who were not interested in "organized religion."

After eating a meal and filling out the forms, the groups watched a thirty-minute segment of *Justice Sunday III*, which included speeches by Rev. Lusk, Tony Perkins, Senator Rick Santorum, and Dr. Alveda King. To conduct the focus groups, I aimed for a flexible style of moderation to allow for changes in the protocol of questions. I began the interview with "ice-breaker" questions (getting everyone's name, favorite food or television show) and then proceeded to ask the participants whether they had heard of, seen, or listened to *JSIII* previously, and then asked their opinions of each of the four speakers featured at the pulpit. As the discussion continued, I asked questions about whether the participants thought it was a good idea for politicians to talk about religion or if they thought most Americans agreed with the principle of separation of church and state. Each of the questions in the protocol was open-ended, and I was able to get through all the questions in each session. In a the first session, the participants' answers prompted questions that had not been included in the protocol, and in subsequent sessions I added those questions in to the conversation.

Once I finished asking all of my questions, I turned off the audio recording equipment, thanked the participants, and invited them to ask any questions they might have about the study. Participants were also reminded that they could contact the Institutional Review Board if they had any concerns. I listened to the tapes immediately after the sessions, making notes. I then sent the tapes to be transcribed, and reread the transcripts for errors while listening to the original tapes. I edited the transcripts, substituting pseudonyms for the participants as I corrected transcriber errors.

Responses from the Audience: Mixed Feelings about
White Republican Speakers' Sincerity

The focus group participants had very different reactions to the black and white speakers. Nearly all of the participants expressed some skepticism about the presence, motives, and rhetoric of the two white speakers, Senator Santorum and Tony Perkins. Most also remarked that each used speaking styles that did not resonate with traditional black church audiences or addressed topics that didn't belong in a church. Santorum especially was singled out as a wooden speaker who wasn't really talking about religion at all, but rather pushing a particular political agenda regarding the Supreme Court. Perkins, on the other hand, was viewed as trying to make a connection with black congregants, but was still suspect due to his political affiliations.

> RODNEY: And in regards to the other speakers, I felt the senator, he spoke well, but that's kind of expected considering he's a senator and he has to speak all the time. His, I don't think he connected to the audience as much on a personal level, like Tony Perkins and the other two.

Another participant was much more blunt in her disapproval of Santorum:

> BEATRICE: My initial reaction to the movie was, to be quite frank, disgust. And particularly when I saw that Rick Santorum was the speaker and it was associated with justice and freedom and liberty, I just find that to be completely, like complete hypocrisy, to associate him with any of that. I think that he is a very hateful person, and, especially when it comes to homosexuality and things like that, and I just thought that all these people were contradictory . . . to like, seeing them, as far as the 1st two speakers go, I didn't really have an opinion, I mean I didn't expect anything really enlightening from what they had to say. I wasn't surprised as far as anything they had to say, as far as the religious thing goes.

Other speakers weren't as affronted by his politics, but agreed that Santorum seemed out of touch.

> ALLISON: Yes, the way he was speaking just seemed . . . he wasn't really fluid with his speech, and he looked down every time he went to say something. And his hand gestures seemed kind of robotic. Those were my 1st impressions.

At the start of our conversations, some of the participants were confused by the event's organization and premise. They weren't sure why this particular combination of religious and political messages was the focus of attention.

KATRINA: I thought it was very unclear when [Lusk] was speaking—it took him a very long time to make me understand what he was talking about. I felt on the edge like what? Towards the end when he introduced the next speaker, then you finally realize the connection between the name of the DVD and what he was talking about.

INTERVIEWER: So what made it clear? What was, in terms of when he introduced, I guess you were saying when he introduced Tony Perkins, what made it clear to you? What was kind of the crystallizing statement?

KATRINA: Just when he began talking about how we're getting away from God and things like that, but before I didn't know what he was talking about. It didn't sound related to religion or liberty or anything, it was just, seemed like a really long introduction of "we're brothers and sisters."

Participants again singled out Santorum as misplaced in this context because of the overt political agenda he laid out in his speech.

MICHAEL: Yeah, [Santorum] seemed like the one person that didn't really fit in with the rest of them because he was a senator, and because the stuff he was talking about, like the other people were talking about religion and he was more talking about senator—Judge—Alito, Judge Alito, or he would become judge later, but he was more talking about him than how, somehow, than all the values that we'd lost over time, back to America.

CHRISTOPHER: I would agree. He kind of lost me at some point, and it more so seemed like he was lobbying for the judge—

ALLISON: Seemed like that was his purpose, and that it was really rehearsed, like I know he had his speech prepared, but it wasn't as though he was there for the actual cause, it was definitely rehearsed, his speech.

The participants were not pleased in general at what they perceived as politicians just going through the motions at churches for political gain. They didn't see the white speakers as sincere in their attempt to connect with black congregants.

CHRISTOPHER: [Satorum] didn't sound really sincere about what he was talking about.

JANICE: Right it was rehearsed.

CHRISTOPHER: It was just like ok I'm going to prepare this speech and talk about this because this is what the event is for. But that's it.

ALLISON: I'm not surprised either. But I think it goes along the lines of you know, candidates and kissing babies. [Laughter from group] . . . I just think that it's more for his agenda than for others.

INTERVIEWER: When you say "more for his agenda than for others," how do you characterize his agenda?

ANDREW: Other agendas would be people who are not . . . white . . . Republican . . . and basically fit among his demographics. So those are the other agendas, but if you have issues that are within his agenda, that coincide with those others, then, you know, things like this would happen, and you have white people and black people who are celebrating Christianity, and you know, they'll go ahead and get those issues dealt with.

While participants could imagine white politicians and black worshippers having overlapping interests, there was disagreement amongst the participants as to whether *any* politician should use a church as a ground for campaigning. Some felt that public displays of religious belief by politicians were always part of a ploy to gain votes.

INTERVIEWER: So, Janice, you said you were sort of skeptical about the whole thing, so would you want your elected U.S. congressmen to show up at *Justice Sunday IV?*

JANICE: If that congressman or woman was there representing him or herself and not speaking from his or her position, then fine. But I don't think that politics should be involved with church. Separation of church and state.

MICHAEL: And I think that if it is, I don't think that they should come out here to get more votes or to get more support behind something they're doing, but you know, if they're heavily involved in a religious organization before they come to that position, then . . . [drifts off, shrugs]

INTERVIEWER: So because prior to being elected they were heavily involved, if they keep showing up at that church or that particular venue then that would be ok?

CHRISTOPHER: I wouldn't, I guess, have negative thoughts about it. But if just out of the blue they just show up, then . . . I don't know.

One participant brought up her own experiences with white candidates coming to her church for political support.

RENEE: Well, I know that during election time, I have been in churches where political figures have spoken before, and I didn't really like it. I know that they're just trying to get their vote out to as many people as possible, but I think just when you get ready to go to church on Sunday, it's not really, you're going there, it's something sacred; it's not really [that] you're trying to push the political. . . . I'm not sure if that was supposed to be like a service or was it an extra thing? If it was going to a picnic or some sort of luncheon thing that the church hosted, I can understand, but in my experience, when I've gone, it's been: you're going to Sunday service, and up pops a political figure.

INTERVIEW: What about you, Katrina? Would you like to see one of your congressional representatives show up at this?

KATRINA: I think it would depend on the person who is running for a particular party and how they present themselves, not at just one moment during the race, but I've noticed that there are some political leaders or people wishing to get in political situations, who automatically come from a certain religious background, and who use those ethics, and those morals, and those beliefs as part of, they want to use them as part of their political campaign because that's essentially what they believe in, and they're thinking that's how they want to establish that certain political leadership role, and I think it's different when you have a person in a certain political position who just, who doesn't necessarily establish first-off that that's the way they're supporting their views. That's different from a political person who right from the beginning states that this is the way I'm approaching things: I'm using the church, I'm using my beliefs, I'm using my morals as something that's going to support me . . .

Another group member questioned whether white politicians were trying to "side-step" race by using religion.

BEATRICE: I feel like that when it comes to issues, especially when it comes to religion, in order to get certain measures passed. . . . Okay, I'm not saying people are racist. I'm just saying whatever personal prejudices they have, they seem to put them aside when it comes to something they believe in. I feel like religion especially allows for people to kind of side-step the whole race issue.

Thus, the white speakers at *JSIII* might still have issues with race, but the participants believed they were able to bracket them in order to garner support for Alito.

Another focus group member agreed, following up with this summation of Santorum and Perkins's agenda:

ALLISON: It's kind of like a planned out thing to get certain votes, to get certain people to go along with what you want, but I agree that there are certain things that people won't pass. They will go out and break down barriers of race so that [the task] gets done, but in other settings, it might not be the same.

Christian Identity and Political Values

Two participants were concerned about the assumptions outsiders seem to have about what it means to be a Christian. They expressed strong beliefs that stereotypes about the Christian Right are mapped onto anyone who is a publicly avowed Christian. As Violet argued, there is much more diversity within the religion, politically and spiritually, than those stereotypes allow.

VIOLET: Well just a quick comment. The Christian vote for me is not necessarily the conservative vote, and that's a distinction that I'd like to make, because that's another stereotype, that the Christian vote is always the conservative vote. In some *states* that's true, but not generally speaking.

She and another member of this focus group argued that they are not swayed by mere proclamations of politicians who claim Christian faith.

Rather, what they want is confirmation that the politicians' political decisions will be in line with Christian doctrine as they understand it. Violet added:

VIOLET: Secondly, if a politician is in a forum—a religious forum—and he's taking a stand on religion, I'd rather know up front those are his beliefs rather than say 2 or 3 months down the line—a lot of people say, "I'm a Christian, this or that." I'd rather know up front what their intentions are, what they are supporting, and how they're planning on going on about doing that. And as far as quoting the Bible or anything like that, I feel the same way. If you want to quote the Bible, that's just another source. If you want to quote Gandhi, quote Gandhi—I won't ask you, "Why you reading Gandhi every day?"

Later, Katrina said:

KATRINA: A lot of people who claim to be Christians—they don't even hold the same beliefs. I could be—one person right here could say they were Christian, and be totally different from me—because a lot of people like to pick and choose: "It's wrong to murder, it's wrong to steal, but I want to have this abortion." You know, and you can't do that. You have to just choose wholly. If you say you want to be a Christian, then you have to believe everything. You can't just pick and choose what you think is right, and the rest of the stuff, you ignore it, so if someone comes against it, you defend it. So I think that's the way I think [Christian politicians] lose a lot of votes, because the audience [of Christians] that they're capturing, whose attention they want, will be very, very small.

INTERVIEW: Allison, what is your call?

ALLISON: If I was to hear a politician, quote the Bible, uh . . . I think—I would hope that that stereotype—of everyone being under the same umbrella of Christianity—I would hope that they would not be under that umbrella where everyone is anti-this, or pro-this, anti-that. . . . If I were to hear that, that's what I would hope for. Another thing that I would think, I would think that it's good that they're quoting something that has really good meanings for morality. And I would hope that they would know about other religions that have good or the same morality. I would assume that they would know that many other religions have the same mode of thinking about things, and I would just hope that they would show respect to other religions.

In their discussion of Christianity, morality, and politics, the participants varied in their belief that religion should be part of politics. What they all seemed to hope for, though, was transparency and consistency from politicians who made public statements about religion. They perceived many politicians—including Rick Santorum—as using religion as a tool to gain voter support. They were also concerned about the ways in which the label "Christian" seemed tied to a narrow stereotype of beliefs and practices. But interestingly, these concerns weren't part of the discussion when we talked about the black speakers.

Reactions to Black Speakers: Ambivalence, Suspicion, and Admiration

Compared to their skepticism about Santorum and Perkins, participants were more ambivalent about the black speakers, Rev. Lusk and Dr. Alveda King. While many agreed that they found King's address passionate and more fitting for a church environment, some were troubled by her use of her family ties to Dr. Martin Luther King, Jr. Likewise, some viewed Lusk as welcoming, but others felt that he was "selling out" his church and trying too hard to embrace white viewers. The following exchange between Renee and Katrina illustrates the mixed feelings about these speakers.

RENEE: For the woman, Alveda King, it seemed like she based a lot of her credibility on her father and on her grandfather when she was speaking. . . .

KATRINA: Alveda King . . . , she was political in that she touched on Martin Luther King and how he addressed [faith] and the words that came out of his mouth, but I'm not sure. It wasn't as formal as Tony Perkins and his address to the crowd. . . .

RENEE: I got kind of a negative aspect from the—Herbert Lusk. I felt kind of, I feel he's sort of selling this church out to these senators and to the media. He was kind of manipulating his church where he was using it as more of a political aspect rather than you know preaching the word of God and trying to do that aspect. I felt like he was trying to work in the political aspect . . . [I think] there should be a separation between church and state. . . . And Alveda King, I felt like, with all the singing and the continuous references to Martin Luther King and her father . . . I felt like she was trying too hard to stress that these are the people I'm related to. I felt like she wasn't using her own credibility and her own voice—more so trying to rely on others and their accomplishments to prove her point

I asked the participants what they thought of Lusk's welcome at the beginning of the program, since it was one of the few moments that racial identity was explicitly mentioned.

INTERVIEWER: What did you think about the Reverend Herbert Lusk—he was the person who opened up the program, who said "I am your brother" and such things. It was his church. What did you think about him?

JANICE: Pretty typical pastor.

INTERVIEWER: "Pretty typical pastor?" Why was he typical?

JANICE: I mean not typical of my church that I'm familiar with, but he has the suit and the voice and the catchy phrases, just things that I hear people describe about their churches.

INTERVIEWER: About what kind of churches?

JANICE: I would say black churches in general.

INTERVIEWER: What did you all think of that "We're all brothers but maybe from a different mother" comment? What do you think [Lusk] meant by that?

KATRINA: I don't think it made sense because normally in a religious setting, in a church setting, if I hear "we are brothers," I automatically think about like, Adam and Eve, but if he says "from a different mother"—I don't know, that kind of threw it off. But maybe he just meant all brothers because they're all related in the body of the church, but that's all I got from it.

BEATRICE: I mean, it made a lot of sense to me because before he was talking about brother from another mother, he was saying well maybe this is your first time in a black congregation. So I felt like he was just trying to bridge that gap and say even though we're from a different ethnicity, we have the same beliefs and common interests, and in that way we're brothers and sisters.

Janice and others picked up on the traditional cadences of black church vocals, and suggested there was something stereotypical about Lusk's performance. But others found his style attractive.

CHRISTOPHER: I guess to me he seemed very welcoming, happy, friendly— kind of similar, same things that she mentioned as well.

ALLISON: And excited that, you know, we were . . . people were coming together for such a good cause.

CHRISTOPHER: And not only just African Americans, but people from all different backgrounds, because he mentioned you know I'm your brother, but we're just from different mothers [laughter from other participants], so, showing I guess, that he embraced not only African Americans, but other races as well.

Since so many of the participants critiqued Santorum's delivery, I asked them follow-up questions to make sure I understood what they meant in terms of the style or styles they would expect in a black majority church.

INTERVIEWER: Now you say that [Senator Santorum] sounded rehearsed, but everyone who was speaking—except for, I think, Reverend Lusk—had notes and you saw, I noticed them looking down at their notes. So what is it about Rick Santorum that seemed more rehearsed than Dr. Alveda King?

CHRISTOPHER: She was more passionate about what she was talking about, like . . . I don't know, she just seemed more passionate than he did about what he was saying . . .

INTERVIEWER: So would you all agree with that assessment: he wasn't really talking about religion in the way that Dr. Alveda King was?

CHRISTOPHER: She was more open with expression I guess, her expression of her spirituality or whatever, because not once did I remember him saying "hallelujah" or "thank you, Jesus" or anything like that, but she was more open to expressing that.

The participants read from the program racial/cultural cues associated with the black church and its civil rights history. As their responses suggest, there were some appealing elements within the *JSIII* program, particularly the presence and style of Alveda King and portions of Rev. Lusk's presentation. Overall, however, they were not impressed by the overtures of the white speakers.

Inroads in the Black Church, or Post-Racial Symbolism for White Voters?

Specialty media such as *JSIII* represent part of a post-racial project that attempts to shift the locus of identity politics from one of identification with a broadly defined, phenotypically visible racial group, to a politics of belonging to a specific religious community. This post-racial strategy may really be for the benefit of white voters, for it provides them with a post-racial means of imagining solidarity with black people. The religion-not-race position provides a means for Republican-leaning white voters to distance themselves from the racist reputation of the party without having to think about the desires of many African Americans to address racial inequality, let alone confront questions of white privilege. As the next chapters demonstrate, the post-racial amnesia that facilitates the idea that religious fellowship will provide a shortcut to racial harmony also encourages the notion that family ties or a single election cycle could profoundly transform race relations without revisiting the past.

3

The Post-Racial Family

Parenthood and the Politics of Interracial Relationships on TV

Network entertainment television has served as one barometer of racial inclusion and sentiment.[1] Although the networks have certainly been conservative in terms of the pace of racial integration—both in front of and behind the cameras—television producers' responses to the challenges of representing diversity provide us with an interesting gauge of what influential, creative people in media think Americans want—or are ready for—in terms of entertainment. For the greater part of this history, this readiness has been translated according to what television executives and creative personnel believe advertisers and white audiences will accept.

In the twentieth century, certain racial inclusion landmarks and landmines became iconic. Nearly all involve African Americans, in a reflection of how dominant television continues to focus on the black/white binary to the exclusion of more representations of Asian Americans, Native Americans, and Latinas/os. Early on, in 1951, the attempt to move *Amos 'n' Andy* from radio to television signaled that the emerging civil rights movement had already changed the calculus of black inclusion in mainstream media: Opposition to that show emerged before the first episode aired.[2] This opposition didn't lead to different approaches to black inclusion, however; rather, it led to continued exclusion.[3] Later, in 1956, when NBC took a chance on a show featuring one of the most popular black entertainers of the day, opposition to Nat King Cole's variety program by advertisers who feared the show would enrage southern affiliates was intense. The assumption that white audiences and consumers weren't "ready" for black representations continued to shape network decisions into the 1960s and 1970s. But as Herman Gray, Robin Means Coleman, and others have documented, the changing racial landscape off-screen finally led to some changes on-screen. Some of the most memorable actors, shows, and characters of the 1960s, 1970s, and 1980s were products of attempts to bring black and brown people on screen: Bill Cosby was suave on *I Spy*; the Lear sitcoms brought us Archie Bunker and the Jeffersons; urban dramas like *Hill Street Blues* and its imitators wove stories of black and white cops, lawyers, and doctors into the mix; and, last but not least, Bill Cosby's triumphant return to TV in the 1980s with *The Cosby Show* made almost everyone feel that they knew a middle-class black family.[4]

Indeed, as some have conjectured, the explosion of black faces on television in the 1970s and 1980s laid the groundwork for whites to feel more comfortable with black people in the workplace, in schools, and in neighborhoods. As *Seattle Times* columnist Jerry Large wrote after the 2008 election, "young voters . . . have seen so many black presidents on TV they don't blink at the idea."[5] Some studies suggest that this could, indeed, be the case: Positive parasocial interaction with television characters can influence perceptions of people in the real world, under certain conditions.[6] Not surprisingly, pundits and observers have compared the Obamas to the *Cosby Show's* Huxtable family and drawn the conclusion that shows like *Cosby* and other vicarious contact with interracial pop culture impacted the youth who voted for the president in overwhelming numbers.[7]

However, post-racial change doesn't simply arise from getting television audiences to see a critical mass of black people on television. Organizations like the NAACP and the advocacy group Children NOW have tried to move away from counting the people of color on screens to thinking more deeply about how and in what contexts these representations occur. Certainly our culture has produced copious representations of African Americans, from minstrel shows to Hollywood's plantation fantasies (epitomized by *Gone With the Wind*). For decades, these inclusions fell within prescribed roles defined by racial hierarchy, thus reaffirming rather than challenging segregation and discrimination. If we are to move toward a post-racial era, we need to examine emerging methods of inclusion to gauge what kinds of messages about people of color are being used to signal racial enlightenment. When, for example, television producers use interracial families as vehicles for racial inclusion, we can't assume the visibility is unambiguously progressive.

The focus of this chapter is the first two seasons (2010–2011) of NBC's prime-time drama *Parenthood* and its representation of the character Jasmine Trussell, one of many mothers on the show. Analyzing how *Parenthood* "integrated" its main family via a troubled inclusion of a black woman and her biracial child, I explore how the inclusion of this black mother to make an interracial family simultaneously amplifies post-feminist and post-racial sentiments and lays bare confusion and discomfort around contemporary race and gender roles. This discomfort emerges out of the invitation to viewers to compare parents—especially mothers—who appear on the show, as well as from the scripting of secrets and lies about sexual relations and parental status in the representation of the interracial couple.[8]

My analysis reaffirms the need to think about sexism and racism as interlocking systems—systems that are sometimes hard to pin down, but that do manifest themselves in our culture and politics. Specifically for this chapter, I attend to the intersections of race, class, and gender in representations of families on television. Here, I examine how "post-racial" and "post-feminist" discourses and sensibilities that have been prominent in the political sphere—see Mitt Romney's joke that he'd do better with poor voters if he was "part Mexican," and the NRA's argument that to stop domestic violence, women should choose to own guns[9]—have influenced a popular representation of family on TV. In particular, post-feminist and post-racial framing of the family deploys strategic depictions of "choices" made by women who are mothers.

To begin, I compare two iterations of *Parenthood*—the original 1989 film and its 2010–2011 TV reincarnation—to illuminate how templates for racial inclusion formed in the 1980s continue to haunt dramatization of interracial family contact and composition in the twenty first century. Then, I discuss the ways in which interracial couples and families have been used to symbolize a post-racial America. Following the work of other critical race and media scholars, I argue that interracial couples and children are key figures in post-racial aesthetics, serving as shorthand for social and interpersonal progress and enlightenment about race. But before delving into the movie, the TV show, and the show's main characters, I will briefly revisit definitions of post-feminism and post-racialism.

Post-Feminism and Post-Racialism, Reexamined

Many scholars have taken on the topic and the trouble of post-feminism. For Mary Vavrus, from' whom I borrow, the most prevalent form of post-feminism found in mainstream media is a "depoliticizing ideology whose claims include that feminism is unnecessary now that women have ascended to high-status . . . jobs and are protected from sex discrimination due to various laws. . . . If women fail to succeed under these conditions, they have only themselves to blame."[10] Post-feminism thus frames women's childbearing and work choices within a neoliberal "individualizing and privatizing rhetoric about social activities (like mothering) and neglect of social programs designed to ease the difficulties of family care."[11] Moreover, this overlapping of neoliberal and post-feminist discourses reinforces and normalizes traditional gender roles in parenting. Characteristic of dominant post-feminist rhetoric is neglect of how institutions, power, race, class, or sexuality still operate to limit the choices of many women,' particularly working-class women and women of color.

Recent revival of the so-called "Mommy Wars" reflects post-feminism's insistence on scrutinizing individual women's choices—with a myopic focus on upper-middle-class women's lives. Susan Douglas and Meredith Michaels skewer the wars in *The Mommy Myth*, where they illustrate how media continue to render harsh judgment on women and girls no matter what choices they do or don't make about sex, parenthood, education, and work. Likewise, philosopher Amy Allen dissects the faulty logic of the media's post-feminist critiques of mothering while framing the struggle as "motherhood versus feminism" rather than as a conflict over the meanings of feminism and the lack of social and structural support for all parents.[12]

As noted in the introduction to this book, the notion of post-racialism can be used by some as a multicultural upgrade for colorblindness and by others to suggest that demographic changes will usher in racial harmony. Eric Watts's consideration of the term reveals why disquiet and disagreement continue to vex our discussions of what race means now that we (mostly) agree that it is a social construction. That is, while race is socially constructed, we experience racial tropes and embody them through "values that are sensually learned and known."[13] Yet, as Watts notes, "post-" suggests a break with the past and creates a gap: A break can separate one from home, from comfort; a break can provide release or relief. In this break one may feel the euphoria of the new or the horror of the unknown. The break can be liberating for those who were oppressed in the old days, and a wound for those who formerly wielded unquestioned power and status. The signs at Tea Party rallies declaring "give me my country back" are expressions of the anxiety in the break of the "post-." Thus, Watts concludes, the eruption of ugly "old-style" racism (for example, online depictions of Michelle and Barack Obama as Dinah and Sambo) reveals that white supremacy is not dead and gone: It is a zombie stalking the land.[14] Thus, one perspective on the post-racial is that it is an era of the "living dead": The racial ideologies and representational strategies that the "post-" declares to be dead and gone refuse to stay buried. They keep cropping up, like zombies, in expected and unexpected places, such as network television.

Drawing on Vavrus's and Watts's conceptualizations of these oft-twinned "post-s," I argue that post-feminist discourses and post-racially revamped stereotypes of black motherhood stalk and shape the character of Jasmine Trussell and infuse the storylines that involve her and her white paramour, Crosby Braverman, as they negotiate their romantic relationship and parenting responsibilities. From this perspective, we can discern how post-feminist understandings of women's choices merge with stereotypes of black unwed mothers that, like zombies, refuse to die and thereby foreclose other possibilities in the story, despite the show's attempt to portray a post-racial family via one of the concept's most popular representational forms: interracial couples and children.

Interracial Couples and Post-Racial Aesthetics

As discussed by many critical race and media scholars, pop culture's recent fascination with and employment of interracial figures and families has a long and varied history. Here, it is important to revisit and emphasize the contributions of scholars such as Mary Beltran, Camille Fojas, and Ralina Joseph to delineate how interracial couplings, and women of color in these pairings, function as post-racial signifiers.[15] Since the 1990s—and most famously in *Time* magazine's "Eve" cover— mainstream media have recirculated and promoted the idea that biological mixing will produce a future America where everyone is blended to some degree, and all exhibit some skin shade of light brown.[16] This intermixture, proponents of this theory claim, will eliminate racial difference by making us all mixed—and therefore all racially the same. By extension, this racial mixing will destroy racial hierarchy as well.

As I and others have argued elsewhere, this is magical thinking at best, for it relocates the responsibility and causality of political and economic inequality in the bodies—in the skin—of individuals rather than in the institutional and cultural practices that define and support the racial hierarchy in the first place.[17] Thus, this approach to "solving the race problem" centers on individual choices and emotions, relying on people's gradual willingness to intermingle, while suggesting that political and social policy has no place in the solution. One need only look to Brazil and other nations that celebrate "mixed" racial populations to see that even centuries of sanctioned multiracial identities can easily result in modes of racial stratification of a different kind.[18] Despite the obvious flaws in the fantasy of racial equality via inter-mating, Hollywood, mainstream news, and Madison Avenue have embraced the multiracial family as a symbol of post-racial progress. In films and TV shows, in ads and feature stores, we see multiracial individuals and families portrayed as proof that we're getting to a post-racial society. In car commercials, movies, and sitcoms, interracial couples and children have become vehicles for expressing to the audience that we have arrived, that the text or product in question is hip—still, perhaps, a bit edgy or exotic, but not threatening.

Yet, as Michele Elam elegantly demonstrates, pop culture representations of multiracial identity need not fall into these categories in her book *The Souls of Mixed Folk*.[19] Elam's investigation of recent novels, comics, and comedy routines that "critique the narrowing of mixed race discourses" to individualistic narratives of self-discovery or apolitical celebrations of the "millennial generation's" ability to blur boundaries shows that there are other choices when media producers aestheticize black-white relationships and biracial children.[20] Likewise, Bambi Haggins also explores some of the possibilities and pitfalls of post-racial entertainment in her analysis of Dave Chappelle's rapid rise on Comedy Central, with routines such as "The Racial Draft" satirizing the ways whites value and undervalue celebrities of color, and questioning the validity of essentialist ties between celebrities of color and their race-matched communities.[21] And, along comparable lines, Jonathan Rossing examines how Stephen Colbert's conservative alter-ego on the *Colbert Report* exposes and critiques the privileges of whiteness, developing a post-racial satirical style that confronts the audience by speaking the tacit understandings about racial politeness and expectations for multicultural tolerance.[22]

Many other television producers, it seems, aren't looking for more critical inclusions of multiracial folk. But they continue these inclusions for economic as well as aesthetic reasons. The world of niche and global marketing requires mainstream media to reconfigure previously all-white casting aesthetics to serve and court multicultural consumers.[23] Within this context, interracial families and individuals provide cost-effective, inoffensive means of representing difference. The increasingly successful careers of multiracial and mestizo/a actresses and actors, such as Rashida Jones, Jennifer Lopez, Halle Berry, Vin Diesel, and Dwayne "The Rock" Johnson, are further proof that producers see benefits in marketing racially ambiguous stars to "ethnic" and "mainstream" markets simultaneously. Moreover, with the entertainers also often portraying love interests or protectors of whites, their stories replicate and update some of the nineteenth- and twentieth-century narratives of interracial contact and conquest.

Jon Kraszewski demonstrates how MTV's desire to rebrand itself as friendly to conservatives and liberals alike led it to an increase in multiracial cast members after 2000. The show's producers saw these individuals as a means to secure white conservative viewers' loyalty to the channel. Fearing the 2000 elections and rising backlash against "liberal media" would scare conservatives from the show, producers shifted their emphasis from encouraging conflicts between conservative, rural, white cast members and black urban participants to bringing in biracial cast members to serve as "bridges" between the races and defuse conflicts.[24] This scripting borrows heavily from 1990s neoconservative framing of interracial families as a vehicle to racial harmony via a colorblindness engendered through the end of racial categorization. For instance, in the science fiction TV drama, *Battlestar Galactica* (2004–2009), Leilani Nishime analyzes how the interracial family—in this case, comprised of a white man, an Asian (and alien) woman, and a biracial child—serves the purpose of bridging cultures, but with a specific twist derived from stereotypes of Asian women.[25] Using alien-human conflict as an allegory for racial/national differences, the show portrays the Asian woman, Athena, as a Cylon (alien) who must prove her loyalty to the humans/whites after falling in love with Helo (a white human soldier) and bearing his hybrid child, Hera. In her analysis of the show, Nishime illustrates how Athena is treated much like Asian women in other dramas—she is understood primarily through her ability to seduce non-Asian men, to reproduce, and to perform punishing labor with no hope of reward. She is continually under suspicion and repeatedly abused, but in a model minority performance, she takes her punishment as a means to prove her loyalty and sever ties with her race, the Cylons.

Post-racial aesthetics are not limited to the inclusion of multiracial cast members or interracial families. Rather, it is also clear that demands for multicultural/racial inclusion have altered the casting expectations for secondary and background actors. One need only look at the roster of guest actors, extras, and recurring characters in NBC's long-running *Law & Order* franchise, ABC's hit *Grey's Anatomy* (2005–present), or its recently retired *Desperate Housewives* (2004–2012) to see that, in addition to a sprinkling of regular characters of color, people of color are in establishment shots, walking through the background, and so on. So while the main cast of shows like CBS's *How I Met Your Mother* (2005–present) or *Two and a Half Men* (2003–present) may be all white, when the cast ventures out into public spaces, people of color are nearly always in the frame, anchoring our sense of a post-racial world where we're all mixing it up.

Post-Racism + Post-Feminism = *Parenthood* 2010

Parenthood's televisual frame incorporates many elements mentioned in the research discussed above. Located in one of the ultimate liberal and multiracial cities—Berkeley, California—the show serves up a white male/black female pairing, replicating what prime time has served up for decades: Uhuru and Kirk had their space-age kiss in the 1960s on *Star Trek*; the *Jeffersons* lived in the same building as the Willis family in the 1970s and 1980s; *Dynasty* revealed a secret biracial sister born to a white corporate head and his black maid in the 1980s, while a Black male lawyer hid his romance with a white female attorney on *LA Law*; and *Girlfriends* and *Sex and the City* explored interracial dating in the 2000s. Heterosexual interracial couples have thus been a convenient device for integrating a cast and/or bringing racial controversy and difference to the small screen. In the post-racial imaginary, the interracial couple (with whom no one has a problem) serves to bridge the gap between the racial past (which forbade such unions) and the future (when this won't be an issue).

The problem is, we're not past it. There is still a significant minority willing to say in opinion polls that they disapprove of interracial marriage and would be upset if a family member married "outside the race."[26] News reports of the Louisiana judge who refused to marry an interracial couple because he feared for the fate of their future children were met with shock in 2009, but any glance at white supremacy websites (and some fraternity prankster pages) shows that women of color are constantly depicted as unsuitable, abominable partners and that desires for white purity persist. We have, obviously, broken with the past, in that the numbers of post-*Loving* interracial families grows larger, and (most) advertisers are not afraid to put interracial couples in their commercials. But as we try to imagine the post-racial future, zombie stereotypes and attitudes from the racial past continue to stalk and shape our cultural output, populating our imaginations with contradictory elements of representation and narration. In other words, post-racial aesthetics of network television often reveal the struggle in the attempt to make something new, to forge what it means to get past our racial past. In this gap between present and post-, *Parenthood* emerges as an illustration of the uncertainty of the "post-," with its dramatic devices leaving many gaps for old stereotypes to flow into the narrative and its characters constantly bumping into the glass walls and ceilings of post-racial, post-feminist America.

Parenthood 1.0: 1980s Hollywood and Integration via Racial Surprise

The TV series *Parenthood* was created by the star director/producer team of Ron Howard and Brian Grazer. The show, which airs on NBC, is an update of the movie Howard directed 1989, wherein Steve Martin led an all-white (save for one) cast. The movie chronicled the hopes and dreams of the Buckmans, a large family living in an affluent suburb of St. Louis. As the Buckman siblings and their spouses (all white, all heterosexual) navigated their dilemmas—how to balance work and family, how to discipline toddlers and teens—one adult son returned with a heretofore unknown child: Cool Buckman. The kicker? Cool was black. In the movie, then, racial difference was injected through a surprise plot turn: A prodigal son returns with a biracial black son in tow, without his black mother (who is never on screen and is described only as a "Las Vegas dancer"). This son eventually abandons Cool to be raised by his father (Cool's grandfather), a crotchety old white guy who embraces his biracial grandson as an opportunity to become the kind of loving, attentive parent he never was to his own sons.

The movie's plot mimics the characteristics of other popular texts of the 1980s that created "integrated" television through the unexpected insertion of African American characters. TV family sitcoms which employed the bodies of young black children deposited into otherwise all-white families to integrate the small screen included NBC's *Diff'rent Strokes* (1978–1986) and ABC's *Webster* (1983–1989), both of which were ratings successes. How do we account for the need for black children to be in all-white milieu? By way of the black parent(s) or potential black guardians being either dead or unfit, and certainly unseen and unneeded.[27]

In the arena of prime-time drama, miscegenation narratives of the early twentieth centuries had more of an obvious influence. *Dynasty*, the hit ABC soap (1981–1989), brought color on screen through the backdoor: Patriarch and oil baron Blake Carrington discovers that Dominique Devereux (played by Diahann Carroll) is his half-sister, born to the family's black maid and his father. Dominique also has a secret: She had a daughter with a white man, a daughter whose existence she kept secret from the man for twenty years. In this way, *Dynasty's* narrative updates early twentieth-century tragic mulatta narratives, wrenching angst and violent upheaval from the exposure of forbidden interracial sex. But unlike the protagonists in most tragic mulatto narratives—tragic because the mixed race individual must die to restore order for white society—*Dynasty's* biracial diva mixes it up in high society, entering the Carrington mansion on equal financial footing with an axe to grind with her half-brother. She and her daughter stick around for the long haul, albeit in less-than-central plotlines after the initial shock of their appearance on the family tree. Both the 1989 film and 2010 television versions of *Parenthood* contain elements of these troubling attempts to integrate representations of interracial families for mass audiences.

Parenthood 2.0: Post-Racial Twenty-First Century Berkeley

In their twenty-first century update of *Parenthood* for network TV, the writers and producers clearly chose to "break" with the original movie.[28] The show, steered by executive producer/showrunner Jason Katims, is also centered on a large family, the Bravermans. But the Braverman siblings are thirty- and forty-somethings (GenXers), and their parents, Zeek and Camille, are aging Boomers. All of them are white, and have white partners and children. Eldest son, Adam, is married to Kristina, a stay-at-home mom who is toying with re-entering the workplace, and they have a teen daughter and a younger son, Max, who has Asperger's Syndrome. Sarah, the eldest daughter, is divorced with two teens and moves back in with her parents. Youngest daughter, Julia, is a high-powered lawyer whose husband, Joel, stays at home with their young daughter. The youngest son, Crosby, is not married, but has a long-term girlfriend who is pushing him to marry her and begin a family. As these descriptions suggest, each sibling's family situation is "different" in terms of work, children, and spousal relationships. The show's storylines milk a lot of drama and plot points from these differences in family situations and the tensions they create between parents and kids, brothers and sisters, husbands and wives.

Rather than living in white-flight suburban St. Louis, Missouri, like the movie family, the TV Bravermans live in multicultural, liberal northern California: Berkeley is their hometown. In their workplaces, in the background, and in establishing shots, we see evidence of the racial and ethnic diversity of California as people of color fill in as extras and tertiary characters like teachers, baristas, and coworkers. Within the family, racial difference comes in the door through two characters linked to the youngest Braverman adult, Crosby. The only sibling who has never married, Crosby finds out in the pilot episode that an old flame, Jasmine, who is African American, gave birth to his son, Jabbar, five years earlier. In the movie, the family finds out immediately about the surprise biracial child when his father, the prodigal son, returns to the family home. In the TV version, Crosby learns of his biracial off-spring while isolated from his family and keeps his son's identity secret for a few episodes. This secretiveness builds dramatic tension around the question of how he will tell his family—and his white girlfriend. This is the first interracial secret used to drive the plot.

Clearly, the TV show is different, and, perhaps, better in many ways. By moving the show to twenty-first century Berkeley, California, and making a black woman a visible and involved mother to a white man's child, the show breaks with the casting and scripting of family dramas and sitcoms of the not-so-distant past. The location of Berkeley is meant to signal to the audience that we're in a different racial place, a liberal, multicultural city. And, unlike the movie, the TV version actually shows the black parent of the secret biracial son on screen. But the placement and treatment of this black woman and the biracial child are not as different as they seem at first glance. This is due in part to the writers' decision to make Jasmine and her son's presence dramatic and unexpected rather than an already-included element of the Braverman family's composition. Of course, one can defend this revision by saying it actually had the effect of creating continuity with the movie's original premises. However, why was it necessary to racially match the unknown son? Beyond that, why make this secret relationship the only biracial family tie? California is home to more interracial marriages and couples than most other states—in 2008, a Pew Center study found the state was third in the nation for interracial marriages. So why didn't the writers make one of the already married couples interracial? Rather than rendering the interracial family distinct—and surprising—why not signal that white-black (or, especially for California, white-Asian or Anglo-Latino) marriages were already all in the family? As the show develops the storylines around the Bravermans and their partners, the contrast between Jasmine and Crosby and the white parental pairs reveals how the decision to replicate the 1989 racial surprise plot encourages additional troubling choices for developing this interracial couple in a TV family.

Meet (and Compare) the Bravermans: Racial and Parenting Differences

Each episode of *Parenthood* moves the viewer from parent to parent, household to household, allowing us to compare the parenting styles, foibles, and lifestyles of each pair. Their coping styles, jobs, home décor, etc., is on display (and under discussion) for us to compare as we move from scene to scene.

Many things make Crosby and Jasmine stand out from the sibling crowd. Crosby is the only Braverman who has never been married. He is like many other thirty-something white male characters in popular media today: living as if he's in perpetual adolescence, with a girlfriend tapping her foot and watching the biological clock tick while he decides if he's ready for adulthood (which here = marriage and parenthood).[29] Crosby is hip and cute—he's a music producer who lives on a houseboat. When we first meet him, his girlfriend, Katie, who is white, gives him an ultimatum: begin a family life with her or she will use frozen donor sperm to strike out on her own to have a baby.

In the first episode, Crosby complains to his siblings about his "baby-crazy" girlfriend. He's uncertain about their relationship's prospects and whether he is ready for marriage and parenthood. Then, Crosby unexpectedly gets a call from an old flame named Jasmine. He describes her to his brother, Adam, as a potential "booty call," saying that Jasmine is "a dancer" who is "really flexible," and implying with his tone, gestures, and expression that their sexual activities were all the more exciting because of her ability to contort her body. However, when Crosby meets up with Jasmine, she has a small boy with her named Jabbar—and she introduces Crosby to Jabbar as his father. Crosby is visibly surprised, and the scene ends with the camera focused on his shocked face. Later, Jasmine explains that she had tried and tried to tell him, calling him on the phone again and again, but that he had never called back. This experience led her to believe that he was not interested in her anymore, and consequently, she figured he wouldn't be a responsible dad. So now he knows, and the audience knows—but no one else in the Braverman family knows for a while. After this initial meeting, Crosby is even more wary of parenting prospects, but is forced to reckon with fatherhood.

Thus, in the show's debut episode, the audience is introduced to all of the mothers in different contexts: as they ready their children for school; as they prepare for work inside or outside of their clearly upper-middle class homes; as they engage in conflict with reluctant kids who don't want to go to a new school, and so on. We see Crosby in conflict with Katie about whether they should marry and have a child. In the show's constant movement across couples and children, homes and workplaces, Jasmine and her "choices" stand out compared to the other mothers. She is the only mother who is *not* white; she is the only mother who has *not* raised her child with a known bio-father in the picture; she is the only mother who did *not* tell the father about his child for five years; she is the only mother who does *not* have a clearly defined home or set of responsibilities. She's the only one who has to confront the father of her child about his lack of interest in her after a night or two of sexual passion, five years earlier.

Revealing the Secret: A Secret Son with an
Unmentioned Racial Identity

Crosby first confesses about Jabbar only to Adam, and then debates whether or not to tell Katie. Indeed, he continues to keep knowledge of his son and Jasmine from everyone but his brother for two episodes—a situation that allows the writers to create a mix of comic and dramatic moments for each impending "reveal" to different members of his family, and to Katie. After Crosby tells his girlfriend the truth, she breaks up with him. After he tells his sister Julia, the lawyer, she advises him to get a paternity test to confirm whether he can be held responsible for Jabbar. When Crosby asks Jasmine to give him a sample of Jabbar's hair, she reacts with anger and hurt: How could he believe she would lie?

He then tells her he won't go forward, yet he akes Jabbar's toothbrush to have it tested for a DNA match, ostensibly without agreement from Jasmine. We are supposed to forgive this action, however, because in the subsequent episode, Crosby is so clearly happy that the test results confirm that Jabbar is his biological child. The fact that Jasmine is in the dark, and that no one seems to find his deception problematic, is the first sign of the latent "father's rights" discourse that rears its head sporadically throughout the show.

While Crosby goes through his journey of confirming and disclosing his fatherhood, viewers can learn a lot about his personality, his emerging relationship with Jabbar, and his communication style, but viewers rarely see Jabbar's mother, Jasmine. Indeed, in the first part of Season one, she is included mainly when she is dropping Jabbar by Crosby's home for father-son bonding or retrieving him from Crosby. When she speaks, she is often criticizing Crosby or expressing skepticism about his sincerity. She does have some reason to be distrustful: Crosby's judgment is questionable, and the writers show his foibles. For example, he takes Jabbar to a parent-child yoga class, but is hard pressed to follow the teacher's instructions because he is so distracted by the derriere of a woman in front of him. Flirting with this woman, he secures a play-date for Jabbar with her son, and then, while at her home, they steal away while the boys play in the pool, watched over by a private lifeguard. As Crosby and the woman begin foreplay, he has second thoughts about leaving Jabbar alone in the pool with strangers, and stops the encounter.

When Jasmine hears about the "pool party" from Jabbar, she is incensed and tells Crosby that she won't be leaving him alone with Jabbar for some time, since he left their child alone in a pool. The camera reveals that Crobsy is crushed by focusing on his expression and protests as Jasmine angrily cancels his next outing with Jabbar. In the first half of the season, this is what the audience can see of Jasmine—that she is warily observing Crosby, giving him the conditions for seeing Jabbar, setting the pace. The scripts don't provide scenes of her being a mother to Jabbar in the ways we see Kristina or Sarah parenting their children in multiple contexts. In contrast, there are tender scenes of Crosby telling jokes to Jabbar, explaining his houseboat, fishing, tossing the ball around, and generally being adorable.

In addition to not providing opportunities to see Jasmine as a parent, the show doesn't locate her spatially outside of Crosby's orbit. Although Jasmine has an apartment, the show doesn't visit its interior until after she and Crosby resume a sexual relationship. Although she has family in Oakland (a space that is coded blacker and poorer than Berkeley), we don't see members of that family until a moment of interracial confrontation late in the season. Thus, the show is set up so that viewers see Jasmine through Crosby's eyes, and she is very isolated from the rest of the characters, even from her own son—the only other person of color with any significant presence on the show—since he is mainly seen with Crosby. Thus, while the audience learns a lot about Crosby's siblings, white in-laws, nieces, and nephews, they learn little about Jasmine. She does not have conversations with other characters about her worries, her concerns, her hopes or dreams for her child. She doesn't have an anchored presence. Rather, she appears and disappears until her relationship with Crosby becomes romantic. This rekindled romance is initially a secret, providing an additional dramatic device to drive plot points.

Guess Who . . .

When Crosby finally tells more of his siblings about Jabbar and Jasmine, he declines to mention race. Within the logic of post-racial television casting, there is no need to mention that either Jabbar or his mother is a person of color—the audience saw it, right? So why talk about it? Race need not be thematized through dialogue, because we're "over it," and only if something very racist happens does racial difference need to be explicitly remarked upon. The first time their racial identity is signaled as different, and perhaps as a possible point of contention, is when Crosby finally tells his parents—in the fifth episode of the season. His father, Zeek, reacts to Jabbar's name with a question: "What kind of a name is that?" Later, when he meets his new grandson, his eyebrows noticeably lift as he sees the boy's skin for the first time. The second time racial difference is explicitly named occurs when Crosby and Jasmine go to a laundromat, and she suggests he needs to separate his white and colored clothes. Crosby responds by joking that it's clear he does not separate whites and coloreds, and jokingly accuses her of advocating segregation as he draws her into a kiss.

It is important to note that only white male characters ever explicitly bring racial difference into the narrative via behavior or speech. Zeek, the elder, has a more ambiguous, but perhaps expected response to having a biracial grandson. When the camera zooms in on Zeek taking in Jabbar's racial difference, perhaps audience members are meant to experience some relief that he doesn't make an issue of it—as other members of his generation might. That is, as a Baby Boomer who grew up through Jim Crow, Zeek could be more likely to have an issue with Jabbar's biracial identity. Crosby, on the other hand, enacts the role of the multicultural-friendly GenXer, who uses humor, musical taste, and dating choices to express his racial enlightenment. He is post-racial: He "gets it"; he makes jokes about race at the Laundromat; he dances to hip hop; he finds women of color attractive. So, he couldn't have had any racial reasons for blowing Jasmine off five years ago: He did it only because he was young and irresponsible. But all of this alleged comfort with race begs a few questions. If the Berkeley-bred Bravermans are so down with people of color, why did the writers deem it necessary to replicate the secret biracial child storyline of the movie and of previous TV shows? Again—why not have one (or more) of the already married pairs be an interracial pair? Why not have a white long-lost son and paramour, or an Asian American, or a Latina/o, either of which would fit the predominant race/class demographics of northern California, as well as the statistics on interracial coupling: White male/Asian female is the most likely interracial pairing in the United States.

More importantly, why wring out so many dramatic moments from disclosure of the secret? One answer is this: While interracial couples are more prevalent today, there is still tension around the issue of interracial marriage, and more importantly, around black-white socio-political relations. As exhibited in the 2008 election, our society continues to rediscover the ways in which many blacks and whites live and experience separate social and ideological realities, separate spaces, separate cultural touchstones. Another answer is that the show is set up from the vantage point of the white family members. Thus, the experience of racial difference is unidirectional: The story sticks to exploring how white people (the Bravermans) react to family situations, including how they are affected by Jasmine and Jabbar's arrival and potential inclusion into the white family.

Balancing the Blame: Jasmine's Choices and Shaming

So, if race wasn't an issue, and if Crosby is so obviously a good guy who just needed a push in the right direction to be a good dad, why didn't Jasmine try even harder to reunite with him five years ago? The writers and actors do a great job of making Crosby look like the ultimate hip dad. So, we need to have a reason for Jasmine's "choice" to keep Jabbar away from this guy. In the post-racial era, it can't be that she was worried that Crosby's neglect of her after they had sex was racially motivated. In the post-feminist era, it can't be *his* fault that he signaled he had no use for her after sex by not returning her calls. Rather, post-racial and post-feminist logics set us up for a reckoning from Jasmine. *Her* choices must be centered as the problem, the generator of the distance between father and son.

As discussed earlier, one of the major elements of post-racial political discourse positions people of color and misguided liberal whites as the real race-card sharks. Black people, especially, are apt to try to make innocent whites feel guilty about race. Likewise, post-feminism posits that women's choices and the feminist movement are to blame for any inequalities or unhappiness women may experience. Thus, while Crosby is at fault for being a jerk to Jasmine, post-racial logic often requires an assertion of white innocence, just as post-feminism displaces patriarchy and centers on (middle-class) women's alleged misuse of their freedoms to "have it all." Add it all up, and a dramatic showdown over the cause of Jabbar's fatherless first five years makes sense, in a post-racial, post-feminist way. Crosby can't be alone to blame for Jabbar's fatherlessness. And any surrogate father or father figures cannot be sufficient, because in post-feminist logic nuclear families are the best choice to make, and post-racial narratives continue to denigrate black extended families and single mothers. So Jasmine needs to share the blame. What rises from the (shallow) grave to make this all make sense is the old, multipurpose zombie of black matriarchy, the emasculating, family-killing power of the independent black mother.

Midway through the season, the writers script a racial confrontation when Crosby's white family finally meets Jasmine's black family. It is a first meeting for the audience as well: As mentioned earlier, up to this point Jasmine is never depicted with any other black relatives or community, only Jabbar. And, in this episode, the writers throw in a doozy of a plotline: On the eve of Jabbar's birthday, Jasmine reveals to Crosby that she lied to her family about him. She told her family that he knew about her pregnancy and refused to be part of Jabbar's life. Thus, she warns Crosby that her family will probably be cold to him, and she is worried that Jabbar's birthday party will be tense. Crosby is aghast, but understanding (he is such a great guy!). Nonetheless, he extracts a promise from Jasmine to come clean with her family after the party.

The party is filmed with Crosby—not Jabbar—at the center of the camera's attention. Even though Jasmine's extended family is ostensibly gathered to celebrate Jabbar's birthday, there is no sense of excitement or care for the boy. Everyone is sitting around, eating snacks with sullen looks on their faces, throwing cold glances at Crosby as he tries in vain to hand out refreshments and start conversations with his son's black relatives. The camera veers from one corner of the house (owned by Jasmine's mother, Renee) to the next, uncovering stony looks and unresponsive black bodies. The house is not well-lit, and it is clearly smaller and less stylish than any of the Braverman abodes, which are all light-filled and well-appointed with chic colors, art, and furniture. When Jasmine introduces Crosby to her mother, Renee only gives him a quick, tight smile and terse greeting before turning her back on him to take a favored black relative to the kitchen. The tension is palpable, and Crosby is visibly relieved when his family arrives.

When the Bravermans enter the house, the camera turns to Crosby who says, *sotto voce*, "Where'd all these white people come from?" This is the fourth moment when a white male cast member acknowledges a racial difference between Jabbar, Jasmine, and the Bravermans. It is followed by a set of shot of the Braverman clan members trying to engage, unsuccessfully, with Jasmine's relatives. The discomfort seems to have a potential end when the camera catches Crosby's mother, Camille, chat with Renee and her son, Sekou.

CAMILLE: Sekou. That's a beautiful name.
SEKOU: Thank you.
CAMILLE (TO RENEE): You must have named him after Sekou Turunga,[30] the African independence leader, I assume.

RENEE: Now, how did you know that?

CAMILLE: Berkeley in the '60s, babe.

RENEE (SMILING, EYEBROWS LIFTED): Well I hear that!

This détente is born of the good will (and liberal bona fides) of a white woman who reaches out and demonstrates she's not a racist—she's culturally aware of African independence movements thanks to her college-era activism and continued Bay Area residency. But Sekou doesn't let the moment last. He cuts in, turning to confront Crosby:

SEKOU: You know what? I'm sorry. This is weird. I know you're tryin' and all that stuff, but where have you been?

CROSBY: I wish I had been here.

SEKOU: Yeah, yeah, that's *your* loss.

CROSBY: No one knows that more than me. No, I'm just glad I get to be in [Jabbar's] life now and hopefully be a role model—

SEKOU: He has a role model, Crosby. I've been here since the day he was born.

JASMINE: Sekou!—

SEKOU: No, I'm just tellin' him how it was. I drove them to the hospital. I stood at the christening. Huh?! Look, I moved apartments just to be closer to him.

RENEE: I'm going to get the cake. Sekou, could you help me?

SEKOU: No, I'm tellin' him how it was—

ZEEK: I would like to say something if I may. [All the Bravermans are caught by the camera looking nervous about what their father is going to say.]

ZEEK: You seem to have a wonderful family. I've met you and I like you all. But why are you treating my son like he's a pariah? Uh, the only reason I can think of is 'cause he's white.

After Zeek makes his statement, his kids scramble to make excuses for him, looking embarrassed and saying, "He didn't mean it like it sounded" and "He has Tourette's." Thus, the fifth time race is made explicit on the show, a white man asserts *reverse racism* to be at work. Renee responds to Zeek's outburst with the observation, "Maybe it's that he's irresponsible." Zeek replies, "Renee, that is not my understanding."⁶

This exchange finally prompts Jasmine to step in, literally, in between the factions. She announces to the families that she lied about Crosby's absence. She follows her confession with an indictment of her choice to be a single mom:

> JASMINE: Look, I was the one who chose to have this baby and not let his father know. It was me. But if you're going to be mad at anyone, be mad at me; don't be mad at him.

Renee and Sekou look shocked. Renee asks why Jasmine would do such a thing, and Jasmine explains that she thought it would be easier if everyone thought Crosby had left her, just as her father left Renee and her children. Renee chastises her with the question, "Easier for who?" Sekou is left speechless. Jabbar then runs back into the room and asks, "Is it time for cake?!" His query breaks the tension, everyone laughs, and Crosby is heard over the happy sounds saying, "Boy buddy, is it ever!" Renee asks "Grandpa Zeek" to help her cut the cake, and everyone relaxes and enjoys the scene as Jabbar blows out the candles. After the party, when Jasmine and Crosby are back at her place, she offers to show him the video of Jabbar's birth. Crosby takes her up on it, and the show ends with a close-up shot of Crosby, tears in his eyes, watching his son's birth in awe. The camera witnesses his joy and pain, and viewers are encouraged to empathize with his emotional response.

The Post-Racial, Post-Feminist Shaming of Jasmine (and Her Black Family)

The Braverman's white liberal identities and Crosby's father's rights are secured in this dramatic crescendo pitting black family against white family. Jasmine's shame is Crosby's redemption. Jasmine's "choice" to be a single mom without Crosby's knowledge is the source of the racial tension at the party. Her lack of honesty has undermined Crosby's ability to be a good father who does the right thing (although one wonders why he didn't return Jasmine's calls five years ago if he's such a good guy). Moreover, the black people at the party are portrayed as unfeeling, not able to put aside a grudge even to make a little boy's birthday party festive. The audience also now knows that Jasmine is part of the stereotypical cycle of single black moms begetting single moms, a cycle that undergirds so much of the discourse of black pathology.[31] Black fathers leave black mothers, and black mothers get all bitter and matriarchal. Jasmine has daddy issues; her brother (like so many black men we see on TV!) is sullen and confrontational. Thus, what could have been framed as an empowered, albeit hard choice to give up on a guy who seemed uninterested in her after sex is now scripted as Jasmine's choice to exclude and impugn a white man by withholding the truth about his son and lying to her family about him. Not only is Jasmine placed in the lineage of perpetual single black mothers; she has also been so adversely affected by the experience of absent black fatherhood that she tells lies to her family about her son's father.

Here is the return of a set of zombie black stereotypes: The broken black family and suspect single black mother are set up in comparison to the intact upper-middle-class white family. Thus, the post-racial and the post-feminist steamroll over Jasmine, leaving the Bravermans' liberal white bona fides and nuclear families in their elevated position. In this comparison of families, the gap of the "post-" opens up, allowing some of the most retrograde ideas about black women and families to flow in through the plot devices and camera angles that the showrunner, writers, and director used to make the birthday party scene dramatic. When race breaks out at the party, it is clearly black people's fault. Sekou's anger, the guests' sullenness, and Jasmine's deception lead to the arguments that precipitate her confession. The showdown between the families is drama that leverages stereotypes instead of offering a more nuanced discussion about why someone would choose to be a single mother, or why there could be tensions when families of different races meet for the first time.

Jasmine, Jabbar, and the other black family members bring race and gender trouble into the script. They are placed in the story to bring in drama, suspense, tension. There is visible tension and discomfort when the "white people" come into the party, and Crosby is the one allowed to mark it with his aside. This discomfort is broken only by whites—by Camille's acknowledgment of Sekou's name and by Zeek's ham-handed diagnosis of the tension in the room, a tension he brings to a head and, ultimately, resolves, since it pushes Jasmine to confess. Once that is done, everyone can be happy and together, eating cake. To paraphrase an early black feminist text, the post-racial post-feminist bridge here is Jasmine's back.[32] The sacrifice of her dignity and the culpability assigned to her individual choices create the space for the white and black family to be together, if momentarily, and for the white family to shine as a liberal, accepting whole.

But the unity is short lived. Other than in this episode, Jasmine's family is not seen again until the very last episode. Their purpose has been served: to bring drama, tension, and resolution for the white father. And an opportunity is lost. Once Jasmine and Jabbar's black family members disappear, we don't get to see how the white and black families interact other than through drama and trauma. The scriptwriters don't show us how they might come to know each other as grandparents, uncles, aunts, and cousins—as family rather than as antagonists. Sekou and Renee aren't invited to Zeek's dinner table where he holds court with the extended family. Thus, the "integration" of the family via black mother/biracial child is incomplete, troubling, a gap still not crossed. Crosby and his siblings never cross Renee or Sekou's thresholds again in Season One. There is never another moment when black people outnumber whites, or are even equal in terms of family representation and interaction.

This aftermath of the party and remaining episodes of Season One suggest that Jasmine's family, her Black/Oakland world and ties, are unnecessary to the composition of extended family support networks. In order to create this interracial union, the only family whose support and love needs to be visible is the white family's. Despite Sekou's testimony about devotion to his sister and nephew since the day Jabbar was born, the writers don't depict this uncle acting like a role model: He is only seen confronting a white father, a confrontation that would have been avoided, perhaps, had his sister told the truth. Audiences do get to see Zeek and Joel and Adam being nurturing towards Jabbar when he interacts with their family, but the only Black male in his life is dismissed from view after he has played his stereotypical role of instigator, aggressor. Sekou's experience is only represented in the context of racially-inflected confrontation and unveiled lies about family. Likewise, Jasmine's mother never gets to act like a grandma after she helps bring in the cake; she, too, is left out, having been exposed as yet another black single mother.

After the Fall: Jasmine amd Jabbar's Integration into the Braverman Clan

Once the ugly confrontation at the birthday party is over, Jasmine and Crosby's relationship develops in the light of day, so to speak, and in full view of the Braverman family. After Jasmine's reckoning, then, she is less isolated from his family, and the couple decide that they are "not just fooling around" anymore. The seriousness of their growing relationship is suggested in the ways Jasmine and Jabbar become more intimately linked to Braverman cousins, aunts, uncles, and grandparents— but there is no such intimacy between Crosby and the Trussells. So, in the episodes immediately following the birthday party, Jasmine and Crosby have a date while Jabbar has a sleepover with his cousin Sydney. Later, Julia recognizes Jabbar's athleticism and recruits him onto Sydney's soccer squad, transforming the team into a juggernaut as the camera follows Jabbar's dominant moves on the pee wee soccer field and Jasmine and Crosby cheer him on with the rest of the Braverman clan. Notably, neither Renee nor Sekou are part of the sideline scene— apparently the black uncle and grandmother weren't able to make it to the soccer game to cheer on their beloved relative; perhaps they weren't invited. Whatever the case, viewers are left without a sense of how Jasmine's black family members might relate to the Bravermans in the absence of conflict. The show, in this way, sets up separate worlds for these families, despite the moments of warmth exhibited at the party after Jasmine's confession. The imbalance in the contributions and presence of the black and white family members is disturbing. In an interview with *Vulture.com*, Katims was praised for portraying a family so realistically. He responded:

> One of the things I find myself saying in the writers' room a lot is, "What would really happen?" A lot of times as writers you want to come up with the best possible story and you bend it according to what you want to happen. I think one of the things that I always try to think about is what would really happen in a situation, what feels real. . . . Everybody has flaws, everybody has demons, everybody has ghosts, but I think you watch people and you see everybody trying to do their best. To me, that's compelling and it sort of reflects what I typically see that happens in the world too.[33]

Apparently, what "really happens" when interracial family is created is that women of color isolate themselves from their family and community of color.

Exit Jasmine, Enter Renee: The Black
Matriarch Gets Her Comeuppance

As the season moves on, Jasmine auditions for the Alvin Ailey Dance Company, and Crosby and Jabbar take her to the audition and cheer her on before she begins. This is the first time we actually see evidence of Jasmine's career as a dancer. For viewers who are aware of the prestige and history of the Ailey Company, it is clear that her dancing is part of an artistic, high-brow professional world, not the "Vegas dancer" career of the (unseen) Black mother in the original movie. Indeed, it would not be surprising if, before this moment, some viewers assumed that Jasmine was a pole dancer or stripper, since almost all the references to her dancing are conveyed through Crosby's sexual desires. In fact, in one episode we hear that Jasmine injured her back during recent love-making because Crosby asked her to contort herself into a titillating position.

The scripts provide audiences with no idea if she was working or looking for work while Crosby and Jabbar have father-son time—the audition scene is the first time we see her in her professional element. This is another thing that makes Jasmine atypical: Other Braverman mothers and fathers, siblings and in-laws are filmed in their workplaces, schools, or wrestling with their career vs. home choices.[34] Jasmine alone has no visible vocation or hopes and dreams until the Ailey opportunity pops up, which soon becomes another plot device to generate tension between her family and Crosby.

Season One ends with a cliffhanger: Jasmine is preparing to move to New York, having landed a spot in the Ailey traveling company. She and Crosby have tense discussions about what will happen to Jabbar. Jasmine has assumed that her mother, Renee, will take care of him at her home in Oakland. Crosby is hurt; he wants Jabbar to live with him on his houseboat. Jasmine is not keen on the idea, since the boat doesn't even have a room or a real bed for their son. When Zeek hears that not only is Jasmine taking the job, but also that Jabbar will live with her mother, he balks. During an alcohol-soaked night on the boat, Zeek tells Crosby he needs to "man up" and tell Jasmine that he's the father, and that he will decide what's happening with his son. Crosby gets angry, and declares his father's advice is not wanted. But it is clear from his facial expressions that he is not satisfied with the situation. Crosby later tells Jasmine that "he has rights" and that she can't make decisions about Jabbar without him. Crosby's outburst in this scene returns us to the theme of father's rights that began with the paternity test, reinforced by Zeek's not-so-subtle suggestions to his son that he needs to take the lead or "wear the pants" in the relationship since he is the man.

In the season finale, Crosby makes up with Jasmine. We later see her at the airport gate, hugging Renee, Crosby, and Jabbar as she prepares to go. The scene ends with the black grandmother, white father, and biracial son waving goodbye, standing together as a unit. But this show of unity is short-lived. When the show returns in Season Two, the initial reintroduction to Renee is via conflict over Jabbar's schedule. In the first few episodes, she and Crosby clash over bedtimes, watching TV, and whether to go to a baseball game or to church. Renee snaps at Crosby, rushes in and out impatiently with Jabbar, and is otherwise portrayed as an impediment to Crosby's relationship with his son. Crosby also complains about this to his own family, including Zeek, who encourages him, yet again, to man up and tell Renee to back off. After getting feedback from Zeek, Crosby does take a stand against Renee. He confronts her about taking Jabbar to church rather than allowing him to go to a baseball game. Then he declares that he will make more decisions about Jabbar's activities because he is his father, and because he wants his son to take part in his family traditions:

> CROSBY: I want my son, Jabbar, to have the same experience with all the other people and the camaraderie [at a baseball game]. So I disagree. And another thing, it's not fair of you to hold some grudge against me for some crap your husband did years ago. I'm here for my son, okay!? And I'm not going anywhere. You're gonna have to deal with that!

Renee is clearly shocked by this speech, and the camera catches her face, eyes wide with surprise and hurt. Between Zeek's advice, Crosby's outburst, and our lack of information about Renee's motives (beyond the stereotype that she is a controlling black mother with man issues) for maintaining her grandson's normal routines, we again are faced with a white father versus black mother situation. As in Season One, where Jasmine berated Crosby for his lack of parenting sense (leaving a child alone at a pool with strangers), Renee also clearly disapproves of his parental choices (baseball instead of church). More importantly, the father's rights theme is amplified here as Crosby asserts his place and power in Jabbar's life against grandma Renee.

The next scene that brings Crosby and Renee together finds them in her living room, sitting on the couch with Jabbar between them, preparing to watch a baseball game. Apparently, Renee has backed down, allowing Jabbar to take in a game rather than go to church or adhere to a regular bedtime. Moreover, she is now being tutored by Crosby in the rules of baseball—she asks a question about the game, listening intently as Crosby describes the players' movements and motivations. As in the birthday party scene of Season One, black mothers are to blame for family tension, and most importantly, are controlling and emasculating. (White) men like Zeek and Crosby need to stand up to them and "find their balls" in order to overcome this negative force that could, of course, distort the childhood of yet another (biracial) black male: Jabbar. Crosby, then, interrupts the pattern of black matriarchal control. As he wrests parental control from Renee, he makes her "see the light" of allowing Jabbar to follow in *his* family's footsteps—and gains her respect in the process.

The latter is reinforced in the next episode, when Renee calls Crosby to ask him to pick Jabbar up from an after-school program. Unfortunately, when he answers his phone, Crosby is in the middle of a party for a band, and he is clearly drunk. But, not wanting to give Renee a reason to re-evaluate her decision to trust him, he declares he will pick up his son. Crosby's solution to avoid driving while intoxicated is to call Gaby, his nephew Max's special education aide, and ask her for a ride. Gaby warns him it is probably not a good idea, but Crosby uses his charm to get her to go along with the plan.

Once they reach the school, they are surprised to see Sekou there, approaching the building ahead of them. Crosby rushes out of the car and confronts Sekou, insisting he leave and let him take care of it.

Sekou observes he is drunk, and that Renee asked him to get Jabbar instead. Crosby tries to push Sekou, who resists, and Crosby topples onto the lawn in disgrace. Sekou turns away, and Gaby gets Crosby back in her car to leave. After this altercation, Crosby assumes that Renee and Sekou will "tell on him" to Jasmine, thereby poisoning their relationship and his reputation as an improving father/adult. When he goes to see Renee and Jabbar, Renee surprises him by saying that neither she nor Sekou will tell Jasmine. She then goes into a speech about how she doesn't need to be in their business, BUT—she hopes Crosby and Jasmine will soon decide what to do with their relationship. She does so through a critique of her *daughter's* work choices.

> RENEE: I know she is doing the best she can. But the truth is, she's been dragging that poor boy all over creation. Summer in New York, then she moves him back here and she goes to Europe. It's not good! . . . So you need to figure it out . . . I mean the both of you together. Children need stability. I know it's modern and fashionable to live your separate lives and split time with your kids, but I think that's a bunch of bull. That boy needs his mom AND his daddy. So either you-know-what or get off the pot.

Crosby is happily surprised by her words, and we are now left with the impression that Renee is "on his side," that side being wanting Jasmine and Jabbar to make a permanent, nuclear family connection with Crosby. Of course, one way of doing this would be for Crosby to move to New York with Jabbar, and start a life there where Jasmine can continue her career. This is never an option, of course, for the show is set up to be centered in Berkeley and the Braverman family abodes. So, the dramatic device of removing Jasmine from the geographic area reinforces the false choice presented by post-feminism: women need to decide whether to have a career OR a family; there is no "having it all"—that was a false promise of second-wave feminism, which set women and their families up for failure.[35] Magically, during her next visit to California, Jasmine announces that she is leaving the Ailey dance company and will stay in Berkeley. This change of heart comes with little discussion and no exposition other than that she missed Crosby and Jabbar.

This sets up the next phase in the relationship: Crosby proposes marriage, and they move into an apartment together. The Braverman family rejoices that he has finally made the right decision to marry his son's mother. Jasmine and Jabbar then join the family at Thanksgiving, where she wows the clan with her athleticism during the traditional turkey-day touch football game. While Renee is also invited to the Thanksgiving feast, Sekou is not. Renee's main function for the Thanksgiving episode is to create tension over whether she can be prevented from trying to take over Camille's kitchen or disrupt other Braverman holiday traditions. Jasmine and Crosby have discussions alone about how to keep Renee from taking over, and when she arrives at the Braverman compound, she tries to join the cooking rituals, but is blocked by Camille and her granddaughter, Amber. Again, the inclusion of this black mother does not create intimacy, but tension between the families. Rather than allowing for an open exchange of traditions, the episode frames her desire to contribute to the dinner as a barely tolerated interruption of Braverman family ritual.

In a subsequent episode, Crosby returns home to find Renee and Jasmine looking over catering catalogues and other wedding paraphernalia. To his surprise, they announce that the wedding date has been changed to accommodate Trussell relatives who have to travel from out of state. Crosby looks bewildered, and becomes more so when he hears the women continue the discussion about various wedding details—details that are apparently new to him and not in line with his vision of the wedding. He leaves the kitchen, chagrined. The wedding—where the Trussells and Bravermans will be together again—is prefaced by interpersonal conflict in which Renee and Jasmine are pitted against Crosby and echoes the discomfort surrounding Jabbar's living arrangements when Jasmine went to New York.

For the remainder of the season, Crosby and Jasmine continue to disagree over their vision for the wedding and their life together. They meet with a reverend, who is black, who will marry them (in Renee's church). As part of a premarital counseling exercise, the reverend asks each of them to draw a picture of their future life, and Crosby has a hard time thinking of that picture, while we see Jasmine eagerly drawing a detailed vision. She presents her picture first, which imagines a house, more children, and her running a dance studio so she can work from home. Crosby looks surprised when he sees what his fiancée has drawn. Crosby's picture, which he is now shy about revealing, consists of stick figures of the three of them, looking happy. The gap between their visions becomes the next bump in the road.

Later on, while doing dishes, Crosby tries to rearrange plates and bowls. Jasmine overrules him that the dishwasher won't get them clean in that configuration. Crosby blows up and declares: "I can't marry someone who will not let me make any decisions! Ok?! I'm starting to realize that you are VERY controlling." Jasmine is quiet, and hurt, and listens as he continues to rant about how she doesn't let him do anything his way. He refers to her drawing, and she replies it was just an exercise. Then she asks him if he wants his ring back, and the argument escalates. She points out that he is often unwilling to make decisions, and that their parental responsibilities require that she step in to make a plan. Crosby then asks if she was going to "drop those kids on my lap like you did Jabbar?!" She is shocked, and yells at him to get out. He then says she is ungrateful for the way he has become part of her life. When they next see each other, she says calmly that they need to spend some time apart to decide what they really want. Crosby begins living on his houseboat again, alone.

Their trial separation sets up a one-night-stand between Gaby—Max's therapist for Asperger's—and Crosby. Promos for the show began to hint at this affair as soon as Jasmine and Crosby had the fight. Jasmine disappears, and Crosby has multiple interactions with Gaby. At Adam's house, he witnesses her have a hard time consoling Max, and takes her for a drink afterwards, where he leans in to kiss her, but they both pull away in time. In the next episode, Crosby helps Gaby set up for Max's birthday party—a party that Jasmine and Jabbar would have attended. However, at the last minute Jasmine calls to tell Crosby that her aunt in Phoenix, Arizona, is ill, and that she wants to visit her to give some help. Their absence provides an opening for Crosby to flirt with Gaby during the party, which leads to sex—and regret.

Gaby and Crosby and Jasmine

In hindsight, viewers of *Parenthood* could have easily guessed that Crosby's attraction to Gaby would lead to trouble eventually. Her character was introduced in Season One as the in-home aide for Max, who has Asperger's. The actress who plays Gaby, Minka Kelly, is a well-known actress who has appeared on other programs, including *Friday Night Lights*, another NBC show that producer/showrunner Jason Katims helmed for the network. When Crosby first meets her in Season One during a trip to Adam's house, he comments to Adam that he finds her attractive. Although Gaby is a recurring character, she does not appear often in Season Two. She is mainly there to assist Max and update his parents on his progress. She is an empathetic, caring, and attractive person. By the time her night of passion with Crosby occurs, the writers have provided plenty of evidence of her allure and the logic of Crosby's temptation.

After Crosby's lapse into infidelity, the next episode begins with Crosby leaving Gaby's bedroom, while she lies asleep, with a regretful look on his face. When he next sees Jasmine, he is drunk and alone on his boat. She wants to end their separation and continue planning the wedding. Crosby is clearly torn as he listens to his fiancée: Should he tell her the truth, or allow this moment to continue into a happier partnership? But he tells her, and she explodes as he tries to apologize. She leaves the boat, yelling that she will never forgive him for what he did to their family.

Having interjected this new level of drama for the interracial couple, the rest of the story is now organized around the question: Can they be reunited? However, instead of devoting time to how Jabbar's parents will repair their relationship—perhaps through counseling? family mediators?—the writers first focus on Crosby and Gaby's side of the love triangle The first episode after Crosby's confession focuses on Gaby's guilt and her relationship with Adam's family, not Jasmine's feelings. We see Gaby tearfully quit her job, and Kristina frantically trying to figure out what she did wrong and what to do without the therapy Max was getting. The episode centers on Kristina's quest to get Gaby to tell her what went wrong, which finally results in the confession that she slept with Crosby. The audience later witnesses the women repair their relationship in a subsequent episode via their shared concern for Max. Gaby, then, is framed not as the typical "home wrecker," but rather as a good person who made a single, costly mistake, which can ultimately be forgiven.

The show details Crosby's range of emotions and tensions with his family in the aftermath of the affair—but not Jasmine's. When Adam finds out Crosby's infidelity caused his son's aide to resign, he is furious and bans his brother from the house. Thus, Crosby and Gaby's affair is mostly used to generate scenes of conflict and angst for Adam and Kristina—not Jasmine, the betrayed party. The episodes revolve around whether Adam will forgive his brother; whether Max can handle knowing he has Asperger's; and whether Kristina can make do without Gaby's help. Jasmine herself is rarely on screen, and when she does appear, she is usually telling Crosby to leave her alone. Only two scenes give viewers a glimpse that Jasmine is experiencing any emotion other than anger. In one, Jasmine has committed to hosting Sydney for a sleepover with Jabbar so Julia and Joel can go out for their anniversary. The camera reveals that Jasmine has been crying: A close-up shot reveals puffy eyes, little makeup, and fatigue. She tries to be upbeat, but dissolves into tears, and Julia hugs her.

The second scene that reveals a more tender side of Jasmine features Crosby and Jasmine together with Jabbar at his school. Jabbar gets to introduce his family to his class, and the kids ask his parents how they met. Crosby jumps in and tells a fairy-tale version of their meeting in New York, ending the tale not with the truth—that he never contacted Jasmine again after having sex with her—but with the statement that as soon as he met her he knew he wanted to spend the rest of his life with her. Jasmine smiles wistfully as she listens to his tale, and doesn't contradict him. Later, Jasmine visits Crosby's houseboat, and tells him she enjoyed the story, but fears it was only a story, and it's time to move on. Crosby is devastated as she leaves the houseboat, but later vows to his siblings that he is going to "get my family back." His plan is to buy a house for Jasmine to prove his commitment.

For the remainder of the season, the camera follows Crosby as he pursues the classic patriarchal proof of providing care: homeownership. He buys the house, fixes it up with Joel, his brother-in-law, and repairs his relationship with Adam in the process. In the last episode of Season Two, Crosby tries to convince Jasmine to see the house. The show ends with Jasmine dropping by with Joel, and the camera follows Crosby touring her around the house. The audience can't hear what they are saying, because the soundtrack takes over, but they are clearly not arguing, and they exchange tender glances as Crosby points out the repairs he and Joel have accomplished. Their future looks brighter, but is still uncertain.

In some ways, Crosby and Jasmine are back where they began: unclear about the nature of their relationship beyond their attachment to Jabbar. And the audience is, in some ways, back where television began with interracial couples. Viewers have been shown an interracial relationship that is unstable and fraught with sexual interactions that are frowned upon by the mainstream: single motherhood brought on by premarital sex, and infidelity on the eve of marital union. Like the mulatto narratives of old and the awkward inclusions of 1980s television, the story of this interracial family is hampered by secrets and lies, and is not equipped to include black family members in ways that enrich our understanding of the interpersonal dynamics of interracial families. Like Dominique Devereaux and her daughter on *Dynasty*, Jasmine and Jabbar are not "with the family" from the beginning as intimate, expected equals. They are introduced via secrets and lies surrounding the sexual relations and knowledge of a black woman and a white man, a white man whose family knows nothing of his interracial sexual dalliance or child. Dominque's mother was a black servant, one who came in through the back door. Though Jasmine and Jabbar didn't come through the back door, they didn't really enter through the front door either. Rather, post-racial and post-feminist logic opened up a side door, created by uncomfortable maneuvers in the script that replicated some old racial stereotypes even as the location and spirit of the show tried to leave them behind. In many ways, then, the show illustrates that TV has not come as far as some have thought in depictions of race and family. The promises of the "post-" to bring women of all colors into the frame ring hollow; in the gaps between past and present, present and future, too many old habits of racial representation continue to stalk this show, zombies refusing to die.

Afterword: Spoiler Alerts, Final Comments

As of this writing, *Parenthood* has finished up its fourth season, with respectable ratings and critical acclaim.[36] The show has also won awards for realistic portrayals of people with special needs, diversity, and other social issues.[37] Crosby and Jasmine are now married and expecting a

new child. But the show continues to include race explicitly as a problem to be solved. For instance, when visiting his dad's music studio,
Jabbar hears a black rap artist use the word "nigga." Crosby agonizes
over how to explain it to his biracial son, but then is offended when his
black wife, Jasmine, lets him know she can handle it. Unfortunately, the
audience doesn't get the full story on how she explains the history and
meaning of racial epithets to a grade-schooler—a lesson many parents
of different backgrounds may want to hear. Her discussion with Jabbar
is overlaid with soothing music, and the camera focuses on Crosby's
face as he admires her words—words the audience cannot hear. Rather
than privilege the black mother's wisdom and experiences with racism,
the show makes the white father's awe the focus. So it goes. Black people on *Parenthood* interject race in problematic ways. Despite the fact
that this episode aired within weeks of Bay Area unrest over police brutality, in the wake of the shooting of Trayvon Martin, and in the midst
of an election campaign where anti-Obama displays of nooses were in
the news, the "problem" of racist terminology was situated in rap music.

 Parenthood is one of a handful of primetime network shows that feature interracial pairs. ABC's *Modern Family*, for instance, has a white
man/Latina pairing as well as gay male parents; *Grey's Anatomy* has at least
two interracial love stories at this writing; and the aforementioned *Battlestar Galactica* featured a white man/Asian woman pair. All of these shows
mobilize interracial families in ways that connect to different aspects of
the post-racial mystique. Where *Battlestar* deploys interracial family as
a bridge between races, *Modern Family* uses broad humor to comment
on racial difference in the manner of the Lear sitcoms of the 1970s, serving up and sometimes skewering stereotypes. Perhaps the jokes about a
Latina's "fieryness" or her accent provoke conversation about interracial
coupling as a part of "modern" American family life, or perhaps they reinforce forever-foreigner stereotypes about Latinas/os. These programs also
continue to position the dual-parent, middle-class family as the correct
means of comparison as they continue to employ stereotypes of women
of color and "domesticate" GLBT parents.[38] Moreover, the women of color
prove their loyalty/acceptability by taking punishment (for Gloria, jokes
at her expense; for Athena, actual torture; for Jasmine, public and private
humiliation) and distancing themselves from their other family members
of color and/or the entire Othered racial group.

Finally, it is notable that these families all "integrate" via the bodies of women of color. Men of color, it seems, are too threatening to become part of the extended family. On *Modern Family*, Gloria's Latino ex-husband, Javier, continually lets down their son. The show pushes Javier out of the family, framing him as an untrustworthy presence. On *Parenthood*, Jasmine's brother Sekou is not included in the sporty outings of the Braverman males, and does not attend Jabbar's school events or soccer games. Her mother Renee is framed as a scold who lives in a run-down part of the Bay Area. The gendered bias for women of color in these post-racial shows reveals yet another zombie stereotype: predatory and untrustworthy men of color who are unable to be domesticated enough to eliminate their threatening sexuality and/or physicality.

These problematic inclusions of interracial couples are examples of the continued discomfort about what race means in what is supposed to be a post-racial era. Clearly, in the first two seasons, the show hesitated to portray racism at work in the lives of the Bravermans' potential new family members, but the show does recognize on some level that it doesn't make sense to cast black people as romantic partners without some gestures that race still matters somehow, if only in misperceptions of motives. Indeed, at the end of Season Two, the eldest daughter of Adam Braverman, Haddie, announces her desire to go on date an older Black teen, Alex, to her parents' initial dismay. She thinks their disapproval may be partly motivated by race, but ultimately, the season ends with Alex telling Haddie he's not ready to date her yet.

The tepid approaches to race in the first two seasons of *Parenthood* leave too much unresolved. Although the show aspires to depict a world where adding a biracial child and his black mother to a white family is not an issue for white people anymore, the absence of dialogue or additional scenes of meaningful contact between the families makes it far too easy for old stereotypes of black motherhood to fill in the gaps. By not committing to doing something more, something different than just bringing in black people to generate drama or affirm the feelings of white characters, *Parenthood*, like the post-, fails to articulate specifically what race does or should mean within this family. It disavows much of the racial past, but continues to depend on some of the racial shorthand of that past when bringing people of color into the frame.

4

Post Racial Audiences

Discussions of Parenthood's Interracial Couple

I side with Crosby and I don't really care for Jasmine at
all and I especially can't stand her mother. I think Crosby
should get some legally established visitation rights—end of
story.
—T. F., "Crosby needs to dump Jasmine," Facebook
discussion thread

As T. F.'s remark demonstrates, fictional television shows can inspire
strong feelings. Viewers connect with storylines and characters, consciously and unconsciously judging the motives of the characters, as
well as evaluating how skillfully the writers develop storylines. It is thus
particularly important for studies of post-racial media to examine how
audiences react when producers inject racial difference into programs
broadcast in an era when race ostensibly matters "less" than it did
before, while advertisers attempt to reach ever-more-diverse consum-
ers/audiences. This chapter takes a look at how some viewers discussed
the post-racial network television drama *Parenthood*. These Facebook
conversations exhibit many of the elements of post-racial discourses
discussed in the previous chapters. Specifically, many audience members felt free to take note of racial difference without seeing any link-
age between difference, on the one hand, and racial stereotyping and
racism, on the other. As they naturalized physical racial markers and
individualized the choices made by characters, their comments resonated with post-racial discourses about interracial families. These post-
racial interpretations were countered by race-conscious understandings
of the show, its characters, and the history of racial representations in
network television.

As I argued in the previous chapter, *Parenthood* is a post-racial update of its movie predecessor. While I ultimately read *Parenthood* as a failed attempt to "integrate" the family, given its recycling of black female stereotypes and inability to provide sufficient depth for black characters, I am clearly not the only one watching the show. Although my reading illuminates where, when, and how black stereotypes, gender stereotypes, and twentieth-century melodramas of interracial relations inform the presentation of Jasmine, Jabbar, and their black relatives, not everyone will share experiences that make these influences salient. Thus, in addition to reading the show's "integration" of its black characters as a cultural critic, I was committed to assessing how others saw these figures as they interacted with the Braverman clan. To gain access to other reactions to the show, I went to Facebook, and read all of the viewer comments in discussion threads that indicated Jasmine, Crosby, and/or Jabbar were the focus of audience talk.

Audiences and Race on TV

Standpoint theory and reception theory remind us how, amongst viewers of a popular television show like *Parenthood*, there will be members of multiple, sometimes overlapping, interpretive communities responding to the program and negotiating its portrayal of parenting from various standpoints. Readings of media are not completely unique or singular: Given our shared cultural heritage, linguistic expectations, understanding of genre conventions, and so on, audiences agree on many facets of meaning, from plot development to which characters are supposed to be good or evil. Beyond this, however, social identities such as age, gender, race, class, sexuality, and their intersections impact how we respond to or evaluate a text; we form "interpretive communities" linked to our social identities. As Stanley Fish wrote, an interpretive community is not merely an aggregation of individuals who share points of view; rather, the interpretive community structures "a way of organizing experience . . . [shared by] individuals in the sense that its assumed distinctions, categories of understanding, and stipulations of relevance and irrelevance [are] the content of the consciousness of community members."[1]

Take myself, for example. My son has Asperger's, and when I watch *Parenthood*, I am particularly interested in comparing my experiences with my son, his doctors and specialists, and others with the Braverman family's experiences with Max. My membership in an interpretive community of parents of special-needs children, then, means I may see the show very differently than people outside of that community. Likewise, I am an African American, biracial woman married to a white American man; my readings of race and gender representations have been shaped by close familial relationships, my scholarship, and personal experiences of racism and sexism. Thus, when I watch the show, I bring my experiences of all-white family gatherings, among others, when I assess scenes between Jasmine and the Bravermans.

To take an historical example of interpretive communities—white audiences generally loved *Birth of A Nation* (1915); black audiences protested the film.[2] All of them agreed on its content: The film portrayed the South after the Civil War and the rise of the Ku Klux Klan. But these audiences disagreed widely over what the film's impact would be on race relations. The NAACP campaigned to have the film edited or banned for fear that its sympathetic portrayal of the Klan would increase anti-black violence and give further validation to Jim Crow laws. In contrast, President Woodrow Wilson called it a masterpiece of history on film; many white film critics lauded director D. W. Griffith's cinematic talents.[3]

Birth provides a stark example of interracial differences in media interpretation, but there are also intraracial disagreements. That is, while interpretive communities do share common frameworks and approaches for understanding media, they don't necessarily share the same opinions about the meaning and impact of particular genres or characterizations. When broadcast on radio, *Amos 'n Andy* garnered both praise and condemnation from black newspapers and individual listeners.[4] More recently, black illustrator Aaron McGruder's comic strip (and now television show) the *Boondocks* has sparked controversy among black audiences. One study of how black readers of the comic discussed its racial content on the *Boondocks* webpage found that comments fell into three categories: (1) debates over whether the strip reinforced or refuted black stereotypes; (2) praise for the strip's relevance to black readers; and (3) questioning whether MacGruder or other black artists have a responsibility to black communities to represent the race positively.[5] Other scholars have likewise found conflicting opinions in black audiences' responses to media that feature racial themes or African American characters.[6]

Discerning differences across and within racial groups can illuminate how a TV drama can spark debates about racial identity, politics, and other issues that impact individuals and groups. Television provides lenses through which we might see other racial/ethnic groups and own identity groupings differently. As Robin Means Coleman summarized, it is imperative for scholars to continue to research audiences because of the "role of media in our domestic settings and daily lives. . . . [E]ntering into a dialogue with audience yields deepened insights into the tastes, . . . interpretations, and political/identity understandings around an important cultural institution."[7]

Popular television can inspire moments for confronting race and racism and, hopefully, lead to transformations of attitudes and actions. Many people credit the miniseries *Roots* (1977), for example, for (temporarily) opening up discussions about the legacy of slavery in the United States[8] How audiences interact with television, then, is important to investigate in terms of the post-racial mystique because therein lies a space where individual, cultural, and institutional levels of racism converge. Although many in critical race theory are concerned that dominant discourses of race reify individual acts and thoughts, Malinda Smith cautions us that we must continue interrogating social *and* individual practices "that are normalized and part of our everyday thinking and acting."[9] Post-racial media texts are often constructed in ways that encourage audiences *not* to notice racism, and instead to see representations of racial difference as mattering only in terms of descriptiveness or novelty, not in terms of power or hierarchy. Post-racial narratives work to "deny, to discount and even to minimize experiences of racism and, thereby, to excuse" audiences from responsibility—moral or political—to act against racism.[10] Smith analyzed official reactions to incidents of on-campus racist spectacles, such as blackface parties that were excused by participants as "just a joke" but not racist. She refers to such excuses as the product of "motivated ignorance," which Cheshire Calhoun describes as self-interested wrong-doing that is supported by social practices that impede individual and group awareness of harm done to others.[11] The post-racial practice of displaying racial difference while denying racial discrimination encourages audiences to "not see" racism in everyday cultural texts—whether on network television shows or in Facebook discussions. Here, I analyze audience discussions to see whether the show's post-racial combination of increased inter-racial visibility and invisibility of racism sparks counter-discourses.

Social media constitute an everyday media context where we can interrogate audience reactions to post-racial television. Many viewers use social media like Twitter or Facebook in tandem with traditional media. We often hear reports or see spoofs of how audience members tweet, post, or chat before, during, and after they watch television shows or movies. It has become commonplace for the TV networks to create official social media portals for fan interaction, attempting to corral viewers into new media spaces that are closely connected to their show and their network's brand. And, of course, these official spaces are more easily tracked than the limitless fan sites viewers can participate in at their leisure. Like communication scholars Patricia Cornwell and Mark Orbe, I am interested in how *Parenthood* viewers use the Internet (in this case, a Facebook page created by NBC) to talk about the show with other audience members. The dialogues of people who may or may not know each other in this online space provide an opportunity to see how they negotiate the racial representations of the show as well as one another's assumptions about race, gender, class, family, and heterosexual courtship.

Looking at the myriad responses of audience members who are motivated enough to post online, we can gain insight into ways that viewers evaluate a character that is still rare on network television: a black woman in a relationship with a white man. Although they are judging fictional figures, it is important to note that our evaluations of entertainment figures may influence our views of people in the real world. Edward Schiappa explains how virtual contact with media characters can impact people's opinions about members of social groups represented by those characters.[12] So, for example, a heterosexual man with no gay acquaintances who watches a show like NBC's hit show featuring gay characters, *Will & Grace* (1998–2005), may feel he is learning what gay people are like from the show, and make assumptions about gay people in the real world accordingly. The question then is, what is he learning? Many critics of the show asserted that the effeminate, over-the-top behaviors of an out gay character, Jack, reinforced anti-gay stereotypes.[13] Implicitly and explicitly, many of these writers assumed audiences for *Will & Grace* would absorb negative beliefs about gay men. However, experiments by Schiappa and colleagues showed that people with little real-world contact with gays and lesbians who watched *Will & Grace* reacted in the opposite fashion: Their anti-gay prejudices were reduced after watching the show.[14] Why would this be the case? Social cognition research suggests some answers.

Psychological and communication researchers have conducted studies that suggest that we describe and evaluate celebrities and television characters in the same ways we describe and evaluate our neighbors and coworkers—even though we don't know them personally, the stars and/or their characters seem "real" to us.[15] Many of us (or our children) cried when Professor Dumbledore died in the sixth installment of *Harry Potter*, or have friends who were incensed that Brad Pitt dumped Jennifer Aniston for Angelina Jolie and angrily condemned those who sided against their favorite actress. Thus, we engage in what social psychologists call "parasocial interactions" with media figures. Our experiences will not be uniform, however: Social identity, level of fan knowledge, and other factors will vary our feelings of closeness to media figures and our judgment of their character. Based on this research on parasocial interaction, Schiappa and colleagues suggest that parasocial contact has the possibility of undermining stereotypes and negative beliefs about a group when the following is true:

1. viewers find the character likable and/or attractive
2. viewers think the character is realistic
3. viewers find the character similar in some way.[16]

Thus, because many study participants found the cast of *Will & Grace* likable, real, and similar somehow, positive evaluations of the characters seemed to mitigate anti-gay stereotypes.

But what about when a character isn't seen as realistic, attractive, or similar? Many researchers and critics assert that the continued employment of unattractive black stereotypes, along with sparse counter-stereotypical characterizations of African Americans, reinforces anti-black beliefs and stereotypes. The theory suggests that anti-black stereotypes are "chronically accessible," and thus unconsciously or consciously affect audience perceptions of black people.[17] While a large majority of whites, for example, report in polls that they do not believe black people are less attractive or smart than whites, studies of implicit attitudes find that the majority of whites do hold anti-black biases.[18] These biases can be primed or activated by media representations, even for people who don't consciously endorse black stereotypes. For example, research on news and political advertisements that use racial imagery or racially coded language prime anti-black stereotypes (e.g., "welfare queen" or "inner city").[19] Less work has been done on reactions to televised entertainment. Such studies as have been undertaken have generally found differences between black and white viewers' interpretations of race, family roles, and gender politics, as well differences between male and female viewers of both races.[20] In some cases, black audiences continue to express worries that black stereotypes in television will have a negative impact on race relations, whereas white audiences don't always share the same concerns.

Although the methods and theories employed by social psychologists and critical race and media scholars are often quite different, they converge in their concerns about the longevity of stereotypes and evidence of continuing racist discrimination in society and media.[21] Observing affinities between critical race theory's interest in narrative and symbols and social psychological examinations of stereotypes, attitudes, and behavior, legal scholar Jerry Kang summarizes, "the scientific consensus is that racial schemas are not of minor significance. Instead, racial schemas are 'chronically accessible' and can be triggered by the target's mere appearance, since we as observers are especially sensitive to visual and physical cues."[22] This means that we are likely to access, and perhaps apply, race or gender stereotypes when we see people of color in the media. And, though much of the bias that results may be unintended or even unconscious, Kang emphasizes that lack of intent "does not magically erase the harm." Studies strongly suggest that this harm takes many forms, including employers prejudging applicants with "black-sounding names" as deficient; police and everyday citizens prejudging black and Latino men as threatening; and strong, agentic women being judged negatively while strong, agentic men are evaluated positively.[23] These judgments occur with people in the everyday "real" world as well as in media contexts. With these studies in mind,

I examine how audience members on Facebook describe and evaluate the interracial family on *Parenthood*.

Facebook and *Parenthood*

I analyzed viewer-created discussion threads on the *Parenthood* Facebook page from the first two seasons of the show. While there are literally hundreds of discussion threads on the show, eight were specifically titled with references to Crosby, Jasmine, Jabbar, and/or racial identity. I gathered all of the discussion threads that focused on those characters and race, and then closely read each for themes, contradictions, and commonalities. I also kept track of the racial and gender identities of discussion participants, using cues such as photographs, explicit identifications of self, and implied identity statements to categorize each participant. In the examples from the discussion threads that follow, I also reproduce participant comments verbatim. My process follows Cornwell and Orbe's study of audience comments on the *Boondocks* website, in which the researchers sorted messages posted to the site by race by using the comments of participants to discern their identity, comments that included comparisons to characters, explicit statements, and the like. In the case of Facebook, some users have photos attached to their screen names. Although those photos, like other visual "evidence" of race, don't guarantee identification, the images do suggest racial identity to other users.

Another point to highlight about my collection of *Parenthood* discussions on Facebook is that I have access only to the responses/debates started by people with access to the Internet and who were motivated to comment in a semi-public forum. Facebook discussions amongst "friends" on other pages that are limited to a network of friends are not part of this study. However, given that race and interracial relationships continue to be touchy subjects for many people, the fact that so many fans were interested in commenting on Jasmine and Crosby's relationship on the public Facebook page that NBC created for the show is in itself notable. Moreover, given its semi-anonymity—one can create a pseudonym, create a fake account, or refuse to post personal identifiers that would suggest race or gender—Facebook is a place where people can be candid (or provocative) without fear of much face-to-face reprisal, although being insulted or hazed online by fellow chatters does occur and can be painful.[24] For this reason, Facebook and NBC's staff could edit or remove postings deemed offensive.

Finally, given the continued segregation of neighborhoods and schools in many parts of the United States, Facebook discussion threads provide a spontaneous space for potential interracial interactions—mediated, but interactions nonetheless. And, given the ability to hide or manufacture an online identity, it is interesting that many of the discussants seemed willing to post personal photos and/or offered descriptions that conveyed their racial identity as they talked about an interracial couple on a major network show.

Parenthood's official Facebook page, which invites its viewers to engage in conversations with each other about the show's plot, characters, and the social issues and dilemmas tackled in various episodes, also demonstrates how social media sites have become integral parts of contemporary television, as the networks look for ways to keep viewers interested as they navigate their multiplying options for screen-based entertainment. Moreover, social media spaces offer opportunities for additional advertising and surveillance of the audience; as people write about the show on the Facebook discussion boards, recommend the page to other Facebook friends, "like" the show, and participate in other ways on the site, Facebook and NBC garner more information about their audience's demographics, tastes, and other data.

Beyond the possible data mining going on, though, the site is constructed to attract audience members, champion the show, and to engage people in discussion about the show's titular topic: parenthood. The most prominent issue for the show and on the Facebook page is autism. The page contains large banner announcements and displays showing parents links to experts, organizations, and personal narratives about autism. Indeed, the show's producers partnered with the organization Autism Speaks to consult on scripts and provide web-based resources to families.

Although the fact that Crosby and Jasmine are an interracial couple was not explicitly thematized by NBC as a social issue on the Facebook page, race was part of the fans' conversation. That is, while the *Parenthood* Facebook page did not invite viewers to see this couple through the lens of race in the way it asked fans to see Max through the lens of

Autism Spectrum Disorder, many discussion threads did comment on how race operated in their relationship and in the production of the show.

Discussing the Interracial Couple and Child

Facebook users' discussions of Jasmine and Crosby's relationship reveal some of the ways in which audience members negotiate post-racial media. I suggest that the comment threads analyzed here reveal moments of "motivated ignorance," as well as moments of intervention wherein other audience members attempt to show their fellow fans how they are "not seeing" racism even as the dominant reading of the show encourages a post-racial sensibility. By reading against the grain of the text, some members of the audience attempt to reframe a black woman/white man relationship as an example of the strength, resilience, and complexity of modern family life. When they contest the arguments of white viewers who see Jasmine as a controlling, unpleasant, and unnecessary character, they invoke their own readings of the show, auxiliary entertainment news, and media history to argue for a more holistic evaluation of this black mother. Moreover, they are "troubling" stereotypes of black motherhood and skin color that some white viewers employ or imply in their critiques of Jasmine and Crosby's relationship. These interventions make it harder for fans to "comfortably coexist with racism even among friends"[25] or at least other fans of the show. As they question the choices of show writers to truncate viewer access to her inner life and minimize her positive attributes, these viewers resist and directly challenge some of their fellow discussants' understandings of racial identification, gender, and single motherhood. In these ways, they subtly and unsubtly call out their fellow viewers for continuing to "not see" racism or sexism.

The eight discussion threads focused on Crosby and Jasmine were often blunt in their expression of support or liking of the characters. From the thread titled "Crosby needs to dump Jasmine" to the one named "Crosby and Jasmine belong together," discussions of these characters were not neutral in their approach to what the couple meant to each other and to the viewers. Four main themes emerged. First, many white participants (people whose photos or self-identifiers marked them as white) characterized Jasmine (and sometimes her mother) as a controlling, manipulative, and unattractive woman who deserved neither Crosby's affection nor his (or viewers') trust. This first theme resonates with my critical reading of the text: that the show frames Jasmine using common stereotypes of black women. Second, and often in response to the first theme, some white participants wondered whether or not Jabbar was truly Crosby's son, using the actors' skin colors to consider whether it was realistic for them to be represented as father and son. As with the first theme, those who doubted Jabbar's parentage seemed influenced by preconceived notions about skin color and racial "biology," as well as negative depictions of single black mothers, both of which influenced their reading of how Jasmine "surprised" Crosby with a biracial son. In these discussions, white participants' declarations about Jasmine and Jabbar echoed post-racial discourses that simultaneously mark racial difference but deny racism. Participants "saw" the differences in skin tone and more, but "didn't see" that their own interpretations of those differences may have been influenced by racist stereotypes.

Third, and often in direct response to the previous themes, participants argued that Jasmine was an attractive, independent, praise-worthy mother who had flaws, but not fatal ones. In this line of discussion, many contributors suggested that negative reactions to Jasmine were exacerbated by how the writing team neglected her character: Jasmine's fans pointed to her shallow back story and meager screen time as a reason why other viewers had such a limited perspective on her motivations and personality. Some implied that black stereotypes contributed to the distrust and disdain felt by white viewers.

Finally, some discussants were concerned that the show's writers—and network TV in general—were incapable of creating and sustaining a complex, caring, and long-lasting interracial relationship. Veering between congratulating the writers for trying at all and second-guessing them as plot twists suggested Jasmine's demise, these participants contextualized their wariness in terms of television history and entrenched stereotypes of black women. In these exchanges, participants invited others to "see" Jasmine through feminist and anti-racist lenses, and suggested that the writers' and some viewers' vision were clouded by racism and sexism.

While one of these themes (Jabbar's parentage) was mainly limited to one discussion thread, the other three were found across the different titles. Indeed, many participants posted remarks on different boards, arguing their points and cross-referencing comments made on different parts of the discussion threads as well as on other fan sites. In these exchanges, participants often brought in new information from industry gossip, teasers for the show, or interviews with the showrunner, Jason Katims. Thus, the discussions wove together a host of media texts, as well as participants' own experiences with race and relationships. In these ways, the Facebook page for *Parenthood* supported a lively, if sometimes contentious, set of intertwined and intertextual discussions of interracial couples on television, limitations on viewers' abilities to identify with black characters, and the sometimes limited imaginations of television producers when it comes to race and family matters.

THEME ONE: JASMINE IS CONTROLLING AND CAN'T BE TRUSTED

Participants who attacked Jasmine's character were ample, and cues such as photos and comments about racial identity suggested that these commentators were all white.[26] Indeed, their intense negative reactions to Jasmine suggests that my reading of *Parenthood's* representation of black womanhood was on target: The writers' choices regarding what to import from the original movie (the surprise biracial son) and how to "balance" Crosby's irresponsibility with women against Jasmine's lie about Crosby framed her in ways that resonate with easily accessible and well-worn stereotypes about black women and families headed by single mothers.

Three discussion threads—all started by a woman, L., who looks white in her screen picture—were generated specifically to argue that Jasmine was neither worthy of Crosby's affections nor trustworthy overall. L. created the threads "Crosby needs to dump Jasmine," "Jasmine," and "Why are Jasmine and Crosby hiding their relationship?" In each of her starting posts, L. asserted her dislike of Jasmine. For example, in her initial post for "Why are Jasmine and Crosby hiding their relationship?" L. wrote, "There's something about Jasmine I don't like and I really don't like her with Crosby." Other participants in these threads agreed, and began building the case that Jasmine was up to something. Either she was lying about Jabbar's paternity or she was a controlling woman who was too focused on her career to truly care about or deserve a relationship with Crosby—or both. In the discussion "Crosby needs to dump Jasmine," L. and two other white women, E. and T. F., argued that Jasmine was untrustworthy to the point that Crosby would need to assert his father's rights through legal action to maintain access to his son.

> L.: She uprooted Jabbar without any thought for a career that came out of the blue. I can't be objective about Jasmine because I don't trust her. Every time something ticks her off she uses Jabbar as a bargaining chip. Waiting five years to tell Crosby he had a son was selfish & cowardly.
>
> E.: Personally . . . I think Jasmine is lying . . . [about Jabbar] . . . Although i like every character in the show and appreciate their perspective Jasmine is hardly a saint. She is beautiful and talented and an opportunist. She wants a bigger life and Crosby isn't it . . .
>
> She is like many women (yes they exist) who . . . drop their kids with their Mom's to pursue themselves, their career goals and even drug habits. No, I am not saying she (jasmine) has a drug habit. So back to the fact that it looks like Jasmine is "away" saint or not (not) the relationship that we will probably be following is the Grandmother and Crosby's which should ultimately end up in a court room I imagine. . . . Looks like a case of Parental Alienation. And, I think Julia [Crosby's sister, a lawyer] should get to work. . . .
>
> T. F.: I side with Crosby and I don't really care for Jasmine at all and I especially can't stand her mother. I think Crosby should get some legally established visitation rights—end of story.

These comments suggest a post-feminist, post-racial tale of an "opportunist" (or gold-digger) black single mother who is looking to "have it all" by shirking her mothering duties.

While many of these participants point to Jasmine's alleged "habit" of dropping Jabbar off and picking him up on a whim as proof of her controlling behavior, when asked by other discussants to explain why she isn't trustworthy, none was able to articulate any links with the show's scripts or plot points apart from her decision to stop trying to contact Crosby when she was pregnant. This decision—concocted by the writers to replicate the original movie's "surprise" of the biracial son—makes her irredeemable in the eyes of many white viewers across all of the discussion threads. On the board "Is Jabbar Crosby's Son?" N. (a woman) snarked on the thread "Jasmine," "Perhaps he would have returned her call if he knew she was having his baby . . . that was a huge part of the message she left out . . ."

Some viewers went so far as to blame Jasmine entirely for the pregnancy, as well as for not telling Crosby. In the thread "Crosby and Jasmine Belong Together," H. (a white woman) told Jasmine's supporters that "Someone not being ready for parenthood is no excuse to not tell him for 5 years. If Jasmine was stupid enough to have unprotected sex with an irresponsible man, she should have dealt with the consequences. No excuse will ever be good enough for what she did." This comment employs the double-bind often used in post-feminist discourse to demean single mothers. On the one hand, Jasmine must take full responsibility for the pregnancy and alleged lack of contraception. On the other hand, she is pilloried for being too self-sufficient and not trying hard enough to get the father involved. Is there a statute of limitations for telling the biological father about a child? Does a woman have a "duty" to do so, even if she has no legal or other solid tie to the father—and he expresses no interest in a relationship beyond sex?

Many discussants stated the obvious: They "identified with Crosby" because he was, as P. (a white male) said, more like themselves. On "Crosby should dump Jasmine," he wrote, "There is something about Jasmine I don't trust. I can't put a finger on it, but I don't see it lasting. Mabey because I have more in common w/ Crosby than anyone else on the show? Time will only tell." White women who said they identified with Crosby did not assert likeness per se, but said that Jasmine was so distasteful, that they had to take Crosby's side, and that the show meant for them to identify with Crosby rather than with Jasmine. In the discussion "Crosby should dump Jasmine," T. F. and M. (a woman) challenged each other about what identifying with a character means.

> T. F.: I gotta wonder why you are so pro-jasmine?!?!?!?! It seems to me the writers want us to identify more w/Crosby.
>
> M.: . . . and i gotta wonder why you are so anti-Jasmine?! In fact i am totally identifying with Crosby, hence the reason why i support him

forgiving Jasmine, supporting her career, and loving her. That's the way it's being written and i am supporting it. This season Crosby appears to be more in love with Jasmine than ever . . . that's what i'm supporting. If jas is who he loves, i am totally identifying with him, it's just what the writers want me to do. How exactly are you identifying with Crosby again?

Here, M. (whose photo suggests she is a woman of color) intervened in the zero-sum framework set up by many of the discussants: To like Crosby is to hate Jasmine. M. asserted that the writers were not necessarily pushing viewers to take sides; rather, they were asking viewers to explore a growing relationship between two imperfect adults who shared a child but not a lot of experience in being a couple. M. redefined identification with a character as making a connection with his/her feelings rather than taking sides. Although some other participants in the discussion appreciated her acknowledgment of the complexity of the characters, none took her up on the suggestion that identification wasn't limited to deciding whose team you're on when a romantic pair has difficulties.

THEME TWO: IS JABBAR *REALLY* CROSBY'S SON?

The second theme was at times interwoven with the first, and was explored mostly in the discussion board (again started by L.) "Is Jabbar Crosby's son?"

> L.: I don't think he is. Jasmine never told Crosby she was pregnant & waited five years to tell him he had a son! And she freaked out when Crosby asked for a paternity test. If she has nothing to hide she would have agreed right away. I'm surprised Crosby didn't ask why Jasmine waited so long to tell him about Jabbar & didn't question her at all.

K. (a woman) replied that she feared "[C]rosby will get very attached, and then he will find out jabar is not his. :(" A. (also a woman) added, "It is very suspicious that she would wait five years to tell him he has a son."

The next commentator, a white man, G., disputed their remarks: "I honestly think that crosby is the father, and that he will stop seeing his current girlfriend and end up having another baby with jabbars mother." To counter, L. shared the following suspicion about Jabbar's skin tone:

> L.: If jabbar is crosby's son, wouldn't he be white or mixed race? He's very dark & his mom isn't that dark. My aunt who is white had two sons with a jamaican man & they are both dark. I always thought if the father is white & the mother is dark, the kid usually is white.

L.'s casual expression of racial "knowledge" illustrates the ways post-racial discussions continue to indulge in pseudo-biological explanations for difference. It also sparked many responses, even though the next episode of the show cleared up the fatherhood issue—Crosby received the results of the DNA test and had proof Jabbar was his son. While a few participants shared their happiness that Crosby wasn't set up for disappointment, others returned to L.'s description of what makes mixed-race people look like their parents. L.'s attempt to use her experience with her aunt's children as proof of what most biracial people should look like hearkens back to the pseudo-science of race and the naïve, misguided, but still prevalent understandings of what factors contribute to skin color variation.

Commentators replied to her posting with with varying degrees of patience. The first response (from C., a woman of color) gently corrected her assumptions with examples and counter-examples of real-life biracial families:

> C.: @L.—I'm late to the party but biracial children's coloring can range from as dark as the dark parent to as light as the lighter parent. The young man who plays Jabbar is biracial; his mother is white and his father is black. Shar Jackson & Kevin Federline's 2 children are very fair (latino/mediteranian looking). While Robert DeNiro & Grace Hightower's son is darker. Genetics is just that funny.
> The only thing I would disagree with is the color of the baby Jasmine gave birth to in the episode last night. The vast majority of "full" black children (regardless of their parents coloring) are very, very light at birth. They darken up later. So I would expect a biracial child at birth to be even lighter. The baby was the only mistake I

would say the show made. Crosby & Jasmine might get together so Parenthood has time to do better research.

Invoking examples from the celebrity world, C. gently informed L. that her single experience with one biracial family was insufficient to form solid expectations for what a biracial child should look like. Simultaneously, C. questioned the use of a "too black" baby for the birth scene, asserting her own type of expertise in skin color variation over time/age and suggesting that the creators of Parenthood need to do more work on the realism of their racial representations. Although her skin color logic is also faulty (kids' skin tones, eye color, hair texture, and so on, can go through many changes as they age), C. makes an important point: The racial appearance of one family member is not sufficient evidence on which to base assertions about how multiracial people's skin "matches" or doesn't match their parents'.

A later response was frank in its disbelief and disdain for L.'s conclusions about skin color within interracial families. S., whose picture shows a black woman standing arm in arm with a lighter-skinned man, wrote : "@L . . . were you born on Mars? Really? Who are you to question what someone's skin color should be? People of color come in all colors, not just dark, or white. Sheesh!" Refuting the oversimplified, faux biologies of race in the discussion more forcefully than C., S. rejected the idea that we can easily map racial identity of parents and children via comparisons in skin color.

Responding to continued claims that Jasmine tricked Crosby about Jabbar's paternity, multiple discussants joined in with textual cues as well as points of physical similarities between the actors that play Crosby and Jabbar. After M. (a white user) predicted a medical emergency would show mismatching blood types between father and son, others argued that the producers made casting and storyline choices so that their family tie was clear to see:

> C. M. (FEMALE): haha i knew he was [Crosby's son] from the beginning! he had to be. each character had to have more than one story line. Crosby was with him and katie, and with him and jabbar. and the shows all about parenting. crosby was the only one that wasn't a parent, and he was the irrisponsible child. . . .

N. (WHITE MALE): The kid is his! The show says that right after crosby left jazmyn she all of a sudden got pregnant! Right after crosby left her and by the way the kid looks like him so theres ur proof the kid is his!

C.: @M.—I HIGHLY doubt a medical emergency is going to arise to show Jabar isn't Crosby's son. That is good for soap operas (a dying breed) not dramatic comedies. I have to agree with [N.] on this one. The kid is his and they casted a child that could pass for Crosby's child. Also the parenthood website listed Jabbar as Crosby's BEFORE the results. . . . If the kid wasn't his then Julia who is a lawyer would have said something. She's the one that told him about his legal and financial responsibilities.

This discussion of what makes TV families "look alike" veered between assumptions about the "real world" of race, genes, and skin color and the world of casting talent and scripting a primetime drama in a "realistic" manner. C., C. M., and N. were quick to reject comments that questioned Crosby and Jabbar's father-son relationship by combining information gleaned from the show, its genre conventions, and comparisons between the actors to reinforce the DNA "evidence" provided by the paternity test episodes. These participants referred both to scenes from the show and to the ways the opening credits, teasers, and website information designated Jabbar as Crosby's legitimate son. They also rejected the idea that the writers of a "quality" show like *Parenthood* would concoct "soap opera" plot twists in order to manufacture more drama.

This work of weaving together multiple media and "real life" resources to support particular interpretations of the show is even more evident in the final theme, wherein mostly women of color viewers devoted significant energy and effort to argue for Jasmine's complexity and humanity to her detractors.

THEME THREE: GIVE JASMINE AND CROSBY A REAL CHANCE
Many women of color fans expressed sadness and frustration at the amount of hatred others directed towards Jasmine. M. and C. N., for example, exchanged exasperated back-to-back posts on L's "Crosby should dump Jasmine" thread:

Figure 4.1. Joy Bryant,
actress who plays Jas-
mine on *Parenthood*.
© Kristen Noseda
./Retna Ltd./Corbis.
Courtesy of Corbis
Images.

M.: CN, i can't believe we are all watching the same show. Some viewers are
just making up things about Jasmine that have no basis in reality; Jasmine is lying, you can't trust her, she'll break Cros' heart, she's up to
something. LOL. The same ones who think Crosby is a model father,
are wishing he has an affair with Gaby; the same ones who claim
to love Jabbar, are wishing his mother would die. Makes no sense
to me. . . . The Jasmine bashing is unreasonable, it's like some feel
personally injured by the fact that Crosby loves Jasmine, despite her
flaws. All the characters on PH are flawed and that's what i love about
them, that's what makes them interesting. Katims is doing a great job.

C.N.: Jasmine could be a clone of June Cle[a]ver and some people will have
issues with her. LOL! I'm still trying to figure out this big lie that

Jasmine is holding. I know, she's an alien from out of space. LOL!
This is so funny to me. What is she up to? Trying to steal his money?
No. Crosby doesn't have a lot of money and neither does his family.
She can't be trusted? Does she work for Bin Laden? LOL! Jasmine is
flawed like the other characters on the show, which makes them all
the more interesting to me.

Both C. N. and M. (whose picture icons suggest they are women of
color) situate Jasmine as one of many complex, flawed characters on
the show. They argue that the anti-Jasmine viewers are unreasonably
magnifying her flaws in ways they do not for other characters. In later
exchanges, they identify race as an influence in this unreasonable
assessment.

M.'s creation of a new thread, "Crosby and Jasmine belong together,"
can be seen both as a reaction to the anti-Jasmine sentiment on the
other discussions and as a way to create more space to appreciate the
show without having to always confront negative comments about the
only major female character of color on the show. Although M.'s thread
was not as popular in terms of the number of different people who
joined the discussion, its 280 postings—most between herself and four
other women of color—provide an extended commentary by audience
members on their hopes for the portrayal of an interracial couple on
primetime "quality" television. Cross-referenced with other postings on
the other threads, discussions between M. and those who shared her
views show that (1) many of these viewers were disturbed by the lack of
complex representations of women of color and their families; and (2)
many believed that well-written television shows can make an impact
on how people see race—for good or ill.

M., P. (a woman of color), C., and others make it clear that part of
their attraction to the show was the inclusion of Jasmine and Jabbar's
storyline. And, as their viewing continued over the course of the two
seasons, their investment in this interracial family's story was palpable
on the "belong together" board.

> M.: I am so excited that PH will return this Tuesday, i like the whole show
> but i really love the Crosby/Jasmine/ Jabbar [storyline]. I hope that
> Cros and Jas have a serious talk about being an IR [interracial]

couple, especially now that they are engaged to be married. They will encounter racism at some point and they should at least talk about how they will deal with it. Yes, IR couples are just like other couples, but they also have unique challenges, which should not be ignored.

M.'s hopes, though, were met with skepticism from P., who predicted the show would not maintain Jasmine and Crosby's relationship once Crosby's niece, Haddie, began to consider a relationship with a black older teen, Alex, in the second season.

> P.: So I read the link "getting involved with Gaby." Have been expecting it. It will be really hard seeing how much a part of the family she is now. I don't know. I'm like A. I don't know if I'll be able to watch it if they split it up. I will tell you, I got really scared with the Haddie/Alex thing because I felt they were not going to have 2 interracial relationships on the show. So the question is, who gets to stay?

As these viewers mused over Jasmine and Crosby's future, they worried about what the writers would do to them—especially given the negative audience opinions they'd read about Jasmine on Facebook and elsewhere. The main concern was that her character was given neither sufficient screen time in her self, nor enough interactions with other Bravermans to overcome the deficit she inherited from the show's set up—namely, not telling Crosby about Jabbar for five years. They feared Jasmine would continue to be portrayed as the villain in the relationship in order for the writers to foster audience sympathy for Crosby.

Thus, it isn't surprising that these viewers often jumped to Jasmine's defense in discussion threads within and outside of the "belong together" thread. These defenses, though, were not knee-jerk assertions of racial sameness or solidarity like those imagined and derided in conservative post-racial discourses. Rather, these *Parenthood* fans articulated exactly where the text revealed to them nuances or possibilities for depth in Jasmine's life story, and reminded their fellow viewers of relevant events, plot twists, and character traits that could provide fodder for different interpretations. On top of these text-oriented interventions, these women also interweaved their own experiences with stereotyping, single motherhood, and television history to make their points.

For example, when other fans lambasted Jasmine for not doing more to inform Crosby of her pregnancy or for being too "controlling," many of her supporters acknowledged she could have done more. But they also asked the critics to consider other elements of the situation. First, as in this exchange between L. (white) and C. (woman of color) on "Why are Crosby and Jasmine hiding their relationship?" the latter argues that people are turning a blind eye to Crosby's poor choices.

> L.: I don't like Jasmine's attitude sometimes, and how she took Jabbar away from Crosby whenever they had a fight. It was immature and mean. Calling him about Jabbar wasn't enough. As soon as she found out she was pregnant, she should have gone to see him and told him in person. It seems like she used that as an excuse to justify her actions.
>
> C.: @L. we will have to agree to disagree. . . . Jasmine should have tried harder at the time of her pregnancy to tell Crosby. But the fact that he didn't call her back showed his immaturity. It appears that Crosby has had commitment issues in the past (ie Katie Pilot episode). . . . Crosby's character has grown on me since the show began but he WAS a flack in the beginning. As far as Jasmine taking Jabbar away she did it twice and one was justified. When Crosby asked for the paternity test she should not have reacted that way but she later apologized. The 2nd time was when Crosby left Jabbar in the pool with the "lifeguard." I wouldn't leave my kid alone with a doctor and he left their child in a pool with some random dude. Sorry but you would have to regain my trust on that one. The behavior was irresponsible and I wouldn't leave my child in your care.

In this exchange, C. redirected the questions of choice and responsibility away from Jasmine's original decision to have a child without a father involved to how parenting should be conducted once the child is out of the womb. Highlighting Crosby's track record, she argued that Jasmine's reactions weren't spiteful but logical because she was protecting their son.

Second, supporters of Jasmine reminded viewers that her labor as a single mother for five years was invisible, yet should be taken into account. For instance, in the "Jasmine" thread, J., a white female viewer, thought that Jasmine deserved more credit for her single motherhood despite her sin of omission.

> J.: I like Jasmine—she screwed up in not telling Crosby about Jabbar, but she also made a good point when he didn't return her third phone call she thought maybe she didn't want him around. Crosby's character is already kind of irresponsible, imagine that five years ago. It's tough being a single mom, she was probably just trying to protect herself and her kid.

Asking her fellow viewers to consider how hard it would be to parent a child alone, as Jasmine did for five years, J. also noted that having to adjust to having a new parent in the picture would be challenging, too.

Discussants underscored how the show privileges the perspectives of Braverman family members and how Jasmine's relative lack of screen time and story development makes it easy for her to look like "the bad guy" since we see her through Crosby's eyes.

> M.: . . . I take issue with the writing. I can't help but conclude that the writing deliberately sacrificed Jasmine's character to tell Crosby's story. Some of the characterisation for Jasmine was just ridiculous, case in point, changing the date of the wedding. No one does that. It was crazy and only served to arouse additional resentment for Jasmine. As written it's easy to erroneously sympathise with Crosby and blame Jasmine.
>
> P.: M., I think people forget about her giving up her dream with Alvin Ailey to be with him. I think part of that is a lot of people don't realize how prestigious a job that is. Also, this show is not necessarily about HER journey but HIS. We are viewing his struggles with becoming a parent.

Here, P. and M. reminded Jasmine's critics of her sacrifices for her son and Crosby. P. surmised that many viewers probably don't have knowledge of the Alvin Ailey Dance Company, which tends to be more accessible to connoisseurs of dance and/or African American cultural history. This comment suggests that the show writers may have done a disservice to the character by assuming most viewers would recognize the prestige of this dance company. Because her career was not clearly outlined, it was easier for audiences to dismiss her choice as an instance of the post-feminist cliché of "career versus family." From this vantage point, Jasmine was merely selfish, and could not be credited with giving up something of significance to return to Berkeley.

Third, once it became clear that Crosby would cheat on Jasmine with Gaby, the fans who posted on "Crosby and Jasmine Belong Together" questioned why the Jasmine haters both supported a man who would cheat and blamed Jasmine for a choice made by Crosby. M. noted how the double standard for sexual infidelity blames women (fiancée pushed him into cheating) and ignores the agency of the men.

> M.: The more i think of it, the more i am puzzled by the writing re Jasmine. I mean why not show Jasmine hurt over the argument, why imply Jasmine pushed Crosby to cheat? Then other things did not make sense, like Jasmine asking Crosby what he was doing there, why would she ask that unless they had agreed to take a break? Then the whole Jabbar issue, obviously they needed to have Jasmine and Jabbar away so that Crosby could cheat, but did they really think the audience would gloss over that and not blame Jasmine AGAIN? I did not get the impression that Jasmine was punishing Crosby by keeping Jabbar away, i do think that she had to go and see her SICK aunt. Coming on the heels of their argument it could look that way but i did not get that she was being spiteful. IMO [in my opinion] the writing was exaggerated to skew things in Crosby's favour . . .

M.'s comment resonates with my reading of *Parenthood*'s post-racial approach to inclusion: It presents characters of color to audiences through the eyes of white characters. Additionally, Jasmine's supporters aired frustrations with how the writers set her up to be compared with Gaby, another under-developed character but one who was clearly sympathetic given her care-taking relationship with Max.

Other fans saw Jasmine as the one to blame and that Gaby as preferable for Crosby. H., a female commenter, told fans on "Crosby and Jasmine Belong Together" that Jasmine's attitude pushed Crosby into sexual betrayal.

> H.: I think Crosby wants to have the responsibilities and baggage that comes along with Jasmine, but she isn't letting him take his share of

it. He got no say in the first 5 years of his son's life, and it appears that he has no say still. I do get that they might love each other or that love is growing, but I think the issues and Jasmine not giving an inch will kill that . . .

More bluntly, M. K. (a man) chimed in on the same thread with the statement: "It's Jasmines fault, she waited 5 years to tell him about the kid. Started off all wrong, women for you." Later, he posted, "Yeah P. They had jungle fever. It's over. Move on, plus Gaby is better. Ha." In response to these types of remarks, M. commiserated with P.:

> M.: i am just as flabbergasted as you are that people think that Gaby is a better fit. You know i'm beginning to wonder if Gaby did not play Crosby, he should have known better than to share details of his private life with someone of the opposite sex, whom he was just getting to know. He was practically ill-speaking Jasmine. Gaby just had sex with someone in a committed relationship, whom she knew was in a vulnerable place, and she will make a good life-partner? P. folks have made up their minds, next week they will sympathise with Gaby and Jasmine will be the evil B#@&! I was surprised when Crosby proposed, and i felt that there was something in the pipeline that had nothing with them being married, i felt it was a plot point for something else, and now i know.

Likewise, A. G., a woman, took issue with folks who asserted that Gaby was more attractive than Jasmine:

> A. G.: So you have seen the good girl Gaby. How do you not know that Jasmine is also loving and sweet? She has done a wonderful job raising her son. I did not see any one avoid her when she intertwined with the Bravermans at Halloween, Thanksgiving, her bridal shower. Just because the writers have her not be social with anyone outside Crosby, you have put this judgment upon her.

Finally, a few viewers questioned why other fans described Jasmine as "controlling" and "mean" instead of "strong" or "responsible." One white woman, K., asked why the commentators who disapproved of Jasmine's choices were so willing to take Crosby's side:

> K.: I don't know why strong women characters are so disliked by audiences
> today. Jasmine kept her baby, she followed her dream of becoming
> a professional dancer and then decided that her child and Crosby
> meant more to her. . . . Crosby's character is immature, irresponsible,
> childish. . . .Why all the love for a loser guy? I don't get it?

For K., Jasmine's plight was related to that of female TV characters in
general: They have few opportunities to be well rounded and strong
without drawing fire for being bitches. Pursuing a related idea, C. S.
wondered why fan evaluations of other women on the show, such as
Sarah Braverman, a single mother who started a romance with her
daughter's English teacher, were not criticized as much as Jasmine.

> C. S.: I can't believe all the things that people are saying. Does anyone
> believe in commitment anymore. Would everyone say the things
> about Sara or Julia. Both have extremely strong personalities. I think
> this is a pick on Jasmine. This woman took care of her son without
> asking Crosby for anything. She is a strong woman who made the
> mistake of having a child with an immature brat. . . .Wow, this makes
> me say Hmmmmm! What is the true story behind the story.

Here, given her other stated concerns about having a successful interracial relationship on the show, C. S. implied that "the true story" behind
the anti-Jasmine comments was racial.

M. also saw Jasmine trapped in a double-bind, and expressed her
exasperation with the hateful remarks she saw on Facebook.

> M.: C. S. after a while i decided to take a break, it is beyond comprehension
> why folks would say the things they do about Jasmine. I knew i had
> to stop when things were being posted about Jasmine/Crosby that
> NEVER happened in the show. I've read that Crosby only proposed
> to jasmine because he did not want her to run off with Jabbar, that
> Jasmine accepted because she wanted a father for Jabbar, that Crosby
> didn't really cheat because he and Jasmine broke up; i mean which
> show are people watching, some don't care about the facts. . . If
> jasmine left jabbar with Crosby for the day, she was using him as a
> babysitter, if she took him somewhere for a day, she was preventing

Crosby from seeing his son. . . . Jasmine isn't allowed to be human like other women, Julia is darn controlling, she belittles her spouse at times and folks don't relentlessly attack her for it. Jasmine can't ever get upset, she should always say yes to Crosby, actually some folks don't want Jasmine to have an opinion.

M.'s comment echoes critiques of media coverage of female politicians and other representations of powerful women—it is nearly impossible for a woman of strength to escape punishment of some sort for not conforming to feminine expectations or for supposedly emasculating men.[27] But these sanctions are more likely for black women, who are already assumed to be less feminine and more emasculating than white or Asian women.[28]

THEME FOUR: WHAT'S UP WITH THE WRITERS?

The main contributors to the "Crosby and Jasmine belong together" discussion thread were incensed and disappointed when Crosby had sex with Gaby. While they credited the writers—particularly Katims—for having the guts to put interracial couples on the show, they were wary about the show's ability to manage Crosby and Jasmine's relationship. They were also concerned that the storyline would veer into stereotypes or repeat other mainstream media depictions of white men/black women and ultimately end or explaining away the relationships. Their fears were exacerbated by their knowledge of other fans' hatred for Jasmine, which they felt was due in part to the underdevelopment of her back story and the way she was perceived by some viewers as a stereotypical "baby mama/angry black woman."

When she first started the thread, M. had high hopes that the writers would avoid this route.

M.: A lot of viewers think that Crosby and Jasmine are stereotypical characters, so they keep expecting Crosby to slip up (by maybe sleeping with Gaby) or Jasmine to break his heart (typical baby-mama goldigger). I don't think katims is going the stereotypical route with Crosby and Jasmine (nor his other characters). They are instead defying those stereotypes and showing that two free-spirited Bohemians can become committed, responsible and selfless as a couple and as parents. Well at least I hope so.

By the time Crosby had sex with Gaby, her hopes were dashed.

> M.: Well the show has created a setup where it's easy for them to bow out of reuniting the couple. . . . Also, BW [black women] in IR [interracial] relationships do not have a good track record in TV, they never get the guy and never make it to the altar; so forgive me if i'm not hopeful this one will.
>
> P.: @C. S.—I felt back in October when he proposed that they would not let them get married and I felt that I couldn't watch it anymore if they broke them up. I'm not as strident as I was then, but it would be really difficult to watch. They are my favorites. I like everyone else, but they are my favorite. And I told you, M. when they had Haddie dating Alex, that I was worried about Cros/jas because I just didn't think they would have 2 interracial couples in the same family. . . .
>
> M.: . . . If Jasmine's character was not invested in when she was with Crosby, one of the central characters, do you think they will invest in her when she is not? It will be totally cruel of this show to have Crosby and Gaby hook up and Jasmine on the sidelines flying her single, independent woman flag.

P.'s, C. S.'s, and M.'s disappointment was not generated solely by the infidelity storyline, but also by their experiences with primetime television's lack of investment in black female characters and interracial romance. Reading reluctance to have two interracial couples in the plot twist that broke up Jasmine and Crosby and reflecting on how little audiences saw Jasmine (even when she was Crosby's fiancée), they were pessimistic that the writers could create anything of interest for her character after the break up. The pro-Jasmine viewers knit together clues from the show, promos, fan sites, and other media hoping to find evidence that *Parenthood*'s writers were not planning to "ruin" Jasmine and Crosby's relationship, or push actress Joy Bryant out of the picture altogether.

> M.: Sometimes i can't see any other purpose for the Gaby thing but destruction of C&J. But Katims said in a recent interview that he wanted to bring to life that irresponsible part of Crosby that we heard a lot about but never saw.

P.: I feel like he did it cause he loves Minka Kelly [from *Friday Night Lights*].

Here, P. and M. traded information from their past acquaintance with Katims's other shows along with interviews with the writer and cast members to try to understand why he would change the relationship so drastically. Reading across these texts and speculating about behind the scenes connections amongst actors and writers, they found additional reasons to explain the probable demise of their favorite *Parenthood* couple.

As they read the tea leaves of entertainment news and fan sites, these viewers were clearly invested in the show's representation of the Crosby/Jasmine interracial relationship and in the inclusion of a black mother and biracial child in the family unit. They were also pleading, in a sense, for the show's writers to resist following the well-worn path to break-ups for black woman/white man pairings in mainstream media.

C. S.: my two cents, I would love to see Jasmine and Crosby together, but it appears as if the people who hate Jasmine have won. When they had Crosby cheat on Jasmine, they doomed the relationship then. If they break them up for good, that is it for me. I would not stop looking at the program because they broke this couple up, but because of the mentality of the writers, directors and producers. They do not see the value in having a child of color with a 2 parent married family. I know this just a drama on tv, but it depicts life situations.

P. then suggested the writers' had made a mistake in deciding which themes to pursue, and that the history between Minka Kelly (the actress who plays Gaby) and Katims contributed to the problematic representations.

P.: I guess I feel they are making [Jasmine] more hard and inflexible. I'm mad that they took an issue—control—and took it off the table and put this stupid one [cheating] on it. You can forgive cheating it just takes time and time is the thing they need. But really, i think Katims loves Minka and wanted her in the show and then thought she was so gorgeous, who wouldn't want to sleep with her. Yeesh! . . . . And

> I saw you [M] post about the angry black woman—that was good. I
> personally think that's why everyone wants Gaby with him. . . .
>
> M.: @P. i don't think we are going to get our couple . . . I've lost hope, TPTB
> [The Powers That Be] will listen to their core audience, i've been here
> done this already.

C. S., M., and P. figured that "The Powers That Be"—meaning the network and the writers—were not concerned about viewers like themselves. They assumed that the "core" viewers were white and likely to
side with the Jasmine-haters.

After the season finale, when Jasmine reconnected with Crosby for a
possible reconciliation, the discussants returned to share their thoughts
of what might happen next. A few were happy that Jasmine seemed to
be willing to let Crosby back into her life and enjoyed a return to scenes
between the actors that were not angry or tense. Others were suspicious
of the show producers and the ambiguity of the ending sequences, won-
dering if they would 'make some sneaky move' during the summer hia-
tus to get rid of Jasmine.

> P.: I agree. I am glad it ended with them looking at the house and talking.
> That's what they need to do. They need to have a season 3. They have
> no other shows and I am sick of two hours of the biggest loser. . . .
>
> M.: C. S. it would also be hard for me to continue viewing. Joy Bryant's
> character attracted me to this show and i have grown to love all the
> story lines. But i don't love the show to the point of seeing my fav
> character relegated to baby-mama status only, especially when i
> was made to buy into the idea of them getting married. Jasmine the
> baby-mama forever just wouldn't cut it for me because it reinforces
> the stereotype that black women aren't desirable life partners. It also
> didn't help that they overdid the controlling issue . . . and it certainly
> didn't help that she was compared to Gaby, a sympathetic character
> from day one. . . . If they break up i will know whose viewership
> TPTB really value.

These fans' distrust of the show's producers ("The Powers That
Be") was warranted given the track record of network TV with interracial families and strong female characters. Except in rare occasions,

primetime dramas give women of color short shrift, relegating them to auxiliary roles and less screen time. Like the audience members in prior studies noted at the beginning of this chapter, the Facebook discussants who rooted for Jasmine and Crosby knew that television history and, perhaps, white audience opinions were against them. Unfortunately, while many women of color and a few white viewers pointed out how the scripts were stacked against Jasmine, most of the white fans who participated in the discussion threads seemed to dismiss any other interpretations of this character. Their reactions correspond with the predictions of the parasocial contact hypothesis—that is, if a character from an out-group (Jasmine) is not perceived to be attractive, likable, realistic, or similar to the in-group (white fans) then parasocial interaction with the character will not challenge stereotypes and may even reinforce them.

Identifications and Disidentifications with Interracial Intimates

Analysis of these comment threads illustrates how fans' views of Jasmine, Crosby, and Gaby clash. As they described and evaluated Jasmine, the great majority of white viewers judgment that she was unlikable, their fixation on the adjective "controlling," and their descriptions of her "dumping" Jabbar on his father but not allowing Crosby to "wear the pants" resonate with the controlling stereotypes of black women delineated by black feminist scholar Patricia Hill Collins. Indeed, some of these viewers even insinuated events and plot points that did not happen on the show to reinforce their case against Jasmine's character.

Other viewers who posted on Facebook—the majority of whom were women of color—challenged the stereotyping of Jasmine and articulated ways to view Jasmine so that she was likable, realistic, and similar to other women characters on the show. They compensated for the lack of screen time and backstory for her character by reiterating and weaving together scenes, experiences, and information across episodes, and challenged discussion participants who brought in false information. Likewise, many reread her single motherhood as an act of strength, not manipulation, and acknowledged the labor and sacrifices of single moms in ways that opposed post-feminist discourses. Some of these commentators also made racism visible. M., in particular, explicitly called out the "baby-mama" stereotype and insisted that the quality of the writers' work—specifically their goal to make characters who are flawed, but not stereotypical—showed Jasmine to be more than that. Finally, Jasmine's supporters wondered aloud why and how viewers could take Crosby's side so easily even when his choices and emotional characteristics did not suggest a flawless individual without any blame. Here, the counter-narrative presented by fans rejected the assumption of innocence for Crosby—a white man—and challenged white viewers to articulate how they came to be convinced of Jasmine's guilt.

Although the participants in the Facebook discussion threads staked claims to particular viewpoints and sympathies with specific characters, the additional conversations on the site did extend the parasocial contact of the television series to an online context, providing another potential vehicle for audience members to (1) interact in virtual space with people of different racial backgrounds via media; (2) reconsider their initial judgment of Jasmine and her family; and (3) consider different information and views about interracial relationships and single motherhood. While the conversations on Facebook I analyzed in this chapter can't tell us whether or not anyone who participated or read these threads changed his or her mind about any of the characters, the discussion board does illustrate audience investment in and interaction with post-racial characters on television. Importantly, the differences between most of the white viewers and women of color viewers suggests that applications of black matriarch stereotypes persist, as do disturbing misunderstandings about the ways interracial families and children are supposed to look and behave. It is heartening to see some viewers challenge such ideas and use their own interpretive lenses and experiences to articulate their desires for more sophisticated treatments of interracial relationships and strong black women. At the same time, further investigation is needed to gauge whether these online discussions can foster reconsiderations of the racial stereotypes and assumptions that were on display in the majority of the Facebook postings.

5

Not "Post-Racial," Race-Aware

Blogging Race in the Twenty-First Century

One troubling omission from the post-racial discourse I have analyzed thus far is the idea of "anti-racism." I thought it reasonable to expect that, in the news, more folks would refer to anti-racism in some way, shape, or form to argue that we were on the verge of a post-racial society. Whether the term appeared in the context of crediting anti-racist movements or anti-racist education, I thought I would see it more often than I did. Indeed, I did a search for variations on "anti-racism" as part of the initial data collection. I used computer searches to see which key terms appeared most often with "post-racial" between 2000 and 2010. I found that in over 4,000 news items, variants on "anti-racism" only appeared in 45; in contrast, "reverse racist" appeared 70 times, "interracial marriage" popped up in 250 items, and "affirmative action" appeared 400 times. This finding is shocking and troubling. Although most people would agree that "post-racial" means that racism has been eliminated, commentators and journalists didn't see fit to extol the virtues of anti-racism as they discussed post-racial politicians or cultural consumption. The focus on personal choices' demographic shifts and gotcha media strategies of the Right seems to have pushed the civic actions of organized, anti-racist people to the margins.

As post-racial discourses are employed by media to reimagine and project an idealized multicultural nation, they are also prescribing how citizens should understand their own and others' racial identities in the public sphere, in public policy, and in private life. These discourses imagine how we citizens should "*do* race"—how we should understand it and perform it in our own lives, as well as how to communicate our racial identity to our fellow Americans. These prescriptions, as the first chapter illustrated, rarely include the term "anti-racism." Post-racial news suggests that citizens and government should do little, if anything, to take action in the public sphere to ensure that the post-racial future actually dawns. In effect, they are implicitly endorsing particular models for understanding the role of race in our society, which involve treating race as a slowly dying social category, a nineteenth-century anachronism that will soon have less influence in our lives than eye color. These dominant discourses largely ignore matters of socioeconomic inequality and evidence of continued institutional racism. They still perpetuate the myth of separate races; the only "positive" difference is the belief they can be joined through biological hybridity. Multiracial people and interracial marriage are proposed as solutions to the problem of the color line, accompanied by calls to get over race, to choose other identities for social organization.

Robert Asen suggests that scholars reorient their "approaches to civic engagement from asking questions of what [citizens do] to asking questions of how" they do citizenship.[1] He suggests we think of citizenship as consisting of "mode[s] of public engagement," which can help us focus on ways in which citizens engage each other and institutions, and produce communications. This theory of citizenship also recognizes that citizenship often entails risk, for in engaging other members of the public in what could perhaps be creative or unapproved modes, rejection or even violence might ensue. In related fashion, this theory of "doing citizenship" sees engaged actors using media discourses to draw lines between public and private, for example, or among genders, races, and classes. As lines—of identification, perhaps—are drawn as citizens engage each set of discourses, Asen argues that "Some participants will be better positioned to draw lines that better represent their interests."[2]

Using Asen's approach, I suggest that post-racial discourses support different modalities of *racial citizenship*, and that with their power to influence and set boundaries for public discourse, media are major players in drawing lines between identity groups and between acceptable ways of doing race, doing citizenship. Furthermore, and importantly, dominant post-racial narratives offer particular modes of doing race and citizenship that do not necessarily represent the interests of people of color. If "racial" citizenship before the civil rights reforms of the 1950s and 1960s meant (fairly) neat divisions between white citizens having extreme social, economic, and political privilege and people of color being brutally oppressed and having access to few, if any, privileges of citizenship, then what does post-racial discourse imagine post-racial citizenship to be? The cases presented in the previous chapters suggest a few ways of doing post-racial citizenship, with preferences for the privatization of race overwhelming ideas for reforming or reimagining public-oriented racial practices or performances.

As discussed in the first two chapters, one of the main ways to be a post-racial citizen is to ask the government to eliminate race as a category for recognizing its citizens and/or organizing its policies. This neo-colorblindness asks citizens to refrain from declarations of discrimination based on race/ethnicity, and to look for race-blind remedies to racial inequalities in education, housing, employment, and so forth. Similarly, as *Justice Sunday III* illustrated, post-racial citizens are encouraged to invest in other, ostensibly more legitimate group identities to organize civic interests. Where race is framed as a destructive and divisive mode of identification, other types of identification, such as religion or nation, are framed as sources of solidarity and healing the scars of race. This approach not only oversimplifies categories of identity as singular rather than intersectional, but also requires amnesia from people of color as they consider overtures and outreach efforts based in shared religion or nation. Moreover, while paying lip service to the social construction of race, this discourse continues to essentialize racial identities.

At the same time that post-racial discourse frowns on political uses of race, it directs post-racial citizens to "do" race through market consumption and interpersonal relations. Fashionistas, music lovers, and movie-goers are congratulated for mixing it up with racial others. In *Parenthood* and in news focused on multiracial families, transformations of family demographics are offered as emblems of post-racial progress, with no explanation of how these interpersonal affinities will translate to social equality. This post-racial paradigm implies that people of color who "blend" with white lovers and spouses will "choose" to immerse themselves in the dominant community, becoming a sort of "bridge" or "model minority" who won't make race an issue. Thus, a kind of neo-assimilation results, where we're all "beige" in the end.

What is largely absent, except in a few outliers in the news, is a sense of how the newly visible multiracial landscape might transform racial politics and interracial relationships. If "old" racial politics were built on essentialism, white supremacy, and extreme legal and physical segregation of different groups, then why not imagine a post-racial politics built on coalitions of groups, forged through regular multiracial interactions? Why not look for examples of people with shared interests in dismantling racial hierarchy, reimagining their modes of identification and goals as they discuss inequality, history, and strategy?

This chapter presents examples of some practical and hopeful race-aware approaches to post-racial citizenship found on news websites and blogs that are focused on racial dynamics. These sites provide not only criticism of the aforementioned ways of understanding and doing race in post-racial America, they also suggest avenues of discussion and action for racial justice. In other words, these sites give visitors tools to critique the post-racial mystique and ideas for practicing anti-racism. In the process, these blogs and webzines reject the "Great Leader" paradigm through features on everyday acts and practices of anti-racism.

Post-Racial Online

Of course, it would be folly to try to catalogue, let alone analyze, all references to "post-racial" and "anti-racism" on the web. For this chapter, I looked at a handful of blogs and web news sites that I encountered as I delved into post-racial references in the news, and sites I knew of from my prior work on race and online news. These sites were *Color-Lines*, *Racialicious*, and *The Black Snob*, and, of course, they represent only a snippet of what might be available online in terms of anti-racist post-racial discourses. Nonetheless, they do provide an instructive contrast to the mainstream news and partisan blogs that made up the bulk of news items analyzed in earlier chapters of the book. As such, these web-based news and opinion resources provide a clear alternative for reimagining racial dynamics in the Obama era.

Each of these sites is slightly different, but all are committed to sustained discussions about race and ethnicity in the United States (although there are sometimes references to other parts of the world). *ColorLines* started as a print magazine, and now maintains a print and online presence. The Applied Research Center (ARC), a non-profit research and advocacy group, provides the home of *ColorLines*. The webzine features investigative reports, interviews, blogs, and updates from a mix of regular contributors and editors. The site also has links to ARC research papers and advocacy projects.

Racialicious is a blog "about the intersection of race and pop culture." Owner-Editor Latoya Peterson, Managing Editor Arturo Garcia, and Associate Editor Andrea Plaid compose and gather a mix of blogs and guest contributions from around the country.[3] Although "pop culture" is the touchstone for discussions of race, as the examples demonstrate, writers incorporate political valences of culture in their dissections of celebrity gaffes. Like *Racialicious, The Black Snob* is also a blog, but is authored mainly by one person, Danielle Belton. Belton characterizes site's focus as "pop culture-meets-politics," and reports a following of two million readers. Many other sites list the *Snob* and *Racialicious* and *ColorLines* on their blog-rolls or cross-post listings to articles on these sites. Additionally, many of the writers represented on all three sites have been interviewed in traditional news media, such as CNN and NPR.

From these three sites, I gathered all of the blog postings and web articles that contained the term "post-racial" in the headline or leading paragraph for the years 2008–2010. After taking out duplicates and articles that were erroneously included in the searches, the total came to 119 articles and blog posts, with *Black Snob* having 15, *ColorLines* having 45, and *Racialicious* having 59. Taking detailed notes on the themes and frameworks in which "post-racial" appeared in each article, I was particularly interested in discovering how writers defined the term, as well as what their discussions suggested that people who are concerned with racism do in an era that has been dubbed "post-racial." Four overlapping themes emerged from my close readings of the blog postings and articles.

Figure 5.1. Danielle Belton, a.k.a *The Black Snob*, blogs on politics and cultural debates. Used with permission.

First, contributors to these websites marshaled plenty of evidence that racist discrimination and violence continue to do harm to significant numbers of citizens of color. This finding is similar to that of many mainstream news commentators, who hedge their bets on post-racial politics by listing existing inequalities and modes of discrimination. Second, along with this information, bloggers included more discussions of how post-racial discourse can minimize racial harms and sidetrack constructive debates about race and public policy. Many argued that the ambivalence of post-racial discourse leaves too much room for those who deny racism to frame the discussion. Writers and bloggers pointed out that, in particular, Obama and his allies' adoption of a post-racial approach (seen as politically expedient) undermined their ability to effectively counter attacks from the Right, let alone advocate for the kinds of policies needed to address racism and inequalities.

Third, having deconstructed post-racial discourses that minimize the significance of race, many of the web contributors focused on proactive means for promoting antiracism. To begin this work, they counseled Americans to be better students of history, utilizing nuanced understandings of the roots and mechanics of civil rights movements, as well as the development of racial hierarchies. Accurate knowledge of our racial history, they suggest, supports a more sophisticated analysis of the contemporary situation and a deeper understanding of the processes and practices that organizations and individuals should adopt to foster anti-racism. Writers advocated intersectional and coalitional approaches to anti-racist work. Whether reporting on the simultaneous effects of race and class on poverty or incarceration, or featuring successful joint campaigns against bigotry by GLBT and Asian American organizations, the blogs present readers with many more examples of grass-roots and individual means for political and personal engagement with anti-racist action. Importantly, these examples go well beyond the black-white framing that continued to dominate discussions of the post-racial in the mainstream news, and, as such, they give readers a sense of the real diversity of political activism around the intersecting issues of inequality and race.

Finally, when bloggers included stories of personal experiences with racism, they usually articulated those moments within larger structural and historical frameworks. They rarely missed a chance to indicate how their stories or the stories of other individuals were just a few examples of a larger pattern with roots in the institutional and cultural aspects of oppression. Adopting the "personal is political" framework, these blog posts and web articles challenged the individualized sensibility of post-racial discourses found in mainstream media. Rather than put the onus on each person to make the "right" choices about race, the blogs analyzed here provide opportunities for readers to rise to the level of the "social imagination," locate their struggles within a matrix of social phenomena, and connect their stories with similarly affected individuals engaged in resistance.

Plenty of Evidence We're Not "Post": Let's Really Talk about Racism

Like some of the left-leaning news items discussed in the earlier chapters, blog posts offered copious evidence from personal experiences, ongoing investigations, and socioeconomic data to debunk the myth that Obama's election engendered a post-racial transformation. For example, when *Racialicious* posted a series of blogs on discriminatory hiring in the adverting industry, guest contributor HighJive wrote a humorous FAQ for "The Culturally Clueless":

QUESTION: Doesn't President Barack Obama prove we don't have to pursue this diversity stuff anymore?

ANSWER: Why do certain individuals view President Barack Obama as some form of reparations—as if his election pays off the bar tab of bias Madison Avenue has amassed over the years? . . .

President Obama assembles a staff reflecting the vibrant variety of brilliance in America. Madison Avenue collects excuses like, "We can't find qualified minority candidates."

President Obama signs his first bill in support of equal pay. Madison Avenue signs diversity pacts and is exposed for paying Blacks 20 percent less than Whites.[4]

On *ColorLines*, writer Channing Kennedy chided mainstream journalists for losing interest in racial profiling and police brutality cases after the Gates affair, especially when sources use the word "systemic." Then Kennedy described a more recent case in which the police unjustifiably Tasered a pregnant Latina and her father and contextualized it within broader institutional practices that reinforce police aggression toward people of color.

Now, you and I spat out the post-racial kool-aid already. We know that "'racism'" can mean something other than a white hood, and that even the most diverse police forces can still practice racial profiling or act on ingrained prejudices. . . . Instead of talking about who is or isn't racist this week, we need to talk about how police are trained, why they're so quick to reach for the mace, or the Taser, or the gun, and why "'non-violent'" and "'non-lethal'" have become sickeningly interchangeable. We need to talk about racism, but not in terms of intent—we need to talk about racism in terms of impacts and outcomes, in which communities of color are more heavily policed by more heavily armed officers with less accountability to the people they serve. We need to talk about . . . why Bushwick kids need to take a class on what to expect during a stop-and-frisk.[5]

In this article, the writer not only critiques the lack of institutional framing in mainstream news about police misconduct, but also provides readers with examples of police practices and vocabulary to explain racial profiling and unjustified force as structural phenomena. Kennedy concludes that discussions of whether an individual was racially motivated is a "red herring" that distracts us from the more important considerations of institutional racism.

Commentators were frustrated—but not surprised—that Obama and his surrogates hadn't used the Gates incident to inject more discussion of institutional racism into the public sphere. Similarly with regard to the nomination of Sotomayor and the rush to blame Shirley Sherrod, they wondered why the administration failed to dispute right-wing accusations of reverse racism. In an interview with *ColorLines* co-founder Jeff Chang, editor Jamilah King asked about the Obama administration's inability to defend itself in racial scandals.

> J. K. : It seems like President Obama was much more willing to speak can-didly about race before he took office. . . . We saw that play out espe-cially during the whole "beer summit" debacle, when he backed down from his criticism of Cambridge police officers. How complicit has the Obama administration been in feeding into the right's race baiting?
>
> J. C.: It's easy to say "very complicit." It's hard to say what Obama himself can do about it. The administration, however, treats race the way it treats "the professional left." It is sensitive to being perceived as too left, too pro-people of color. So when Attorney General Eric Holder began speaking about dealing with race, he was quickly pulled back to the right. The Shirley Sherrod incident illustrated definitively that the administration is on a hair-trigger on the public perception of being cast as a "pro–people of color" administration. There is no doubt that, behind the scenes, the administration is pushing forward with needed reforms.[6]

A *Racialicious* guest blogger, Andrew Grant Thomas, had harsher criti-cism for the president's avoidance tactics. Thomas characterized the 2010 State of the Union speech as a lost opportunity to help the public understand the intersections of race and class that make it unreason-able to expect that race-blind policies will ameliorate racial disparities.

> As a matter of political calculus, the silence was unremarkable and unsurprising, coming as it did from a president reluctant to publicly tread the ground of race except, at times, in the context of his personal biography. However, with respect to on-the-ground realities and the opportunity presented for social transformation, a continued failure to engage race would be devastating. . . .
>
> He pointed out that in the 21st century "one of the best anti-poverty programs is a world-class education." However, the president neglected

to mention that young Latino adults earn bachelor's degrees at one-third the rate of their white peers, and that African Americans earn degrees at only half the rates of whites. . . . [I]t would have been crucial that he also offer informed insights into the underlying [structural] dynamic. . . . The president could have educated the American people about the many young African Americans and Latinos who live isolated from decent opportunities in neighborhoods that provide access only to underfunded, low-performing schools, unsafe streets, a limited number of unpromising jobs even in "good" times.[7]

This critique recalls Stephanie Li's characterization of Obama's post-racial rhetoric as "signifying without specifying." Obama can gesture to race and suggest he "gets it" via his life story, biracial family, and the symbolism of his phenotype without clarifying how these factors link to public policy. He rarely delves into the details of how race/ethnicity/class/gender influence society, not just biography. Thomas counters this strategy by highlighting all Obama *could* have said to explain entrenched, recurrent outcomes of marginalization for people oppressed by race and class.

This and other blog posts offer examples of important types of questions to ask and issues to raise when post-racial evasiveness is the dominant mode of operation. A roundtable response to an *Atlantic Monthly* article titled "The End of White America?" illustrates the importance of posing challenging questions that expose the assumptions that support post-racial discussions in the mainstream media. One of the respondents, Fatemah, commented as follows:

Hsu's "The End of White America?" (cue scary music) essentially aims to hash out the following: "Hey, white people are freaked out that people of color are becoming the majority in the U.S. Why's that? Don't worry, guys. It's cool."

. . . Hsu hints at a "white panic" caused by the racial demographic shift, but doesn't explore it, question it, or even attempt to assuage it (except for a few paragraphs in the last section). He quotes Bill Imada, who states that whites are worried about "losing control," which is the reason for all this "white panic" over shifting ethnic demography. But instead of analyzing this point ("What do they mean by 'losing control'?

What do they think this means for them?"), it serves as a transition at the end of a section, and is quickly glossed over in a comparison of different "types" of whites (the seemingly conservative and liberal camps) that still doesn't tell us what white people are afraid of.

Fear can't be assuaged or overcome without an assessment of what it is you're afraid of, which Hsu hints at in the next section but never actually plainly states: "The coming white minority does not mean that the racial hierarchy of American culture will suddenly become inverted. . . ." As if people of color will suddenly disenfranchise whites, confiscate their assets, and force them into slavery.[8]

Fatemah and other roundtable participants pointed out how Hsu's article, which is supposed to "go deep" on race, succeeds only in recycling shallow stereotypes and vague assertions about whiteness and fear. There is no serious attention to power, or sufficient discussion of whether white fears have any basis in actually existing social, economic, or political contexts.

In another *Racialicious* article, a writer reposted an open letter to University of California San Diego Filipino American students from Dr. Jody Blanco. Blanco, a professor of Comparative Literature and Spanish, wrote the letter in response to a "Compton Cookout" hosted by a majority white fraternity which featured blackface and costumes mocking African Americans. The event sparked protests, but also provided conservatives with another opportunity to assert that offended students and faculty were too sensitive and opposed free speech. Dr. Blanco's letter, in contrast, provided a template for countering those who try to silence protests against racist acts by invoking the First Amendment:

The scandal isn't that the right to free speech might even include the right for individuals to denigrate and stereotype people: I can turn the TV to Fox News Channel and see the proof of that for myself any given day. The scandal is that an event like this could only happen in or around a university or institution that has failed in its commitment to academic and cultural diversity. The scandal is that many students at UCSD consider black people and communities as a product of their imaginations and consumer habits: an entertainment commodity we pay to watch on

MTV, or hear on the radio. A stereotype we have the "right" to enjoy and take pleasure in, because we have paid good money to possess and consume it in the privacy of our homes and TV screens. The scandal is that many whites—and even Asian Americans—do not belong to a community that involved and involves the active participation and vital humanity of another person or community of color, another historically underrepresented minority.[9]

In this letter, readers have a powerful example of someone redirecting the conversation back to the harm done to those who are mocked. Dr. Blanco underscores how an appeal to a "universal right"—free speech—can be used to devalue the speech of marginalized groups when they speak out against discrimination. The spotlight is on the roots of that mockery in media systems that continue to exploit racist imagery and educational institutions that have not yet made good on the promise of integration. Reminding students of the widespread availability of speech venues for people who value the speech rights of racists more than the rights of people of color to defend themselves against hateful speech acts, Dr. Blanco assembles a clear rebuttal to those who argue anti-racist protest violates the speech rights of the white fraternity brothers who exploit racist stereotypes for fun.

Taking the Intersectional View: Activism and History beyond Black and White

Twin deficiencies of mainstream news items' post-racial reportage are the continued focus on black-white relations and the lack of historical context. While black-white dynamics certainly are important to address, discussions of race restricted to this dualism do not provide a comprehensive framework for understanding racism in the United States. Moreover, this focus continues to displace the issues faced by Latina/o, Asian, and Native American communities, while also failing to account for coalitions that are often built at the grass roots level across and within different identity communities. For instance, when he introduced Dr. Blanco's letter to Filipino students, blogger Ninoy Brown noted that the NAACP had spoken out on the "Compton Cookout" and that Dr. Blanco's letter "was important for more folks to read, as well. Dr. Blanco was an inspiration for many of us, student of color organizers, while attending UCSD."[10] Ninoy creates a sense of an inter-racial community of student leaders who will be inspired by the letter even though it was originally sent only to one specific group.

Returning to the letter itself—in it, Blanco provides context for explaining why it has historically been important for communities of color to support each other's struggles against racism:

> For those of you who have close friends in the black community, you may have witnessed . . . students weeping in the halls and on Library Walk at their helplessness and inability to represent themselves against the violence of having other people represent them. If you are like me, you are familiar with this feeling. . . . I'm asking you to become or stay involved, first and foremost, because as historically underrepresented minorities we are directly implicated in both acts of racial hate speech and the university's responses to it. . . . [W]hen the US conducted a near-genocidal war against the Philippines at the beginning of the twentieth century . . . both US soldiers and commanders often referred to Filipinos as "niggers." In the 1920s and 30s, . . . [Filipinos] were identified as "niggers," and they were lynched, beaten, and murdered without any recourse to the law. To this day, the word retains the same popular meaning as it did at the turn of the century: to be a "nigger" means to be identified as an available target for extra-judicial violence and social exile, without right of appeal to an established or legitimate authority.[11]

Drawing a picture that includes personal and historical details, Blanco calls attention to similar experiences with white supremacy endured by Filipinos and African Americans. The combination powerfully testifies to the importance of history to understanding the present and empha-sizes the need for coalitions. Blanco's definition of "nigger" also under-scores the importance of contextualizing speech in terms of the relative power of speakers and listeners—an aspect often overlooked in facile discussions of who is "allowed" to use racist, sexist, or homophobic epithets in the post-racial world. While in popular humor and some arenas of rap music, the word is tossed around as an artifact of a hip, post-racial sensibility, Blanco reminds readers of its origins and uses as tool accompanying violence.

Other writers were likewise committed to making connections between marginalized groups in ways that refocused attention on power and privilege, not post-racial visibility and individualism. For example, writer Daisy Hernandez emphasized in a piece for *ColorLines* that attacks on one group's civil rights can easily lead to setbacks for other marginalized groups. In an article on legal arguments supporting California's anti-gay marriage law, Proposition 8, she underlined how a win for conservatives would potentially harm not only GLBT communities:

> The legal fight to overturn Prop. 8 took a scary turn yesterday for communities of color. The defenders of hetero marriage argued that gays and lesbians don't need the state to protect them from discrimination because they have political clout. . . .
>
> "Gays and lesbians are able to achieve positive outcomes in the political process" and can "attract the attention of lawmakers," according to Kenneth Miller, a political science professor who testified as a witness for the defense of the same-sex marriage ban. . . . What Miller and the pro-Prop. 8 side really did yesterday in court was to argue that the United States is post-gay. But you can't be post-gay without also being post-racial. If the judge buys Miller's argument, it would give legal support to the idea that Blacks, Latinos and other people of color are also too empowered to deserve the state's attention and protection.[12]

Hernandez's concern about the broader implications of Proposition 8 reflects the advice conveyed in an article about a speech at ARC's racial justice conference by scholar Melissa Harris-Lacewell:

> Harris-Lacewell told the crowd of racial justice activists . . . that our movement must stop compartmentalizing itself. Harris-Lacewell . . . urged progressives to see how race, gender, LGBT issues are all interconnected. . . . The Shirley Sherrod incident, and the white farmers who came to her defense, forced us reexamine how we see our allies—not as "who looks like us," but more about "who sees us," said Harris-Lacewell.[13]

In a similar vein, HighJive's first answer to another "Culturally Clueless FAQ" rejected zero-sum racial logic that supposes a "win" for one group means a "loss" for or neglect of other oppressed groups.

QUESTION: Why do all the diversity discussions focus on Blacks—what about Latinos, Asians, Native Americans, People With Disabilities, Gays, Lesbians, Women, Veterans, Older Employees, Pit Bull Lovers, Mutants and The Rest Of Us?

ANSWER: Get in line. Unfortunately, the deeper you dig into Madison Avenue's corporate closet, the more skeletons you'll find. Recent years have seen work and deeds demeaning everyone listed above. . . . Blacks are in the spotlight for a few reasons. First, the group has been officially fighting for change since the 1930s. To understand the details, read Madison Avenue and the Color Line by Jason Chambers. . . . [A]ttorney Cyrus Mehri is building a class-action lawsuit focused on the inequities Blacks seemingly always face in the ad game. However, it's important to realize the real battle is not being waged exclusively for any single group. The Bendick and Egan Economic Consultants, Inc. report stated the following:

> . . . the same issues of employment bias in the advertising industry simultaneously affect other "outgroups"—race-ethnic minorities such as Latinos and Asians; women; older workers; persons with disabilities; and even White males who do not share the cultural or stylistic characteristics of the White males who dominate the industry. These other groups would benefit alongside African Americans from a reformed, inclusive advertising industry culture.[14]

HighJive's long-term, multiracial view of the struggle on Madison Avenue demonstrates how historical insight and making connections between groups that struggle against discrimination encourage us to see the ad industry as a system with a legacy of practices that discriminate against people of color.

Although many writers illuminated the need to understand history and look more closely for inter-group affinities, these discussions recognized that forging coalitions takes time and effort, and often engenders some discomfort. They also didn't shy away from acknowledging prejudices within and across marginalized groups. In a roundtable with lesbian and gay bloggers of color, *ColorLines* editorial director, Kai Wright, asked each to comment on the "conventional wisdom" that

Latinas/os and African Americans are more homophobic than other groups.

> PAM: I give an honest answer: yes and no. In black and Latino commu-
> nities, the matter is not completely about race, per se, it's about
> whether you're talking churched or unchurched. Religion is by far
> more important than race when it comes to fomenting homophobia,
> however, the black and Latino communities at large have not held
> publicly accountable the pastors stoking anti-gay sentiment. That's
> going to take time to change.
>
> MIRIAM: What gets me most about this blame game around homophobia
> is the role that white communities—primarily through the history of
> colonization—have had in the homophobia that exists in the com-
> munities of color. You can see this even more clearly internationally,
> but in immigrant communities here as well. In many (if not most)
> communities of color, there is a vibrant history of sexual and gender
> diversity. Think of two spirit folks in Native American communi-
> ties, hijras in India, etc. It was often the colonial powers that came in
> (with strong religious agendas) and stamped out much of that culture
> of diversity and acceptance. Now white folks are coming back around
> to sexual diversity and they're finger pointing at communities of
> color? Oh hell no.[15]

In their thoughtful responses, Pam and Miriam took time to discuss other intersectional identities—religion, nation—that come into
play when discussing people of color and attitudes toward sexuality. Whereas Pam suggested that religion is actually the more relevant
influence, Miriam referred to histories of colonization that suppressed
gender diversity in indigenous communities. Their exchange opens the
lens of identity much wider than most mainstream news discussions of,
say, black pastors such as Herbert Lusk who urge fellow worshippers to
vote against gay rights. In so doing, the round-table participants didn't
excuse the homophobia that comes out of particular black churches or
neighborhoods; rather, they contextualize homophobia as a stance that
emerges from a variety of influences, not just shared racial identity.

A few commentators used electoral politics as a means to suggest
more border-crossing and coalition-building would benefit multiple

communities of color. In these postings, most referred to intersections of race, ethnicity, and class. For example, in an interview with *Color-Lines*, David Ochoa, who is Latino and was a delegate to the 2008 Democratic National Convention, responded to the idea that Obama's presidency means the country is on the cusp of a post-racial era by noting the need for people of color to act in solidarity around class more often when voting.

> That [post-racial idea] is complete b.s. People of color make the least, pay the most, and suffer the worst. Let's not kid ourselves, the people who harvest the crops and clean the bathrooms are people of color. The problems in this country largely are carried by low income people, and another commonality is that they most often are people of color. The anthem of Barack Obama's presidency is not going to be Kumbayaa. That's not pragmatic to think that way. But what I think Barack Obama has a capacity for [is] bridge-building, and I'm hopeful about that. But you know, I'm ashamed to say we were late, the Latino community, to come around to Barack Obama. That's due to racism. This campaign offers us a new possibility, and I know that without the Black vote, there would be no Tony Villaraigosa in LA.[16]

Here, Mr. Ochoa admitted to tensions and racism between Latinas/os and black Americans, but then also took a moment to recognize that the first Latino mayor of Los Angeles, Antonio Villaraigosa, was elected with black voters' help. Like HighJive, he presented a case for people to reject zero-sum thinking about political or economic benefits, and encouraged a coalition-based approach to solving the race/class conundrum.

The Personal Is Political—When We Make It So

Personal experiences were often used by bloggers and contributors to illustrate a larger problem, or just to vent about recent media firestorms about race or Obama. But unlike post-racial stories in the mainstream news which isolated individuals from structural factors, the blogs and articles on these sites almost always made links between personal frustrations and institutions, racial history, or widespread public practices.

Thus, for instance, in reflecting on the Cambridge Police Department's decision to charge Dr. Gates with disorderly conduct even after he proved he was in his own home, *The Black Snob* shared memories from her family's brushes with racist law enforcement:

> Personally, I think Gates was arrested for having a normal, human reaction as opposed to the reaction my Grandpa was taught to have living in segregated Arkansas. Meaning, be humble and apologize even when the police are in the wrong. My grandpa, while in his 60s was once stopped because he and his brother, also in his 60s, had a bunch of furniture in the bed of their truck and the officer, young enough to be one of their grandkids asked, "What are you *boys* doing with this stuff?" . . .
>
> Black people are not allowed it seems, under any circumstances, to ever have a human reaction to police error or harassment. Even in Post-racial America. . . . You are not allowed to get mad. You are not allowed to voice your opinion. . . . You are supposed to be *apologetically black.* Sorry for being an obvious target of racism. How dare you be born this color and attract this negative attention? *I'm so very sorry for being born black in America. How can I make this up to you, Mr. Officer?*[17]

Recounting two generations of police harassment, *The Black Snob* undermined the post-racial myth that "old-style" racism is gone, and also took aim at the white innocence narrative that posits people of color are at fault for making white people uncomfortable with their presence, or when they notice racism happening. This is one of the "pendejo games" (feigning ignorance about one's power and impact) that critical race scholar Aida Hurtado skewers as a move meant to silence people of color and maintain the fiction of white racial neutrality. *The Snob's* breakdown of the Gates event and her family's experiences uncovered the faults in the innocence narrative, and revealed the absurd blame-the-victim assumptions that often underlie official responses to police racism.

"The Violence of Revulsion": Confronting Everyday Cultural Racism

Many of the blog entries focused on the continued employment of racist caricatures and stereotypes in entertainment and media. In these posts, bloggers didn't end their critique with historical accounting of the origins of old-school representations of black or Asian people; rather, they pushed further to delineate the real harm done when people assume that their personal fascination with or profit from racial stereotypes doesn't hurt anyone except the "over-sensitive." After seeing one too many New Orleans storefronts with racist paraphenalia for sale, *Racialicious* blogger Fiqah had to text a friend to make sure she wasn't alone thinking that pickanninny dolls and the like were offensive. She emailed a friend a picture of one doll. The text conversation went as follows:

HIM: WHAT THE FUCK! Where did you find that at?
ME: At a gallery
HIM: Was it a Klan gallery? That's some racist shit.[18]

When one of the artists told Fiqah that he didn't realize the dolls could be seen as racist, and other storeowners told her how popular the postcards of grinning Mammies were with tourists, she pondered why these good-natured folks didn't seem bothered by the images. The answer was that they had grown up with them all their lives. The continued popularity of such images in a "post-racial modern society" speaks to "a diabolically sophisticated narrative that combines tenets of 'colorblindness' and 'tolerance' with post-racialism. The result: a system of rhetorical gaslighting that permits individuals to indulge in the most blatant kinds of old-school racism while simultaneously denying its existence."[19]

The feeling of having been "gaslighted" by whites who deny any racial or racist elements to their collectibles was shared by other bloggers. For example, in response to white Dutch models being dressed up with blackface makeup in French *Vogue*, Min-ha wrote a post for *Racialicious* titled "Blackface and the Violence of Revulsion." There, Minh-ha described how she came upon the photos in the course of her daily fashion reading—photos "violently interrupting" her day. These images, she argued, are a product of "racial arrogance" that does not stop to consider the visceral responses of people of color who feel "anger, exasperation, disappointment, and a feeling I can only describe as racial fatigue." This is one of the privileges of whiteness: to not think about the damage inflicted when one "plays" with race.

The bloggers put the pain experienced by people of color front and center, spotlighting the carelessness of fashion editors and gallery owners who look to the bottom line without much care for the emotions or cultural heritage of consumers of color. These blogs echo Malinda Smith's deconstruction of on-campus racism, in which white privilege is shown to be "ignorant" of—or unconcerned with— the pain experienced by people of color when they encounter racist images, speech, and behaviors on the street, in the classroom, or in the media.[20] Like the Facebook fans who rushed to Jasmine's defense on the *Parenthood* discussion boards, these writers offer criticism of the seemingly inexhaustible supply and tacit endorsement of racial caricatures in media.

Other than protesting how and why people profit from racial caricature, what can be done to educate people beyond exposing the pain caused—pain often dismissed as "over-thinking" or "political correctness"? When things get personal, how to respond? Many writers addressed the nexus of the personal and political, musing over recent racial controversies and interpersonal interactions that left them less than satisfied with their spouse's, colleagues', or friends' response to racism. Some bloggers who were part of interracial couples or families acknowledged that when intimates make racial jokes or ignorant remarks, "the best course of action isn't actually obvious. Do you go ahead and try to have an anti-racist 'teachable' moment knowing full well that Americans SUCK at talking about race or let it go?"[21] These pieces testified to the fact that the upswing in interracial marriage hadn't made much of a dent in improving racial discussions. As Ope Bukola wrote for *Racialicious*, "If we're really going to be anti-bigotry, then we need to have the back of those we care about" and take a risk in confronting racism from in-laws and others, even if we don't have clear rules of engagement.

Other columnists provided insight and advice from their own navigation of treacherous racial waters with their families. Terry Keleher, for example, offered "Four Tips for Interracial Parenting" on *Color-Lines*. Step number two is "Learn to understand and challenge institutional racism." Keleher then explained the need for white individuals to make it a priority to be anti-racist allies through an understanding that racism isn't just personal prejudice, but a systemic phenomenon.

It's not enough to try and change yourself or other individuals. We also have to change institutions that have biased practices and unfair policies. Schools are a great place to start challenging institutional racism, since most families have direct experience with them. . . .

If the advanced placement classes are filled with mostly white students, if the curriculum is perpetuating stereotypes, if there aren't many teachers of color, you can do something about it. Ask questions, talk with students about their experiences, request public documents, organize parents, talk to elected officials, notify the media and take public action. If you're white, you don't have to wait for people of color to complain first. You can be change agents and . . . allies to people of color. [22]

These "tips" articulate the intimate act of caring for one's children with the politics of race and social change. Dismissing colorblind and postracial paradigms that privatize race or compartmentalize racism into feelings and individual acts, Keleher gives readers clear examples of why it is imperative to move beyond the personal to affect the structural to make a better world for children of all races. More importantly, each of the tips suggests a specific anti-racist intervention that could be implemented by any parent, anytime, anywhere. Finally, the blog post presents the idea of whites being agents and allies in facilitating anti-racist solidarity.

What is inspiring about these websites and blogs is how they offer a very different orientation toward racial citizenship than mainstream media. While many writers describe how communities of color have reasons to be allied with each other, they don't articulate solidarity in terms of "we're more alike than different," or by suggesting a more "universal" identity grouping (like class or nation) to use as an organizing principle. Rather, these bloggers illustrate how people of color, GLBT, and white allies share similar experiences with and analyses of racial hierarchy, discrimination, and abuses of power. It is through these shared experiences, they argue, that shared investments in organized struggle develop. This doesn't mean that people become "colorblind" or forget the uniqueness of their own histories in the United States and elsewhere in order to facilitate interracial cooperation. Rather, the postracial visions advanced in these websites acknowledge the pitfalls any movement faces if it identifies itself as either colorblind or associated with a singular identity to the exclusion of other intersecting identities. While those monolithic movements are vulnerable to the post-racial mystification practiced in dominant discourses, the blogs give us a wider variety of ideas of how to move from and between shared histories and shared struggles to find common ground and relevant tactics without insisting on common identity.

Conclusion

Back to the Post-Racial Future

On February 27, 2013, two events occurred that together caught the attention of news commentators' irony detectors. One was President Barack Obama's dedication of a statue of civil rights activist Rosa Parks. The other was the U.S. Supreme Court's hearing of arguments against the 1965 Voting Rights Act. Indeed, many television news outlets moved from footage of the President's remark that without movement pioneers such as Parks, he "would not be here," to Supreme Court Justice Antonin Scalia's condemnation of the VRA as "a racial entitlement." But the juxtaposition of Obama's reverence for civil rights history with Scalia's disdain was not the only peculiar instance of racial histories remixed in the early weeks of Obama's second term.

In the wake of the Sandy Hook school shootings, white neoconservative gun advocates like Ted Nugent argued for their rights to unlimited assault weapons by alluding to Rosa Parks and Martin Luther King, Jr., lamenting that gun owners weren't seated "at the front of the bus."[1] Others declared January 19, 2013—the date of the Martin Luther King holiday—Gun Appreciation Day, and held rallies.[2] They argued that if Dr. King were alive, this pacifist, non-violent leader who was slain by a gun-wielding racist would have marched with gun owners to assert their rights. Others proclaimed that if African slaves had had free access to guns, emancipation would have come sooner than 1865.[3] As Larry Ward, the organizer of Gun Appreciation Day, told CNN, had blacks had "the right to bear and keep arms . . . perhaps slavery would not have been a chapter in our history."[4]

The absurdity of these statements would be almost laughable had so many right-leaning news sites and talking heads not recirculated and, in some cases, adopted the claims about slavery and civil rights and guns. From Fox News to the blogosphere, many who argued against gun control measures used these spurious comparisons to lay claim to victim status and assert consonance with civil rights resistance. Some even turned to the Holocaust, saying that Hitler was able to decimate the Jewish population because he "took their guns."[5] Worse still, these fantasies of gun ownership and liberation were put forth both with seriousness and without any regard for the actual history of legal, social, economic, and physical violence that combined to oppress black slaves and free blacks, and Jews throughout history as well. As one reader commented in response to Ward's comments, "Yes. If Africans brought to America had been given the rights of free citizens, they wouldn't have been slaves. Funny how it didn't work out like that."[6] Nevertheless, the idea that somehow black people would be granted free access to guns during the brutal, racist rule of white citizens—citizens who were rewarded for turning in escaped slaves, citizens who rioted through black neighborhoods and left orphanages burning—was actually a subject of debate for at least a week on television and beyond that on the Internet.

Research on the most recent presidential and midterm elections have found disturbing evidence of a resurgence of "old fashioned racism"— meaning endorsement of explicit anti-black stereotypes, such as beliefs in black intellectual or moral inferiority—as well as a continuation of "modern racism" or "racial resentment" amongst white voters. One such study found that old-fashioned racism was a stronger determinant of white voter preferences in the 2010 election than in the 2006 election.[7] Other studies found that racial resentment[8] and ethnocentrism[9] were strong predictors of white voting preferences in 2008. In addition, researchers and observers have shown that many Tea Party members (who are seen as having had significant influence on Republican electoral politics during the 2010 and 2012 elections) are more likely to express racial resentment *and* old-fashioned racism at rallies and in their publicity campaigns.[10]

As discussed in the introduction, GOP strategists were more than willing to admit that they were going for "the white vote" in the past two election cycles, and didn't seem very concerned about how some of their messages could be viewed as being racially coded, if not outright racist. Much ink and many data bytes have been employed to deride Republicans for "delaying the inevitable" demographic change where whites will no longer be a majority of voters. Importantly, many of those strategists who counsel the GOP to makeover the image it has long had as a white, intolerant party have focused on finding "standard bearers"—Senator Marco Rubio (a Cuban American) or Governor Bobby Jindal (an Indian American)—who reflect the "new" multicultural America. Unfortunately, the reduction of people of color's political affiliation to simply matching skin color or ethnicity still seems in place. The idea that millions of voters of color who stood in agonizingly long lines in Republican-controlled states would soon forget so many important parts of history is appalling. Would they remember which party made it harder for them to vote? Would they forget the antics of prominent members of the party who want to prohibit gay marriage? Would they recall which party wants to restrict contraception access, or which party wants to allow unlimited access to deadly firearms that kill hundreds of young people of color every month? Would their memories be so easily wiped out by the affinity neoconservatives imagined between Rosa Parks and the opponents of gun control?

Remember How Obama Got Here? Wasn't It . . . the Civil Rights Movement?

In a 2009 essay for *ColorLines*, whiteness scholar Tim Wise laid out some of the repercussions for allowing others to rescript histories of anti-racist struggle in ways that erase painful conflict and simplify notions of racial justice.

> It's been a rough year for Martin Luther King, Jr., and for his legacy. . . .
>   We have turned King into a milquetoast moderate whose agenda went little beyond the ability to sit next to white people on a bus. We've

stripped away from the public remembrance of this man his calls for income redistribution . . . his proclamation that poverty, racism and militarism are the "triple evils" that America's rulers have not the courage to confront. When conservatives can effectively twist King's singular line about judging people on the "content of their character" rather than the color of their skin into a reason to oppose affirmative action, even though he openly supported such efforts in his writings and interviews in 1961, 1963, 1965 and again in 1967, it ought not surprise us that folks are a bit confused about who King was, and about the principles for which he stood.[11]

As Wise observes, detaching King's image from his work is dangerous. Such a move muddies the waters of collective memory, making it hard for new generations to understand the full scope and meaning of freedom struggles, to learn from the past, or to generate interest in sustaining or extending the legacy of activists like King. The post-racial mystique is dependent, in part, on the kind of racial amnesia—or racial arrogance—that enables crass stunts like holding a "Gun Appreciation Day" during the Martin Luther King holiday. As more than a few commentators infamously said on election night 2008, people of color can't "complain" anymore about racism now that the United States has a black president.[12]

But many have gone beyond telling people of color they can't say racism exists; they have further declared an inversion of racial subjugation, whereby it is now whites who need a Dr. King to safeguard their rights and privileges. For instance, after the strong turnout during the 2012 presidential election of black, Asian American, and Latina/o voters (despite voter suppression tactics) many on the Right began expressing fear about the end of the "white establishment."[13] Just a few weeks before the election, a white student at Towson University sought to create a White Student Union in order to fight an alleged "inherent anti-white bias in academia and mainstream society." He argued that it was no different than black or Asian students creating a student union to represent their interests in the face of discrimination.[14]

People who so easily reconfigure the meaning of social movements in ways that facilitate these sorts of delusions of a racial power reversal operate from a space where they cannot "see" racism in its twenty-first century forms, let alone read the past for wisdom on how to combat racial injustice. I am particularly intrigued by the kind of amnesia—or the practices of "not-seeing" race—that made many people so surprised at the number of racist jokes, gaffes, and defamatory statements made by President Obama's opponents almost weekly, if not daily. And to me the recurrent "surprise" and dismay suggest that we really are behind in thinking about racial politics and should have listened more closely to those who were publicly unsure about Obama's chances to become the first president who was not white.

In 2007 and early 2008, many astute observers of racial politics predicted that Barack Obama had no chance of winning the Democratic nomination, let alone the White House, in the upcoming election. Many scholars and pundits—black and white—said America wouldn't be ready until at least 2012 or even 2016. Obviously, their predictions regarding the outcome of the 2008 election were wrong, but few have revisited these forecasts and explored their sources. Doing so here, and exploring ways in which the "readiness" of the white American public to vote—or not vote—for a man of African descent was construed, I will argue that peculiar patterns of memorialization and forgetting created grounds for undue optimism about our "readiness," as well as misunderstandings of the reasons many black scholars and voters had for thinking that Obama could not win in 2008. If we fail to understand these dynamics of public memory, we are in danger of losing opportunities to ready ourselves for pluralist politics.

In reviewing why it was that many observers—particularly African Americans—felt pessimistic about Barack Hussein Obama's chances at getting the nomination (let alone winning) in 2008, we can see their awareness of certain deep cultural assumptions about race that seem to anchor some white voting behavior. Pessimists used history as well as diagnoses of the dominant white culture's treatment of black politicians and everyday people of color to frame his chances. So I would like to suggest not only that their predictions were rational, based on existing empirical evidence of white political behavior, but also that their diagnosis of the depth of the cultural anchor of white supremacy helps us to see how the Birthers (who believe Obama is not a native-born citizen of the United States and therefore cannot be president) and others were not so unexpected after all.

To begin, let's look at the two most common reasons why many political observers thought it was too early for Obama to win the presidential election and why 2012 or 2016 were seen as more "realistic," especially in allowing time for him to gain more experience in the Senate and the country to "progress" more in terms of race relations.

Reason #1: Hillary's Turn

If we go back to 2007, the case against Obama was pretty tight. After all, he was running against a white woman with at least six advantages over him: (1) national name recognition; (2) incredible fund-raising and plentiful personal coffers; (3) a popular former president husband; (4) more "experience" and powerful allies; (5) a good reputation with black elected officials—ostensibly the same officials whom Obama should have been courting;—and, of course (6) whiteness. Yes, she had gender working against her, but if we look at the relative successes of white female candidates for state-wide offices such as governor—as well as in the Senate and the House of Representatives—we find that many more white women have been elected than black men or women. Thus, electoral evidence suggests that white female candidates are not as hampered by gender as black candidates are by race. This is not an argument about the "oppression Olympics," but just an observation based in actual electoral data.

Reason #2: White Voter Behavior

Studies of actual races for state-wide or national offices as well as experimental studies of white voter preferences show strong evidence that despite improving statistics in opinion polls that say a majority of whites are "ready" and willing to vote for "qualified" black candidates, white voters don't actually vote for black candidates as often as their stated beliefs suggest. Analysts and pundits referred to cases where black candidates polled well with white before the election, only to end up losing or winning by a very slim margin. These examples included references to: Harvey Gantt's U.S. Senate race loss in North Carolina; the infamous—and ill-named—"Bradley Effect," where Mayor Tom Bradley barely won his seat in Los Angeles after polling well ahead of his white opponent; and the recent loss Harold Ford, Jr., suffered after polling strongly in the 2006 Tennessee senate race, only to have some last-minute race-baiting ads released on the eve of the election. Studies of racial cues in political ads find a strong correlation between exposure to racial cues and anti-black sentiment. Together, these stories and studies suggested that the U.S. white majority did not yet contain the critical mass of voters who would not be susceptible to race-baiting and that there still remained an influential subgroup of bigots or racists who would never vote for a black person. Under these conditions, an Obama candidacy did not appear realistic.

Moreover, no Democratic candidate for president has won either the majority of white votes or the South since the Republicans launched their infamous Southern Strategy (courting the votes of Southern segregationists) in the wake of Lyndon B. Johnson's support for civil rights legislation. With these stats, who would expect a black candidate to win as many white votes as John Kerry, the losing 2004 candidate, had, let alone former Arkansas governor President Bill Clinton? If we couldn't expect white Democratic candidates to win the majority of white votes, how could we reasonably expect a black one to do it—and especially one who has a Muslim middle name, Hussein, at a time when a majority of white Americans said it was okay to racially profile Muslim Americans at airports and other public places?

Amnesia and Dreams

So these are the reasons why many people thought that Obama should wait another cycle, or be satisfied with a good showing and drop out of the primaries as soon as Hillary's campaign crushed him. These reasons are based on both measurable phenomena, including black candidates' recent losses even when it looked good for them in the polls, and the unavoidable reality that there still exists at least a significant portion of the white electorate that endorses black inferiority stereotypes. Some people still have a white supremacist mind set, and others are ready to exploit racial fears and misgivings about race-based policies to prime white voters to turn on Democratic candidates of any color. Though these were solid reasons to question Obama's chances, obviously predictions that he would lose were wrong. Many people said, "I told you so," and argued that the pessimists themselves were out of touch, overly consumed by race, and unwilling to believe in the fulfillment of King's "Dream."

While I disagree with those commentators who alleged Obama's victory was the culmination of Martin Luther King's "Dream" (narrowly interpreted), I think it is ultimately to our benefit that they did make that connection, because it directed public attention to the uncanny overlap of multiple racial/national commemorations. In January of 2009 the inauguration of a new president; the King national holiday and newly built monument; and preparations for the one hundred and fiftieth anniversary of the Civil War were underway. The intersection of these events provides us with coordinates for recurrent conflicts over the meaning of race in America, specifically elements of racial domination that grew out of slavery. As Kenneth Bindas wrote, all Americans, at least since the Civil War, have "had to deal with the structural and generational memory of slavery, Jim Crow, and its corresponding historical paradigm of subordination, which helps to construct a collective memory."[15]

From November of 2008 to January of 2009, the process of memory construction was in overdrive, with a mass media frenzy of congratulatory coverage of the first black president, along with intimations of the real end of race, the final crushing of the nation's "original sin" of slavery, all under the gaze of the angelically characterized martyrs of the 1960s: MLK, JFK, and RFK, the last of whom said before he died that there could be a Negro president in forty years. However, this optimistic discourse was shadowed by a soon-to-explode, parallel narrative of national crisis. In this retelling of American milestones, the crisis was precipitated by the fraudulent election of a non-citizen, a secret Muslim, a rabid anti-white double agent of blackness destined to seek revenge against a now shrinking white population for the sins of slavery and Jim Crow. The existence and force of this second narrative, and its roots in deep cultural understandings of race, citizenship, religion, and nation, are major reasons why many black observers not only feared Obama would be easily beaten by Hillary Clinton, but also, once he got the nomination, feared for his life.

That some were surprised at the post-election expressions of white racism and xenophobic nationalism is indicative of the failure of our society to further interrogate the collective memory of racial subjugation and to take accountability for the lasting effects of racial apartheid that structured not only law and policy, but culture and society. In particular, our increasingly mediated remembrances of the eras of slavery, segregation, and draconian restrictions on immigration encourage a sort of selective collective memory and a truncated practice of remembrance, crowding out and discouraging the counter-memories of African Americans and others brutalized by these systems of dominance.

What is exciting and hopeful about the convergence of the anniversaries I listed earlier and the subsequent outpouring of white rage, conspiracy theories, and appropriated histories in the public sphere is that together they blew open a hole in the post-racial argument, a hole wide enough to fill with counter-memories and discourses that include those who were excluded. If the fears expressed by those whites who declared "I want my country back" and the greasy kaleidoscope of racist images displayed in private emails "between friends" that were made public, in white power websites, and on Tea Party rally signs and bumper stickers teach us anything, it is that the idea of a man of African descent in power provides at least enough symbolic juice to reinvigorate and expose the continued strain of white supremacy that refuses to go away quietly.

Their fantasies of race war and health care as reparations lay bare the fact that any "racial reconciliation" that has occurred since the ebb of the mass movements of the 1960s has been terribly incomplete, and that our dominant displays of collective memory have been horribly inadequate to the task of democratic renewal. We need to discuss more deeply the causes and effects of the long civil rights movement, and the ways our mediated remembrances do not provide sufficient context for conversations about and approaches to racial reconciliation. It requires us to attend seriously to culture and the stories we tell ourselves—or ignore.

So first, I would like to describe what I mean by the "deep meaning" and "deep narratives" of culture. Building on the arguments of scholars in sociology, rhetoric, and memory studies, I illustrate how dominant white culture and media production have created two enduring—and often contradictory—deep narratives of slavery, class, Jim Crow, and the civil rights movement that are evident in representations of the racial past and contemporary interracial interaction. I contend that the dominant white-oriented "progress" narrative attends only to triumph and glosses over the pain, struggle, and losses—losses that are the product of white supremacist domination. This approach to our history perpetuates the myth that scores of racially "innocent" whites vastly outnumbered a smaller number of "bad"—and usually poor Southern—whites in the past. Now that the bad guys are vanquished, we can all be friends. Rather than listening to and fully incorporating the counter-memories of people of color, the dominant racial progress narrative employs a paltry type of multiculturalism in the service of national unity, which, however, is exposed to be quite tenuous, especially in moments of crisis. Second, I sketch out suggestions of what we might do in the midst of this revival of the "culture wars"—in some ways an extension of the Civil War—if we can get the excluded histories back into the frame. In this environment of increasingly vicious public discourse and cynical deployments of identity, we have some room to maneuver, to engender dialogues, and to present alternative pathways towards a future that learns more lessons from our collective past.

Culture and Deep Assumptions about Race

Collective memories are part of the "social imaginary." As Darrel Enck-Wanzer writes, the social imaginary informs and is "informed by factual and normative commitments about 'how things usually go' and 'how they ought to go.'"[16] Collective memories, then, and commemorations of significant events, comprise part of our understanding of how things "usually go," because we know the story, and its lessons suggest how we should behave in the future. The factual and normative aspects of commemoration draw "attention to . . . social practices and civic habits . . . political doctrines . . . and circulating symbols."[17] King's "Dream" is one such symbol; marching in Washington and voting are civic habits; racial segregation and democracy are political doctrines. Our attention is drawn to these and more when events call on us to collectively remember the civil rights struggle.

Thus, collective memory and commemorative practices provide a field within which we recognize the "deep meanings" that circulate—often without notice—in our culture. Following the work of Durkheim, Robert Wuthnow notes that commemorations are part of the periodic renewal of democratic society. At these times, we transmit core values, reinivigorate our associations, and engage in public advocacy.[18] We can view the presidential inauguration, for example, as a performance of democratic renewal, wherein the peaceful transition of power between administrations occurs in the public eye after the votes have been tallied and verified and the figure of the executive unifies the nation. Obama's inauguration was an exceptional moment of expectations and hope for renewal of a nation in economic crisis, at war, and in the throes of post-racial discourses that suggested *this* president would serve as a conduit for our "better angels" to finally make good on the promises of the Declaration of Independence that all its citizens are created equal. This hope hedged against fears that the United States was on the path to becoming a "society in which the narrow self-interest Tocqueville warned about has become so rampant that we find it difficult to work together for the common good."[19] Many voters and commentators hoped that Obama would inspire people to embrace a form of citizenship that emphasized public spirit rather than private gain. In his rhetoric, people heard a call for a return to attention to the public sphere, to consensus building and civic pride.

But even as folks drew upon a common store of cultural meanings about democracy, some of the other deeply held meanings served as barriers to social cohesion, even as people yearned for change. Wuthnow writes that though deeply held cultural assumptions are evident when "society mobilizes itself to achieve some laudable end," as the mobilization occurs, the same society may find itself puzzled that it is "a long way from achieving its ideals."[20] For example, even after investing significant human, legal, and monetary resources to ending segregation, racism and racial inequalities persist. Wuthnow argues that we should acknowledge that this isn't just about finding the right legal or policy remedy; rather, "there is more to the problem than just rolling up our sleeves."[21] To achieve the sort of democratic renewal that would get us past what Obama once called a "racial stalemate" requires a redefinition of culture "at the level of deep meaning; for instance, by reinterpreting old narratives or constructing new ones that tell how a person should behave in order to be regarded as morally responsible" and in whom we can trust.[22]

Cultural assumptions about behavior inform our sense of trust; but "trust is rooted in tacit knowledge about such matters as affinity (who am I like?) and responsibility (who will be there when I need them?)."[23] So race, class, religion, nationality—all of these facets of identity factor into deep meanings about trust and the common good. When it comes to race, there is little trust to be had. Stark evidence of racial profiling, unequal and unjust sentencing procedures, redlining in real estate and lending, draconian anti-immigrant policies and violent acts against undocumented workers paint an ugly picture of an untrustworthy society. Moreover, public opinion polls strongly suggest that a majority of whites see no link between these facts of racial life and racism. Only 32 percent of whites in a recent poll agreed that racism is still a problem, even though a majority admits inequalities still exist.[24] If a large portion of our society doesn't even see that racism still operates, that it contributes to the "racial stalemate," and that it serves as a deep anchor keeping us from moving faster away from the murky waters formed in cultural narratives of race and fear, superiority and Otherness, then we will continue to find solving the problem of the color line a Sisyphean task.

One way to start is by excavating and deconstructing the ways in which dominant collective memories of racial "anniversaries," so to speak, are anchored to problematic deep meanings of race, individualism, innocence, government, and responsibility. Paul Shackel suggests that public memories are established through three types of activity: (1) forgetting or excluding certain narratives of the past; (2) "creating and reinforcing patriotism"; and (3), "developing a sense of nostalgia to legitimize a particular heritage."[25] I follow his argument that dominant groups often use collective memory in ways that naturalize inequalities—but that collective counter-memories can be deployed as well to challenge that process. Importantly, he notes that collective memories are more reflections of "present political and social relations" than "accurate" representations of the past.[26] So we should attend to what elements of our political present are served by particular renderings of our collective racial past.

So now I turn to the dominant, competing collective memories that media have circulated and normalized in two particular versions of the nation's racial past. The first is the "lost cause," wherein the memories of the daughters and sons of the Confederacy hold the South was wrongly invaded and abused; that slavery actually benefitted black people (as did subsequent Jim Crow segregation); and that the federal government regularly oversteps its bounds in state sovereignty.[27] This version of history posits that the racial troubles of today stem from the tyranny of government and, for some, the inferiority of non-white groups.[28] The most rabid pro-Confederacy supporters imagine that a race war is inevitable and that the South will rise again. The more temperate believers argue that individualism and states' rights trump any attempts to legislate racial equality.

The second is the "white civil rights heroes" and white innocence narrative, which centers on the experiences and feelings of whites who contributed to or witnessed moments in the civil rights movement.[29] The innocence part of this collective memory posits that good white people (usually in the North) were either unaware of, unconnected to, or not implicated in slavery, Jim Crow, or other racial oppressions, and thus remain untouched by racism in the present and future. For these groups, the remnants of racial oppression and racial tensions are caused either by folks who "play the race card" to gin up white guilt to get concessions, or by the remaining "rednecks" who still lurk on the fringes of society but will soon be gone due to generational change. Through the perpetual progress brought by education and the limited integration efforts of the past forty years, eventually we will get to an approximation of King's "Dream" of a world where we're judged not by the color of our skin, but the content of our character.

Mainstream media have dramatized both of these collective memories, and their main themes are easily found in a host of Hollywood productions. From *Birth of a Nation* (1915) to *Gone With the Wind* (1939) and a host of other depictions of a genteel Southern elite, the "lost cause" narrative has structured depictions of Blacks as savages tamed only by the firm white hands of Southerners.[30] Likewise, Confederate monuments lionize the generals and soldiers who died fighting the North, and replicate the idea that slavery was good for blacks, as in the South Carolina monument to the "faithful slaves" who allegedly stood by their masters during the war.[31] While not directly connected to the specifics of Confederate nostalgia, sitcoms like *Beulah* (1950–1953), which featured a black maid happily serving a white family, and 1980s "buddy" movies reinforced the idea that blacks are happiest when in servitude to or managed by whites.[32]

Today, images of passive, happy slaves and black sidekicks are not as prevalent as they once were, and clearly there are voices raised in protest as well as counter-representations available to audiences. But simultaneously there are specialty media—DVDs, websites, blogs— where the "lost cause" lives on, chock full of "old school" white supremacy ready to be discovered or recirculated with the push of a button. The racist caricatures of Barack and Michelle Obama that sprouted up are evidence of how accessible and relevant the Sambo, the Mammy, and the Brute remain.

Public memories of white heroism and innocence are more widespread and available to mass audiences. Kelly Madison, Kristen Hoerl, and others have described how Hollywood created a slew of civil rights–themed films that focus on the heroic acts of individual whites, shunting generations of black activists and everyday participants to the margins.[33] Just as in the "lost cause," the pain and loss that white supremacy caused black Americans is muted. And, more importantly, their agency is dissolved when they are framed as being perpetually dependent upon the good graces of white people.

When the everyday indignities and violence of racist domination are erased from the frame, people can deny that it was all that bad, or that they had anything to do with that racial stuff. As generations witness "the nationalization of the movement, the street names, television specials, books and movies," they are usually introduced to the people and events in ways that suggest we're past racism, and that it was inevitable that the nation would come together to right all racial wrongs.[34] Even those who were alive during the movement seem to have taken on this notion. For example, historian Kenneth Bindas found in his oral history projects with aging whites that they were reluctant to name or describe any of the obvious impacts of segregation in their lives—even though they came of age in the midst of Jim Crow. Participants claimed they never even saw any black people, or they rationalized that any racial segregation they witnessed was "just how it was," as if some invisible force field once separated white from black and was lifted away "naturally," not by struggle and painstaking changes in the law.

Figure C.1. Tulsa, Oklahoma, Red Cross workers after race riot.
Courtesy of the Library of Congress, Prints and Photographs Division.

The idea of racial innocence is reinforced in contemporary media, which suggest that there really is no more work to be done by the everyday citizen to reduce inequalities. At the same time Hollywood renderings of the Jim Crow era reassure us that good white people were in sufficient supply to ease any suffering felt by blacks (see *Mississippi Burning* [1988] and *The Help* [2011]), advertising and entertainment television have specialized in creating multiracial vistas that assure us we are so different from our segregated ancestors. From McDonalds commercials to *Grey's Anatomy* to *Glee*, race rarely flares up at all. And when race does rear its head, jokes are made, feelings are not hurt too badly, and everyone goes back to normal in their multicultural schools and workplaces by the end of the hour.

Likewise, other scholars have demonstrated how anti-affirmative action activism and news framing helped construct whites as the real victims of racism, having *their* opportunities reduced as part of a remedy for Jim Crow.[35] At the same time, black politicians who argue for race-conscious remedies are framed as reverse-racist hucksters who cry discrimination at the smallest provocation. These narratives of white innocence/black intransigence allow for the reverence of the white heroes of the past—who somehow felt a responsibility to contribute to ending racial segregation without being implicated in racial hierarchy— and denial of any complicity or accountability for the cumulative effects of centuries of white supremacy.[36] And, they continue to center on the motives and actions of whites, and ignore the initiative and creativity of blacks and other people of color who create tactics to fight against and survive racial domination. The deep meanings of whiteness and civic responsibility, the hero/innocence dominant collective memories of the Civil War and civil rights movement enable a kind of forgetting and passiveness about racism in the present. That is, these narratives suggest we just need to wait for the right leader to emerge, and he (because it's always been a he!) will let us know where to march, what slogans to adopt, and so forth, so that we can find our way out of the stalemate.

The faults of this approach are easy to see when it is confronted by the resurgence of the "lost cause" collective memory and its visions of (white) American renewal. Recent calls for a monument to be erected in Selma, Alabama, to honor Bedford Forrest—the man popularly credited with founding the Ku Klux Klan—is only one of the most recent incidents of this desire to reclaim the Confederacy without coming to grips with the reality of white terrorism. In the gaps between these two dominant, white-centered narratives—the passive wait for the next leader versus the anxious vigil for the redemption of the Confederacy—black Americans and other people of color are held at arm's length, in civil rights limbo. When added to the empirical evidence of racist inequalities and white voter reluctance to cast a ballot for black candidates, the predictions of Obama's loss made in 2007 don't seem so crazy, do they? And, I can't help but want to say "I told you so" to the many people who seem bewildered by the stark displays of racist iconography and vicious racist humor that have found their way into all corners of the public sphere. Yes, they are usually met with condemnation, but also with denial of racial import—as in the case of the Montana judge who apologized for circulating a racist joke about Obama's parents via email to "private" "friends," while claiming that he isn't a racist, just "anti-Obama."[37]

The harshness of the racist, xenophobic responses to Obama's presidency was a sharp slap in the face, a surprise to many well-meaning people who were sure that we were on the cusp of a post-racial America. But one leader cannot bring about deep cultural change overnight. And the pervasive narratives of civil rights movements being over, being dependent on the charisma of the right kind of black leader, obfuscates the long-term activism, mundane actions, and everyday bravery that must accumulate over time to develop a new sort of civic consciousness. Many historians, activists, artists, and archivists strive to record and publicize the memories of those who survived segregation, xenophobic policies like Japanese internment, broken treaties and genocidal violence against Native Americans, and various and sundry means of terrorizing those who cross the border to the South. In these counternarratives of what civil rights movements mean and what fighting for justice means, the struggle and the pain are clearly visible. The cultivation of oppositional consciousness and self-determination is central. And, always, we hear and read that survival was not guaranteed even for the fittest and the smartest, and that white allies were not often in view.

Oral and written histories of people of color who did survive the atrocities of racism often emphasize "the sacrifices necessary to challenge" racism,[38] and not the feel-good moments afterwards. In these counter memories, we see how the most mundane acts—riding a bus, writing a letter, reading a book, speaking in one's native language, looking someone in the eye on the street—were potential seeds of change, moments of resistance. Think of what it would do to the dominant narratives of civil rights if we focus on these counter-public memories when we commemorate Dr. King, or inaugurate the first biracial president. If these memories were more accessible when the pundits were debating Obama's chances to win, how many more would have been skeptical, or more cautious, predicting a post-racial win? More importantly, what would they say was important to analyze in the electorate? Which voters would have gotten more attention as they gauged people's desire to renew America again through electoral change? I would argue that if these counter-memories were in the minds of news media makers, there would have still been concern about what white voters would or wouldn't do in the ballot box. But, the focus on "will they or won't they" vote for Obama would not have completely crowded out some of the most heartening and interesting things happening in the electorate.

As political scientist Cathy Cohen reminds us, in 2004 and 2008, young voters of color increased in numbers that far outstripped the growth of white voter participation in their age group.[39] But the agency and initiative of young voters of color were not consonant with the narrative of white-led progress in U.S. democracy, not part of the story of progress wrought not by the masses, but by enlightened black leaders whose eloquence moves us all to moral action. Likewise, some poor white voters' dismay with Mitt Romney and other Republican candidates got little attention.[40] And, some studies—as well as recent incidents of racist graffiti on college campuses—suggest that middle class, college-educated whites are sometimes *more* likely to express racial resentment.[41]

The narrative of a finite, no-longer-necessary civil rights movement still resonates in mainstream media and beyond. This collective memory draws attention to a limited set of social practices and civic habits that focus on the charisma of leaders and the spectacular display of mass marches. The focus on short timelines and singular leaders creates a blind spot for the other practices that occur at less lofty heights. Joined by other narratives that write off certain sectors of the voting public—i.e., youth of color—and hyperventilate over the motives of others—i.e., white college students hip to Obama—these deep narratives make it harder to imagine other avenues for change in the racial landscape of America. If we can't see and value the participation of young Latina/o, Asian American, and black voters now, when will we ever? If we can't remember that the majority of white votes continue to go to Republican candidates who play on racial fears every election, how can we start a conversation about making a post-racial America?

But if we center attention on the collective memories of struggle, then we are drawn to different social and civic practices. If we look at the increasing involvement of youth of color through the prism of the memories of struggle, then we need to acknowledge that they voted in 2012 against very high odds—confusing voter ID laws, stop-and-frisk harassment, cuts in public education, and anti-immigrant fervor. To understand how they were able to get to the ballot box, we must turn our attention to the long-term involvement of communities of color in fostering care and passion for justice. There, we learn something we can't from the narrow horse-race focus on the "moderate white voter" whom the political and press elites say Obama and the Democrats must

Figure C.2. Seattle, Washington, Martin Luther King, Jr., Day March.
Courtesy of Seattle Municipal Archives.

lure into his camp. If we stop to consider that a "great leader" and "toler-ant" white voters are *not* the most important factors in our democratic outcomes and improvement of race relations, then we can tell a new story, craft a different narrative that challenges the conventional wis-dom and transforms the deep meanings of race in our culture. Listen-ing to and learning from the experiences of everyday people who sur-vived Jim Crow and struggled for justice not just on one shining August day, we have a better chance to value a set of experiences that call for accountability, that don't play down the brutality and devastating con-sequences of racial domination. We also have to remember that the descendants of the oppressors and the oppressed are often still sizing each other up with wariness. Attention must be paid; reparation must be made. How can we hear these stories, see the evidence of the contin-ued legacy of Jim Crow, and not feel any accountability, any urgency to make amends?

If we begin to recraft our collective memories, to reconfigure com-mon assumptions about the meaning of the civil rights movement and of race in our society, then we can't just blame Obama for not being truly "post-racial," as many have done. We can't wait for him or someone else to save us from our history. A community-centered, multi-racial approach to public memory exposes both the democratic and undemocratic processes in our past. We can't let ourselves off the hook if we recognize that it was people just like us who did or didn't act, did or didn't trust each other. There were people who decided that their identity didn't have to rest on being superior to another group of people. There were people who believed in their ability to work collectively for change. People like us expanded our democracy; and people like us fought to retain the status quo of inequality. We are their daughters, grandsons, and great grandchildren. We should start acting like we know from whence we came.

NOTES

NOTES TO THE INTRODUCTION

1. So many books and programs from the 1980s and 1990s (and about those eras) could be in this list, but here are a few notable ones: Nelson George, *Post-Soul Nation* (New York: Viking, 2004); Toni Morrison, ed., *Race-ing Justice, En-Gendering Equality: Essays on Anita Hill, Clarence Thomas, and the Social Construction of Reality* (New York: Random House, 1992); Cornel West, *Race Matters* (New York: Vintage, 1994); bell hooks, *Yearning: Race, Gender and Cultural Politics* (Boston: South End Press, 1999); Mark Anthony Neal, *Soul Babies: Black Popular Culture and the Post-Soul Aesthetic* (New York: Routledge, 2001); The Black Public Sphere Collective, eds. *The Black Public Sphere* (Chicago: University of Chicago Press, 1995); Marlon Riggs, dir., *Black Is, Black Ain't,* DVD (California Newsreel, 1995).

2. Again, while this list will not be all-inclusive, a sampling of work discussing these emergences includes: Paula Massoud, ed., *The Spike Lee Reader* (Philadelphia: Temple University Press, 2008); Paul Taylor, "Post-Black, Old Black," *African American Review* 41 no. 4: 625–40; Jennifer Harris and Elwood Watson, eds., *The Oprah Phenomenon* (Lexington: University Press of Kentucky, 2009); Maureen Mahon, *Right To Rock: The Black Rock Coalition and the Cultural Politics of Race* (Durham: Duke University Press, 2004); S. Craig Watkins, *Representing: Hip Hop Culture and the Production of Black Cinema* (Chicago: University of Chicago Press, 1999); Jacqueline Bobo, *Black Women as Cultural Readers* (New York: Columbia University Press, 1995); Toni Morrison, *Playing in the Dark: Whiteness and the American Literary Imagination* (New York: Vintage, 1993); Michael Eric Dyson, *Reflecting Black: African American Cultural Criticism* (Minneapolis: University of Minnesota Press, 1993).

3. Patricia Williams, *The Alchemy of Race and Rights: Diary of A Mad Law Professor* (Cambridge: Harvard University Press, 1992); Shelby Steele, *The Content of Our Character* (New York: Harper Perennial, 1991); Ellis Cose, *The Rage of A Privileged Class* (New York: Harper Collins, 1993); Michael P. Rogin and Robert Post, eds. *Race and Representation: Affirmative Action* (New York: Zone Books,

1998); Melissa Harris-Lacewell, *Barbershops, Bibles & BET: Everyday Talk and Black Political Thought.* (Princeton: Princeton University Press, 2006); Jayne O. Ifekwunigwe, ed., *"'Mixed Race'" Studies: A Reader* (New York: Routledge, 2004); Michael O.Emerson and Christian Smith, *Divided by Faith: Evangelical Religion and the Problem of Race in America.* (New York: Oxford University Press, 2001).

4. Eric K. Watts, "The Nearly Apocalyptic Politics of Post-Racial America: Or, 'This Is Now the United States of Zombieland,'" *Journal of Communication Inquiry* 34 (2010): 216–17.

5. See, for example, discussions in the following recent books and articles: Ralina L. Joseph, *Transcending Blackness: From the New Millenial Mulatta to the Exceptional Multiracial* (Durham, NC: Duke University Press, 2012); Roopali Mukherjee, "'Bling–Fling': Commodity Consumption and the Politics of the ' Post-Racial,'" in *Critical Rhetorics of Race*, eds. Michael Lacey and Kent A. Ono (New York: New York University Press, 2011), 178–96; Catherine R. Squires, *Dispatches from the Color Line: The Press and Multiracial America* (Albany: SUNY Press, 2007).

6. Squires, *Dispatches from the Color Line.*

7. Amy A. Hasinoff, "Fashioning Race for the Free Market on *America's Next Top Model*," *Critical Studies in Media Communication* 25 no. 3 (2008), 324–43; Joseph, *Transcending Blackness*; Mary Thompson, "'Learn Something from This!': The Problem of Optional Ethnicity on *America's Next Top Model*," *Feminist Media Studies* 10 no.3 (2010): 335–52.

8. Hasinoff, "Fashioning Race," 335.

9. Catherine R. Squires, "Coloring in the Bubble: Perspectives from Black-Oriented Media on the (Latest) Economic Disaster," *American Quarterly* 64 no. 3 (2012): 543–70.

10. Jonathan Rutherford, *Identity: Community, Culture, Difference.* (London: Lawrence & Wishart, 1990), 11.

11. Henry Giroux, "Consuming social change: The 'United Colors of Benetton,'" *Cultural Critique* 26, (1993): 5–32.

12. Jon Krasewski, "Multiracialism on *The Real World* and the Reconfiguration of Politics in MTV's Brand During the 2000s," *Popular Communication* 8 (2010): 132–46.

13. Squires, *Dispatches.*

14. Nasar Meer and Tariq Modood, "The Multicultural State We're In: Muslims, 'Multiculture' and the 'Civic Rebalancing' of British Multiculturalism," *Political Studies* 57, no. 3 (2008): 1–25; Tariq Modood, "Is Multiculturalism Dead?" *Public Policy Research* (June–August 2008): 84–88.

15. Susan Searls Giroux, "From the 'Culture Wars' to the Conservative Campaign for Campus Diversity: Or, How Inclusion Became the New Exclusion," *Policy Futures in Education* 3, no. 4 (2005): 314–26.

16. Evelyn Alsultany, "Selling American Diversity and Muslim American Identity through Nonprofit Advertising Post-9/11," *American Quarterly* 59, no. 3 (2007): 28.

17. See discussions in: Alsutany, "Selling"; Barbara Biesecker, "No Time for Mourn-ing: The Rhetorical Production of the Melancholic Citizen-Subject in the War on Terror," *Philosophy and Rhetoric 40*, no.1 (2007): 147–69; Giroux, "From the 'Cul-ture Wars'"; Bruce B. Lawrence, "Conjuring with Islam, II," *Journal of American History* 89, no. 2 (2002): 485–97; Melani McAlister, "A Cultural History of the War Without End," *Journal of American History* 89, no. 2 (2002): 439–55.

18. See studies summarized in Marta Tienda, Sigal Alon, and Sunny Niu, "Affirma-tive Action and the Texas Top 10 Percent Admission Law: Balancing Equity and Access to Higher Education," February 2008, http://theop.princeton.edu/reports/wp/AffirmativeAction_TopTen.pdf. See also Nicholas Webster, "Analysis of the Ten Percent Plan," Kirwan Institute for the Study of Race, 2007, http://kirwanin-stitute.osu.edu/wp-content/uploads/2012/05/Texas-Ten-Percent_style.pdf.

19. David Roediger, "White Workers, New Democrats, and Affirmative Action," in *The House That Race Built,* ed. Wahneema Lubiano (New York: Vintage, 1998) 48–65. See multiple essays on and analysis of economic and social data that sug-gest that class-not-race approaches have failed to shrink racial gaps in education, jobs, and wealth in "Revisiting William Julius Wilson's *The Declining Significance of Race*," *Journal of Sociology & Social Welfare* 39, no.1 (2012).

20. Liddy West, "A Complete Guide to Hipster Racism," Jezebel.com, April 26, 2012,http://jezebel.com/5905291/a-complete-guide-to-hipster-racism.

21. Channing Kennedy, "Understanding Hipster Racism: Lester Bang's 1979 'White Noise Supremacists,'" ColorLines.com, April 27, 2012, http://colorlines.com/archives/2012/04/hipster_racism_isnt_new_read_1979s_white_noise_suprema-cists.html.

22. Bangs's article was reproduced at http://www.mariabuszek.com/kcai/PoMoSemi-nar/Readings/BangsWhite.pdf.

23. West, "A Complete Guide."

24. Kennedy, "Understanding Hipster Racism."

25. There are many discussions and investigations of the impact of race on society and individual life chances, from research on the racial disparities in public health (e.g., the Kaiser Foundation provides regular updates on minority health, accessi-ble at http://www.kff.org/minorityhealth/index.cfm) to racial bias in the criminal justice system (e.g., Michelle Alexander, *The New Jim Crow: Mass Incarceration in the Age of Colorblindness* [New York: New Press, 2012]), the "achievement gap" in K–12 education (e.g., Jessica Rebell and Michael A. Wolf, *NCLB at the Crossroads: Re-examining the Federal Effort to Close the Achievement Gap* [New York: Teach-ers College Press, 2009]); and employment discrimination (e.g. George Wilson, ed., *Race, Ethnicity, and Inequality in the U.S. Labor Market,* Annals of the Ameri-can Academy of Political and Social Sciences Series, vol. 609 [Thousand Oaks, CA: Sage, 2007]).

26. Bambi Haggins, *Laughing Mad: The Black Comic Persona in the Post-Soul Era.* (New Brunswick, NJ: Rutgers University Press, 2007). See especially discussion of Chappelle's spectrum of conciliatory to confrontational racial humor, 192–99.

27. Jonathan P. Rossing, "Critical Intersections and Comic Possibilities: Extending Racialized Critical Rhetorical Scholarship," *Communication Law Review* 10, no.1 (2010): 10–27, 15.

28. Edward Schiappa, *Beyond Representational Correctness: Rethinking Criticism to Popular Media* (Albany, NY: SUNY Press, 2008).

29. Betty Friedan, *The Feminine Mystique* (New York: Dell Books, 1963/1983).

30. Squires, *Dispatches*.

31. Thomas Holt, *The Problem of Race in the Twenty-First Century* (Cambridge: Harvard University Press, 2000), 23.

NOTES TO CHAPTER 1

1. Peter Goldman, "Sizing up Carter: The Question of Character," *Newsweek*, September 13, 1976.

2. My research assistants and I searched for items in the Lexis/Nexis English-Only News database. The assistants read through the items to eliminate articles that were repeats, as well as articles that were captured due to idiosyncrasies such as having the *Washington Post* moniker situated next to the word "race." I created a codebook based on previous research, and then the assistants read through each item to identify explicit assumptions, themes, and people associated with "post-racial." I also read through the items to identify other unexpected themes or issues associated with the term.

3. See analysis of news reports on Tiger Woods in Squires, *Dispatches from the Color Line*, 189–92.

4. Tom Teepen, "We're Red, White, Blue and Lots More," *South Bend Tribune,* April 27, 1997. This piece was syndicated by Cox News Service, and also appeared in five other newspapers in the West and Midwest.

5. Gordon Dillow, "Their Race? Some Students Just Won't Say," *Orange County Register,* March 19, 1998.

6. "Recent Case Argued Before the Supreme Court Regarding Redisctricing," *Talk of the Nation*, NPR, May 18, 1999.

7. Jim Schutze, "Taking It to the Street: Want to Get Elected to City Council in Southern Dallas? Forget the Race Card and Patch that Pothole," *Dallas Observer,* April 22, 1999.

8. Ibid.

9. Noemie Emery's essay was part of the special segment of the *Weekly Standard* titled, "Is There a Worldwide Conservative Crack-Up? A Symposium," August 25, 1997/September 1, 1997.

10. Squires, *Dispatches*, 175–78.

11. Bradley Jones and Roopali Mukherjee, "From California to Michigan: Race, Rationality and Neoliberal Governmentality," *Communication and Critical/Cultural Studies* 7, no. 4: (2010) 401–22.

12. For example, Illinois Representative Joe Walsh (R) was caught on camera at a 2012 town hall meeting telling the crowd that "[t]he Democratic Party promises

groups of people everything. They want the Hispanic vote, they want Hispanics to be dependent upon government, just like they got African-Americans dependent upon government. That's their game. Jesse Jackson would be out of work if they weren't dependent upon government. There'd be no work for him." See "Joe Walsh: Democrats Want Hispanics, African Americans "Dependent On Government,'" Huffington Post.com, May 30, 2012, http://www.huffingtonpost. com/2012/05/30/joe-walsh-hispanics-african-americans_n_1557480.html. During the 2012 primaries, candidates Newt Gingrich and Rick Santorum argued that Obama wanted black people to remain dependent, and falsely claimed his policies had made more Americans dependent on food stamps than during any other administration. And, after a speech to the NAACP, front-runner Mitt Romney implied that black voters who supported Obama just wanted other citizens to give up precious tax dollars so they could get "free stuff." Susan Brooks Thistlethwait, ""Free Stuff?' The message from Romney's NAACP Speech," Washington Post. com, July 12, 2012, http://www.washingtonpost.com/blogs/guest-voices/post/free-stuff-the-message-from-romneys-naacp-speech/2012/07/12/gJQAFNhGgW_blog. html.

13. The Joshua Generation is a reference to a passage from the Old Testament which has to do with a younger generation who benefit from the struggles of their parents. Obama dubbed himself and other young politicians the "Joshua Generation" who followed the "Moses Generation" of civil rights activists whose actions created the context for his successes in college and politics. He used the term in his March 4, 2007, speech in Selma, Alabama, to commemorate the 1965 "Bloody Sunday" march for voting rights. "It was left to the Joshuas to finish the journey Moses had begun, and today we're called to be the Joshuas of our time, to be the generation that finds our way across the river." Full text of the speech available at http://blogs.suntimes.com/sweet/2007/03/obamas_selma_speech_text_as_de.html.

14. See, for example, Charles Payne's enlightening history of civil rights from the grass roots level, *I've Got the Light of Freedom*, as well as in Nikhil Pal Singh, *Black Is a Country: Race and the Unfinished Struggle for Democracy*. (Cambridge: Harvard University Press, 2004). For discussions of the erasure of women's leadership, see Bernice McNair Barnett, "Invisible Southern Black Women Leaders in the Civil Rights Movement: The Triple Constraints of Gender, Race, and Class," *Gender and Society* 7, no. 2 (June 1993): 162–82. For analysis and commentary on the problematic focus on male leadership, see Belinda Robinette, *How Long, How Long? African American Women in the Struggle for Civil Rights* (New York: Oxford University Press, 1997), and bell hooks, *Salvation: Black People and Love* (New York: Harper Perennial, 2001). For discussions of the problematic way the civil rights movement—and Martin Luther King, Jr., in particular—is memorialized, see Renee C. Romano and Leigh Raiford, eds., *The Civil Rights Movement in American Memory* (Athens: University of Georgia Press, 2006); Jacqueline Dowd, "The Long Civil Rights Movement and the Political Uses of the Past," *The Journal

of American History 91, no.4 (2005): 1233–63; and Ronald Turner, "The Dangers of Misappropriation: Misusing Martin Luther King Jr.'s Legacy to Prove the Color-blind Thesis," *Michigan Journal of Race & Law* 2, no.1 (1996): 101–30.

15. Matt Bai's *New York Times Magazine* cover article, "Is Obama the End of Black Politics," gathered together the entire elected body of "Joshua Generation"—i.e., post-racial politicians—in one feature published August 10, 2008. Prior to that, however, each of the men listed in this section were repeatedly associated with the term "post-racial," but none more than Booker between 2002 and 2005.

16. Dave Russakoff, "In Newark Race, Black Political Visions Collide," *Washington Post*, May 14, 2002.

17. Alexandra Marks, "New Game in Urban Politics," *Christian Science Monitor*, May 10, 2002.

18. This narrative was also reflected in the now-famous documentary made about the campaign, *Street Fight*, dir. Marshall Curry (Magnolia Home Entertainment, 2005), reviews of which allowed reporters and commentators to revisit and reinforce the theme of black generational conflict. The film premiered at the Tribeca Film Festival and then was aired on PBS's *Point of View* on July 5, 2005. It was nominated for an Academy Award for best documentary, guaranteeing more coverage by the media.

19. Marks, "New Game in Urban Politics."

20. Russakoff, "In Newark Race."

21. Ellis Cose, "What the Revolution Was For," *Newsweek*, May 13, 2002.

22. Jonathan Tepperman, "Complicating the Race," *New York Times*, April 28, 2002.

23. Chris Smith, "Brooklyn Bantustan," *New York Magazine,* July 24, 2006.

24. Houston Baker, Jr., "Critical Memory and the Black Public Sphere," in *The Black Public Sphere*, ed. Black Public Sphere Collective (Chicago: University of Chicago Press, 1995), 5–38.

25. See Turner, "The Dangers of Misappropriation." Ron Walters, "Keep King's Words in Context," *Baltimore Sun*, January 19, 1998.

26. For a bracing, thorough set of discussions on the ways in which popular representations of black power are limited and limiting, see V. P. Franklin, ed., *New Black Power Studies: National, International and Transnational Perspectives*, special issue of, *Journal of African American History* 92, no. 4 (2007).

27. See Clare Jean Kim, "Managing the Racial Breach: Clinton, Black-White Polarization, and the Race Initiative," *Political Science Quarterly* 117, no. 1 (2002): 55–79; and John Brenkman, "Race Publics," *Transition* 66 (1995): 4–36.

28. Examples abound of Republican appointees, supporters, and elected officials who made public statements or pursued policies that clashed with basic ideas of civil rights or racial equality. See, for example, defenses of the Confederate flag in many Republican-led states such as South Carolina throughout the early 2000s; Senator Trent Lott's 2002 speech lauding Strom Thurmond and wishing he had won the presidency in 1948, when running on the segregationist platform; the anti-interracial dating policies (not ended until March 2000) at Bob Jones

University, a regular stop on the speaking circuit for any Republican presidential hopeful; and the widespread stereotyping of Muslim and Arab Americans as terrorists-in-waiting, deserving of extra surveillance and/or harassment, exemplified most recently by Representative Peter King's much-criticized hearings on Muslim American "radicalization" in 2011.

29. Andrew Sullivan, "The Left and Condoleeza Rice," *New York Sun*, November 19, 2004.

30. Luiza Savage, "Senator Miller's Angry Keynote Divided Listeners," *New York Sun*, September 3, 2004.

31. Jonah Goldberg, "Only Time will Zell," *National Review*, September 2, 2004.

32. See Steven M. Teles's account of the racial strategies of "compassionate conservatism" in the 1990s and early 2000s in "The Eternal Return of Compassionate Conservatism," *National Affairs* (Fall 2009), 107–27.

33. "The Politics of Tokenism," *Economist,* August 12, 2004.

34. Keyes notoriously said in one debate and in ads that Obama wasn't a "real" black man (or a real Christian). See commentary on the debate in Richard Thompson Ford, "Name Games: The Folly in the Attempts to Define African American," Slate.com, September 16, 2004, http://www.slate.com/articles/news_and_politics/ jurisprudence/2004/09/name_games.html.

35. Steven Malanga, "Reagan's Unlikely Heir," *City Journal*, Winter 2006.

36. Frances Fitzgerald, "Holy Toledo! Ohio's Gubernatorial Race Tests the Power of the Christian Right," *New Yorker*, July 11, 2006.

37. Kathryn Jean Lopez, "Meet 'Jesse Jackson's Worst Nightmare,'" *National Review,* February 15, 2006.

38. Ibid.

39. Many academics and political observers have observed the contradictions in the strategy of using conservatives of color to legitimate racially coded rhetoric and policy measures. See, for example, Angela Dillard, "How the New Black Elite Peddles Conservatism," *New Labor Forum* 13, no. 1 (2004): 31–38.

40. O'Connor wrote: "The Court takes the Law School at its word that it would like nothing better than to find a race-neutral admissions formula and will terminate its use of racial preferences as soon as practicable. The Court expects that 25 years from now, the use of racial preferences will no longer be necessary to further the interest approved today," *Grutter v. Bollinger*, 539 U.S. 306 (2003).

41. George F. Will, "The Supreme Court Made No Sense Here," *Charleston Daily Mail*, June 28, 2003.

42. Colbert I. King, "Truth from Justice Ginsberg," *Washington Post*, June 28, 2003.

43. Susan Herbst, *Rude Democracy: Civility and Incivility in American Politics* (Philadelphia: Temple University Press, 2010), 150, n. 14.

44. We double-coded a subsample of 25 percent of the stories for coder agreement. All results reported here had at least 90 percent inter-coder agreement.

45. Stephanie Li, *Signifying Without Specifying: Racial Discourse in the Age of Obama* (New Brunswick: Rutgers University Press, 2012).

46. See, for example, Enid Logan, *At This Defining Moment: Barack Obama's Presidential Candidacy and the New Politics of Race* (New York: New York University Press, 2011); various contributions to Heather Harris, Kimberly Moffit, and Catherine Squires, eds., *The Obama Effect: Multidisciplinary Renderings of the 2008 Campaign* (Albany: SUNY Press, 2010); Catherine R. Squires and Sarah J. Jackson, "Reducing Race: News Themes in the 2008 Primaries," *International Journal of Press/Politics* 15, no. 4 (2010): 375–400; Siobahn Stiles and Carolyn Kitch, "'Redemption for Our Anguished Racial History': Race and the National Narrative in Commemorative Journalism about Barack Obama," *Journal of Communication Inquiry* 35 (2011): 115–33.

47. Enid Logan, *At This Defining Moment*, 31.

48. Stiles and Kitch, "'Redemption,'" 128.

49. Daniel Schorr, "Wright Hurts Obama's Notion of a Post-Racial World," *All Things Considered*, NPR(Washington, DC, April 29, 2008).

50. Mohammed Ali Salih, "A Son's Wisdom on a Post-Racial World," *USA Today*, February 22, 2008.

51. Richard Rodriguez, "Black, White, and Shades of Grey," *Newsweek*, June 2, 2008 (emphasis mine).

52. Mark Dolliver, "Double-Vision: The Race Issue Revisited," Adweek.com, July 14, 2008.

53. James A. Bacon, "Put Race Behind Us?" *Deseret Morning News*, November 11, 2008.

54. Ibid.

55. Emily W. Pettus, "For Ole Miss, Debate Marks School's Progress," Associated Press, September 20, 2008.

56. Michael Crowley, "Post-Racial," *New Republic*, March 12, 2008.

57. Dana Cloud, "To Veil the Threat of Terror: Afghan Women and the Clash of Civilizations in the Imagery of the U.S. War on Terrorism," *Quarterly Journal of Speech* 90, no. 3 (2004): 285–306.

58. "From Slavery to Obama," *Chicago Sun Times*, November 5, 2008.

59. Justin Ewers, "An Enviable Position for Civil Rights Advocates," *US News & World Report*, December 1, 2008.

60. See Robert Spicer, "The Obama Mass: Barack Obama, Image, and Fear of the Crowd," in Harris, Moffit, and Squires, eds., *The Obama Effect*, 190–208.

61. Ibid. Public endorsements from Senator Ted Kennedy and Caroline Kennedy, the daughter of President John F. Kennedy, came early in the campaign, along with numerous comparisons between JFK and Obama—both were elected senators at a young age, both were Harvard educated, etc.

62. There continue to be superhero memes inspired by Booker. Recently, see the Twitter hashtag fest "#corybookerstories" after the mayor rescued someone from a burning building in April 2012. Twitter users imagined other humorous and not-so-humorous rescues Booker might be involved with in the future, such as "Cory Booker caught N. Korea's missile launch with his bare hands #corybookerstories."

63. Dan Spencer, "Would an Obama Victory Prolong the Racial Divide?" *California Yankee*, February 28, 2008.

64. Ron Feldman, "Letter to the Editor: Obama Has Invited Legitimate Criticism," *Chicago Daily Herald*, March 28, 2008.

65. Pamela Gellar, "The Real Racism in Obamanation," Atlas Shrugs.com, November 17, 2008, http://atlasshrugs2000.typepad.com/atlas_shrugs/2008/11/the-real-racism.html.

66. The Southern Poverty Law Center, as well as the FBI and other organizations, have charted increases in white power organizations and their activities since Obama was elected. See SPLC summaries of white hate groups at http://www.splcenter.org/get-informed/intelligence-report/browse-all-issues/2012/spring/the-year-in-hate-and-extremism. See also the Leadership Conference's discussion of white power groups and hate crimes at http://www.civilrights.org/publications/hatecrimes/white-supremacist.html, and *Democracy Now!* special report on white supremacist group activities at http://www.democracynow.org/2010/1/11/white_power_usa_the_rise_of.

67. Annette John-Hall, "Race Still Matters in Obama's Post-Racial America," *Philadelphia Inquirer,* January 26, 2009.

68. Ibid.

69. DeWayne Wickham, "Post-Racial Era? Go Tell Victims of Police Shootings," *USA Today*, January 13, 2009.

70. Ryan McAuliffe Straus, "Racism Is Still among Us," *Albany Times-Union*, January 21, 2009.

71. "The Post-Racial Conversation, One Year In," *Talk of the Nation*, NPR, January 18, 2009.

72. Andrew Breitbart, "No More Apologies from Sotomayor," *Washington Times*, June 1, 2009.

73. In 2012, the issue of racial profiling became a hot topic in the news due to high profile shootings in Oakland, CA, and in Florida. This prompted more discussion of data and studies that strongly suggest police use racial profiling extensively and without cause in cities such as New York, Philadelphia, and Chicago. See, for example, editorials in the *New York Times* on the "stop and frisk" laws (e.g. "Injustices of Stop and Frisk," , *New York Times, May 13, 2012*, http://www.nytimes.com/2012/05/14/opinion/injustices-of-stop-and-frisk.html?_r=1); articles and editorials in TheRoot.com and Colorlines.com on the racial impact of so-called "stand your ground" laws in states such as Florida (e.g., Jenée Desmond-Harris, "Florida, Black Victims, and Stand Your Ground," TheRoot.com, June 5, 2012, http://www.theroot.com/buzz/florida-black-victims-stand-your-ground; Sean Thomas-Breitfeld, "Could I Be Both Trayvon Martin AND George Zimmerman?" ColorLines.com, April 11, 2012, http://colorlines.com/archives/2012/04/could_i_be_both_trayvon_martin_and_george_zimmerman.html.

74. "President Obama Shows Race Baiting Lessons Learned from Wright, et al.," Weapons of Mass Discussion, July 23, 2009, http://massdiscussion.blogspot.com/2009/07/president-obama-shows-race-baiting.html.

75. John Yoo, "Court's Push Toward Post-Racial America," *Providence Journal-Bulletin* (Rhode Island), July 11, 2009.

76. Roger Simon, "What Happened to Post-Racial America?" Politico.com, August 7, 2009, http://www.politico.com/news/stories/0809/25890.html.

77. Glenn C. Loury, "Obama, Gates, and the American Black Man," *New York Times*, July 26, 2009.

78. "Black Intellectuals Decry 'Beer Summit': Say Notion of a Post-Racial America is a Myth," States News Service, August 6, 2009.

79. "Whose "Post-Racial" America?" *Tell Me More*, NPR, July 22, 2009.

80. Lillian Morgeau, "Gaining Ground: Getting to Post-Racial by Way of Pop Culture," *Sunday Oregonian*, March 29, 2009.

81. Lenox Magee, "Post-Race USA—Are we There Yet?" *N'Digo*, February 19, 2009.

82. Glenn Gamboa, "Jackson: About Face on Race?" *New York Newsday*, July 5, 2009.

83. Andrew Dansby, "Michael Jackson 1958–2009: Legacy Lies in his Art, not Scandals," *Houston Chronicle*, June 26, 2009.

84. "A New Post-Racial Political Era in America." *All Things Considered*, NPR, January 28, 2008.

85. Shelby Steele, et al., "The President is No Redeemer, Post-Racial or Otherwise," *Wall Street Journal*, November 9, 2010.

86. Pam Spaulding, "Ring in the Post-Racial New Year: Obama Effigy in Plains, GA," Pam's House Blend, January 3, 2010, http://pamshouseblend.firedoglake.com/2010/01/03/ring-in-the-postracial-new-year-obama-effigy-in-plains-ga/. The story was also posted on Therawstory.com on January 5, 2010.

87. Charles J. Ogletree and Johanna Wald, "A Little Less "Post-Racial," a Little More Listening," *Washington Post*, July 24, 2010.

88. Bonnie Goldstein, "A Child Will Lead Us: Post-Racial Attitudes," *Politics Daily*, July 22, 2010, http://www.politicsdaily.com/2010/07/22/a-child-will-lead-us-post-racial-attitudes/.

89. Lauri Apple, "Liveblogging the Apotheosis of Michelle Bachmann," Wonkette.com, August 10, 2010.

90. Di Hall, Letter to the Editor, *Fresno Bee*, 2010, http://wonkette.com/417300/liveblogging-the-apotheosis-of-st-michele-bachmann-of-minnesota-and-other-midterm-primaries.

91. Steve Dickler, "Tea Party New Source for Hope, Change," *Island Packet*, September 14, 2010.

92. Ron Todt, "Conservative Blogger says Obama Not 'Post-Racial,'" Associated Press, July 31, 2010.

93. "Shirley Sherrod and a 'Post-Racial' America," *Los Angeles Times,* July 22, 2010.

94. See images and footage at "Slideshow, Offensive Tea Party Signs, YouTube video, 2:15, posted by "naacpvideos," September 2, 2010, http://www.youtube.com/watch?v=uPKhH7tYIj8; "Tea Party Racism: What the Media Won't Show You About Teabagger Racism," YouTube Video, 5:28, posted by "ronaldjacksonX," February 9, 2010, http://www.youtube.com/watch?v=S38VioxnBaI&feature=re

lated; "10 Most Offensive Tea Party Signs and Extensive Photo Coverage from Tax Day Protests," *Huffington Post,* April 16, 2009, http://www.huffingtonpost. com/2009/04/16/10-most-offensive-tea-par_n_187554.html?ref=tea-party; and Arian Campo-Flores, "Are Tea Partiers Racist?" *The Daily Beast,* April 25, 2010, http://www.thedailybeast.com/newsweek/2010/04/25/are-tea-partiers-racist.html.

95. See, for example, t-shirts and bumper stickers for sale with the slogan "Obama: African Lion or Lyin' African" at zazzle.com. Or do a Google search for "Obama pimp" and see the many ugly Photoshop mash ups of the president and first lady as pimp and prostitute.

96. Mary Sanchez, "Post-Racial U.S.? Not Happening," *Modesto Bee,* July 26, 2010.

97. Ibid.

98. David Dante Troutte, ""Post-Racial' Blame Games," Politico.com, July 22, 2010. http://www.seattlepi.com/national/politico/article/post-racial-blame-games-896291.php.

99. Pam Spaulding, "More Post-Racial America: Blacks Still Barred from Juries, KY Segregated Clubs Still Live On," Pam's House Blend, June 2, 2010, http://www. pamshouseblend.com.

100. Ibid.

101. Tim Barker, "Campus Hate Crimes Defy Idea of Post-Racial America," *Salt Lake Tribune,* April 10, 2010.

102. Brian Gilmore, "We Need a Post-Racial and Post-Poverty America," *Modesto Bee,* January 17, 2010.

103. Ibid.

NOTES TO CHAPTER 2

1. See, for example, Todd Gitlin, *Twilight of Common Dreams: Why America Is Wracked by Culture Wars* (New York: Henry Holt, 1996). See critiques of the "class over race" approach in Aldon Morris and Carol McClurg-Miller, eds., *Frontiers in Social Movement Theory* (New Haven: Yale University Press, 1992).

2. See, for example, Samuel Huntington, "The Clash of Civilizations," *Foreign Affairs* 72, no. 3,(1993): 22–49. For discussion and critiques of the "clash" paradigm and assumptions about the benefits of assimilation to Western values, see Tariq Modood, "Is Multiculturalism Dead?" *Public Policy Research* 15, no. 2 (June–August 2008): 84–88. See also Douglas Hartmann and Joseph Gerteis, "Dealing with Diversity: Mapping Multiculturalism in Sociological Terms," *Sociological Theory* 23, (2005): 218–40, on competing definitions of multiculturalism and how assimilation is one of many mechanisms for managing diversity of groups in society.

3. See Douglas Hartmann, Xuefeng Zhang, and William Wischstadt, "One (Multicultural) Nation under God? Changing Uses and Meanings of the Term 'Judeo-Christian' in the American Media," *Journal of Media & Religion* 4, no. 4 (2005): 207–34, on the increasing use of "Judeo-Christian" as a term to describe a narrowing sense of common moral foundations for citizens in the United States.

For a defense of the notion that the United States is essentially a Judeo-Christian, conservative, free-market ordered, and *superior* country, see Dennis Prager, *Still the Best Hope: Why the World Needs American Values to Triumph* (New York: Harper Collins, 2012). Also see discussion of how the Christian Right frames liberals and Democrats as degraders of Judeo-Christian and free market values in Chris Hedges, *American Fascists: The Christian Right and the War on America* (New York: Simon & Schuster, 2008).

4. Harris-Lacewell, *Barbershops, Bibles, and BET*, 255.

5. Ibid., 38.

6. Birgit Meyer and Annaliese Moore, "Introduction," in *Religion, Media and the Public Sphere*, ed. Birgit Meyer and Annaliese Moore (Bloomington: Indiana University Press, 2006).

7. Ibid., 1.

8. John T. McGreevy, *Parish Boundaries: The Catholic Encounter with Race in the Twentieth-Century Urban North* (Chicago: University of Chicago Press, 1998).

9. Henry Goldschmidt, "Introduction," in *Race, Nation and Religion in the Americas,* ed. Henry Goldschmidt and Elizabeth McAllister (Oxford: Oxford University Press, 2004), 5.

10. Michael Omi and Howard Winant, *Racial Formation in the United States: From the 1960s to the 1990s,* second edition (New York: Routledge, 1994), 56.

11. Robert Fanuzzi, "Frederick Douglass's 'Colored News Paper': Identity Politics in Black and White," in *The Black Press: New Literary and Historical Essays*, ed. Todd Vogel (New Brunswick: Rutgers University Press, 2001), 55–70.

12. Charles Payne, *I've Got the Light Of Freedom: The Organizing Tradition and the Mississippi Freedom Struggle.* (Berkeley: University of California Press, 2007). See discussions of black churches and responses to LGBT rights in Cassandra Chaney and Le'Brian Patrick, "The Invisibility of LGBT Individuals in Black Mega-Churches," *Journal of African American Studies* 15 (2011): 199–217; Christopher Lisotta, "Homophobia of All Hues," *Nation*, May 17, 2004; and Eric Daniel, "Black Clergy in the 2000 Election," *Journal for the Scientific Study of Religion* 42, no. 4 (2003): 533–46.

13. Numerous news outlets and activists have noted, in hindsight, that initial reports that African Americans had "tipped the balance" for Prop 8 in California were wrong, and that in polls African Americans report more support for gay marriage than other groups. See, for example, Jorge Rivas, "People of Color More Likely to Support Gay Marriage," Colorlines.com, May 23, 2012, http://colorlines.com/archives/2012/05/people_of_color_more_likely_to_support_gay_marriage_than_whites_abc_poll_finds.html; Scott Keyes and Jay Legum, "Two African American Pastors Explain Why they Support Gay Marriage," ThinkProgress.org, July 12, 2012 http://thinkprogress.org/lgbt/2012/07/12/515269/african-american-marriage-equality/?mobile=nc; and Jenee Desmond Harris, "Blacks and Gay Marriage," TheRoot.com, May 24, 2012, http://www.theroot.com/buzz/african-american-support-marriage-equality-higher-general-pop.

14. Dorothy Roberts, *Killing the Black Body: Race, Reproduction and the Meaning of Liberty* (New York: Random House/Pantheon Books, 1997); Harriet A. Washington, *Medical Apartheid: The Dark History of Medical Experimentation on Black People from Colonial Times to the Present* (New York: Random House, 2008).

15. See discussions of outrage over the billboards that stated things such as "Black children are an endangered species" in Miriam Z. Perez, "Past and Present Collide as the Black Anti-Abortion Movement Grows," *Colorlines.com*, March 2011, http://colorlines.com/archives/2011/03/past_and_present_collide_as_the_black_anti-abortion_movement_grows.html; Sarah Ostman, "Women Speak out Against Anti-Abortion Billboards Targeting African Americans," Austin Talks.org, July 1, 2011, http://austintalks.org/2011/07/women-speak-out-against-anti-abortion-billboards-targeting-african-americans/.

16. "Controversial Ad Links MLK, GOP," *Washington Post*, October 19, 2006, http://www.washingtonpost.com/wp-dyn/content/article/2006/10/18/AR2006101801754.html.

17. E.R. Shipp, "Black Republicans Have Gall to Call King One of Their Own," *New York Daily News*, October 8, 2006, http://articles.nydailynews.com/2006-10-08/news/18351594_1_national-black-republican-association-michael-steele-democratic-party.

18. Tali Mendelberg, *The Race Card: Campaign Strategy, Implicit Messages, and the Norm of Equality* (Princeton: Princeton University Press, 2001).

19. Sharon Schmickle, "Christian Coalition Sets Sights on Broader Racial Appeal," *Minneapolis Star Tribune*, January 31, 1997.

20. Reed, quoted in ibid.

21. Although Warren's views on these issues lean progressive, he is also known for being anti-abortion and anti-gay marriage. President Obama was heavily criticized for inviting him to give an invocation at his 2008 inauguration. See Alexander Mooney, "Obama's Inaugural Choice sparks Outrage," CNN.com, December 17, 2008, http://articles.cnn.com/2008-12-17/politics/obama.warren_1_gay-marriage-gay-equality-gay-rights-proponents?_s=PM:POLITICS.

22. For reports on racial reconciliation events and mergers, see postings in the *Baptist Press*, such as this article on churches in Louisville, KY, that merged in 2009: David Winfrey, "2 Churches, in Uniting, Envision Model for Racial Reconciliation and Changing Lives," September 2, 2009, http://www.bpnews.net/bpnews.asp?id=31185. Also see commentary on racism and religious separation in David Van Biema, "Can Megachurches Bridge the Racial Divide?" Time.com, January 11, 2010, http://www.time.com/time/magazine/article/0,9171,1950943,00.html.

23. Although this chapter focuses on media outreach by a particular coalition of faith-based groups and conservative politicians, I mention these other initiatives to note that black audiences of Christian faith may or may not discern differences between mediated appeals like *JSIII* and the aforementioned desegregation efforts. Perhaps people who have engaged in intra-faith, anti-racist initiatives would be more or less skeptical of the billboards and commercials mentioned in the earlier section.

24. Rove and his operatives were linked to an attack ad that claimed that John McCain's adopted daughter—who is from India—was actually a secret black love child born to a black mistress. See Jennifer Steinhauer, "Confronting Ghosts of 2000," *New York Times,* October 19, 2007, http://www.nytimes.com/2007/10/19/us/politics/19mccain.html?pagewanted=all.

25. For an interesting look at Republicans' racial code word strategies, see Stefan Forbes, dir., *Boogeyman: The Lee Atwater Story,* (Interpositive Media, 2008). See also Mendelberg, *The Race Card.*

26. Teles, "The Eternal Return of Compassionate Conservatism," 109, my italics.

27. Ibid.; Tasha S. Philpot, *Race, Republicans and the Return of the Party of Lincoln* (Ann Arbor: University of Michigan Press, 2007).

28. Tracy Van Slyke, "Bush Meeting Black Clergy: Will Try to Mend Some Fences while Seeking Help on Social Issues," *Pittsburgh Post-Gazette,* December 20, 2000.

29. David Kirkpatrick, "Black Pastors Backing Bush are Rarities, but not Alone," *New York Times,* October 5, 2004.

30. Teles, "The Eternal Return of Compassionate Conservatism."

31. Laurie Goodsteing, "Minister, a Bush Ally, Gives Church as Site for Alito Rally," *New York Times,* January 5, 2006.

32. Tom Krattenmaker, "A 'War' on Christians? No," *USA Today,* March 27, 2006.

33. Kimberly Hefling, "Conservatives to Rally One Day Before Alito Hearings," Associated Press, January 6, 2006.

34. Michelle Hiskey, "Herb Lusk II: First Prayer," *Atlanta Journal Constitution,* February 4, 2006.

35. Hefling, "Conservatives to Rally."

36. Ibid.

37. Max Blumenthal, "Who Are Justice Sunday's Ministers of Minstrelsy?," *Huffington Post,* January 6, 2006, http://www.huffingtonpost.com/max-blumenthal/who-are-justice-sundays-m_b_13348.html.

38. Italics mine. Note: all example quotations from the *Justice Sunday III* broadcast come from the official transcript that I downloaded from the FRC website. I watched the entire DVD while reading through the transcript to ensure there were no significant changes to the text as spoken.

39. Kevin Coe and David Domke, "Petitioners or Prophets? Presidential Discourse, God, and the Ascendancy of Religious Conservatives," *Journal of Communication* 56, (2006): 309–35.

40. Blumenthal, "Who are Justice Sunday's Ministers?"

41. Many scholars have written about the patriarchal biases in some strands of black nationalism. See Toni Morrison, ed., *Race-ing Justice, En-Gendering Power;* Patricia Hill Collins, *Black Sexual Politics: African Americans, Gender, and the New Racism* (New York: Routledge, 2004); bell hooks, *We Real Cool: Black Men and Masculinity* (New York: Routledge, 2004). For specific discussion of black feminist responses to the billboard campaigns that posited black mothers' wombs were the "most dangerous place" for black children, see Kimala Price, "What is

Reproductive Justice?: How Women of Color Activists Are Redefining the Pro-Choice Paradigm," *Meridiens* 10, no. 2(2010): 42–65.

42. James Bennett, *Religion and the Rise of Jim Crow in New Orleans* (Princeton: Princeton University Press, 2005); Michael Emerson and Christian Smith, *Divided by Faith: Evangelical Religion and the Problem of Race in America* (Oxford: Oxford University Press, 2000).

NOTES TO CHAPTER 3

1. See, for example, Herman Gray, *Watching Race: Television and the Struggle for "Blackness"* (Minneapolis: University of Minnesota Press, 1995); Robin R. Means Coleman, *African American Viewers and the Black Situation Comedy: Situating Racial Humor* (New York: Garland, 1999).

2. Melvin P. Ely, *The Adventures of Amos 'n' Andy: A Social History of an American Phenomenon* (Charlottesville: University of Virginia Press, 1991).

3. Means Coleman, *African American Viewers*; Janette Dates and William Barlow, eds., *Split Image: African Americans in the Mass Media* (Washington, DC: Howard University Press, 1990).

4. In addition to Gray, Means Coleman, and Dates and Barlow, see also Christine Acham, *Revolution Televised: Prime Time and the Struggle for Black Power* (Minneapolis: University of Minnesota Press, 2004); Sut Jhally and Justin Lewis, *Enlightened Racism: The Cosby Show, Audiences, and the Myth of the American Dream* (Boulder, CO: Westview, 1992); Darnell Hunt, ed., *Channeling Blackness: Studies on Television and Race in America* (New York: Oxford University Press, 2004).

5. Jerry Large, "A New Era Begins: The Significance of the Barack Obama Victory for America," Blackpast.org, n.d., http://www.blackpast.org/?q=perspectives/new-era-begins-significance-barack-obama-victory-america-and-world.

6. Schiappa, *Beyond Representational Correctness*.

7. Tim Arango, "Before There was Obama, There was Bill Cosby," *New York Times*, November 7, 2008.

8. The British movie *Secrets and Lies*, directed by Mike Leigh (October Films, 1996), tells the story of a black optometrist who seeks her birth mother—only to find she is white and uncomfortable telling the rest of the family the story. The birth mother keeps her daughter a secret until she lets slip at a party that the black woman she'd been pretending was a colleague is actually her daughter.

9. Romney's "joke" was part of the infamous "47 percent" remarks he made during a fundraising event for wealthy donors. See David Corn, *47 Percent: Uncovering the Romney Video that Rocked the 2012 Election* (New York: Harper Collins, 2012). In the wake of the Newtown, Connecticut shootings, gun advocates—including some Republican lawmakers—widely suggested that women would be better protected from all kinds of violence if they had guns, at the same time that they refused to support the reauthorization of the Violence Against Women Act. See Madeline Morgenstern, "GOP Rep: 'I Wish Elementary Principal Had an M4 in her Office,'" TheBlaze.com, December 16, 2012, http://www.theblaze.com/

stories/2012/12/16/gop-rep-i-wish-elementary-principal-had-an-m4-in-her-office-takes-his-head-off-before-he-can-kill-those-precious-kids/. Fox commentator Dana Perino was one of many who argued that domestic violence victims would be well served by guns and by making "better choices" in their lives. See Melissa Jeffersen, "Dana Perino: 'Female Victims of Violence Should make Better Decisions,'" *Huffington Post*, December 6, 2012, http://www.huffingtonpost.com/2012/12/06/dana-perinovictims-of-vio_n_2251761.html.

10. Mary Vavrus, *Postfeminist News* (Albany: SUNY Press, 2007) 49.

11. Ibid.

12. Amy Allen, "Mommy Wars Redux: A False Conflict," *New York Times*, May 27, 2012.

13. Smith, quoted in Watts, "Nearly Apocalyptic Politics," 217.

14. Watts, "Nearly Apocalyptic Politics."

15. Mary Beltran and Camille Fojas, eds., *Mixed Race Hollywood* (New York: New York University Press, 2008); Ralina Joseph, "Tyra Banks is Fat: Reading (Post-) Racism and (Post) Feminism in the New Millennium," *Critical Studies in Media Communication* 26, no. 3, (2009): 237–54;

16. Suzanne Bost, *Mulattas and Mestizas: Representing Mixed Identities in the Americas, 1850–2000* (Athens and London: University of Georgia Press, 2002); Carolyn Streeter, "The Hazards of Visibility: 'Biracial' Women, Media Images and Narratives of Identity," in *New Faces in a Changing America: Multiracial Identity in the Twenty-First Century*, ed. Loretta I. Winters and Herman L. DuBose (Thousand Oaks, CA: Sage, 2003), 194–221.

17. Squires, *Dispatches from the Color Line*; Kim M. Williams, *Mark One or More: Civil Rights in Multiracial America* (University of Michigan Press, 2008); Kathleen Odell Korgen, ed., *Multiracial Americans and Social Class: The Influence of Social Class on Racial Identity* (New York: Routledge, 2010).

18. G. Reginald Daniel, "Multiracial Identity in Global Perspective: The United States, Brazil, and South Africa," in *New Faces in a Changing America*, 247–86.

19. Michelle Elam, *The Souls of Mixed Folk: Race, Politics and Aesthetics in the New Millennium* (Stanford: Stanford University Press, 2011).

20. Ibid., xix.

21. Bambi Haggins, *Laughing Mad: The Black Comic Persona in Post-Soul America* (New Brunswick, NJ: Rutgers University Press, 2007).

22. Jonathan P. Rossing, "Deconstructing Postracialism: Humor as a Critical Cultural Project," *Journal of Communication Inquiry* 36, no. 1 (2012): 44–61.

23. Leonard M. Baynes, "White Out: The Absence and Stereotyping of People of Color by the Broadcast Networks in Prime Time Entertainment Programming," in *Media Diversity and Localism*, ed. Phililp Napoli (Mahwah, NJ: Lawrence Erlbaum, 2007), 11–26; Robert Entman and Andrew Rojecki, *The Black Image in the White Mind* (Chicago: University of Chicago Press, 2000); Leon E. Wynter, *American Skin: Pop Culture, Big Business and the End of White America* (New York: Crown, 2002).

24. Jonathan Kraszewski, "Multiracialism on The Real World and the Reconfiguration of Politics in MTV's Brand during the 2000s," *Popular Communication* 8, (2010): 132–46.

25. Leilani Nishime, "Aliens: Narrating U.S. Global Identity through Transnational Adoption and Interracial Marriage in *Battlestar Galactica*," *Critical Studies in Media Communication* 28, no. 5 (2011): 450–65.

26. Squires, *Dispatches*.

27. This television strategy updated the token/only tactics of the 1960s, exemplified by *I Spy* and *Julia*. The difference here, especially in the case of *Diff'rent Strokes*, is that the black children became vehicles for racial difference not only via skin color but behaviors, such as the use of black vernacular.

28. On the heels of the success of the 1989 film, a TV version of the movie was launched in 1990, but it was cancelled after twelve episodes. This chapter does not draw from that incarnation of the program.

29. For a good critique of the Judd Apatow universe and similar humorous takes on extended male and female heterosexuals' adolescence, see Chris Lehmann, "HBO's Female Regression Analysis: American Pop Culture Teems with Characters Afraid of Adult Responsibilities," *In These Times*, May 17 2012, http://inthesetimes.com/article/13184/hbos_female_regression_analysis_girls_and_veep/. Also see Hilary Radner's discussion of the differences between Apatow's "homme coms" and "chick flicks" in *Neo-Feminist Cinema: Girly Films, Chick Flicks, and Consumer Culture* (New York, Routledge 2010).

30. It seems the writers were trying to make a reference to Sekou Toure, but in the reading of the line, it sounds like Camille says "Turunga." To catch the error, one must have knowledge of the actual African leader Toure; if not, the African-sounding name is, it seems, sufficient to do the work the writers sought, which is to show Camille as a racially/ethnically hip Baby Boomer.

31. Hill Collins, *Black Sexual Politics*; Wahneema Lubiano, "Like Being Mugged by a Metaphor: Multiculturalism and State Narratives," in *Mapping Multiculturalism*, ed. Avery F. Gordon and Christopher Newfield (Minneapolis: University of Minnesota Press, 1996), 64–75.

32. Cherie Moraga and Gloria Anzaldua, eds., *This Bridge Called My Back: Writings by Radical Women of Color*, second ed. (Boston: Kitchen Table/Women of Color Press, 1984). Some of the essays in this collection speak to the pattern in some feminist circles wherein women of color are pressed to "solve" or suppress their feelings about race problems which white feminists won't address.

33. Willa Paskin, "The Showrunner Transcript: Parenthood and Friday Night Lights' Jason Katims on Portraying Families Realistically," Vulture.com, May 20, 2011, http://www.vulture.com/2011/05/jason_katims_showrunner_transc.html.

34. For example, Joel experiences internal conflict about being a stay-at-home dad, and is featured in scenes where he navigates play dates and school performances; Julia is often seen preparing for work at her law firm in her office or at home; Kristina has angst about whether to return to the workplace or is occupied with

the day to day planning of the household as well as Max's special needs. The camera follows Sarah as she searches for jobs, visits her kids' schoolteachers, and laments her failure to find steady employment. Even the patriarch and matriarch, Zeek and Camille, have many scenes where they voice concern about financial deals (Zeek) or what careers or vocations to pursue in semi-retirement (Camille).

35. This sensibility is also reinforced during Season Two through a storyline focused on Joel and Julia and the issue of who makes decisions about childbearing. Adding on to the existing thread of Julia's inability to consistently bond with their daughter, the post-feminist theme develops further as Joel pines for a return to his (manly) construction work, his feelings exacerbated by emasculating remarks from Zeek. Joel's anger toward Julia for assuming he'd continue being a stay-at-home dad with a second child suggest that, like Jasmine, Julia has chosen work at the expense of family, endangering their happiness.

36. The show has gotten sparkling reviews in the traditional press, (e.g., "NBC's Parenthood makes a case for itself," *Los Angeles Times*, April 7, 2010) and online (e.g., *Grantland*'s Juliet Litman and David Jacoby told readers "Why It's Time to Binge-Watch Parenthood" in a January 23, 2013 post after the season finale.) According to ratings posted on TVbythenumbers.com, *Parenthood* has done well with viewers in the 18–49 range, and its numbers improve when DVR recording data is included. In November of 2012, it was tied for first among adult viewers 18–34 for Tuesday primetime dramas. In 2011, the show was credited with bringing NBC back into second place in primetime viewers after lagging behind CBS and ABC for years.

37. In 2012 the show won a PRISM Award from the Entertainment Industries Council for realistic portrayals of mental health issues, as well as the award for Best Drama of 2012 from the National Association of Multi-Ethnicity in Communications.

38. Kelly Kessler, "They Should Suffer like the Rest of Us: Queer Equality in Narrative Mediocrity," *Cinema Journal* 50, no. 2 (2011): 139–44; Christina M. Laveccia, "Of Peerenting, Trophy Wives, and Effeminate Men: Modern Family's Surprisingly Conservative Remediation of the Family Sitcom Genre," *Harlot: A Revealing Look at the Arts of Persuasion* 6, (2011), http://harlotofthehearts.org/index.php/harlot/issue/view/6.

NOTES TO CHAPTER 4

1. Stanley Fish, *Doing What Comes Naturally: Change, Rhetoric, and the Practice of Theory in Literary and Legal Studies* (Durham, NC: University of North Carolina Press, 1989), 141

2. It is also notable that the Ku Klux Klan used showings of the film to recruit members. Catherine Squires, *African Americans and the Media* (New York: Polity Press, 2009); Thomas Cripps, *Slow Fade to Black: The Negro in American Film, 1900–1942* (New York: Oxford University Press, 1977).

3. Cripps, *Slow Fade to Black*.

4. Ely, *The Adventures of Amos n Andy.*
5. Nancy Cornwell and Mark Orbe, "'Keepin' it Real' and/or 'Sellin' Out to the Man': African-American Responses to Aaron McGruder's *The Boondocks*," in *Say It Loud!* ed. Means Coleman (New York: Routledge, 2002), 27–43.
6. See chapters in Means Coleman, *Say It Loud!*, especially Debbie A. Owens, "Media Messages, Self-Identity and Race Relations," 77–93; Leslie B. Inniss and Joe Feagin, "*The Cosby Show*: The View from the Black Middle Class," 187–204; Squires, "African Americans and the Media."
7. Means Coleman, *Say It Loud!* 19
8. Kenneth K. Hur and John P. Robinson, "The Social Impact of 'Roots,'" *Journalism Quarterly* 55, no. 1 (1978):19–83; Richard G. Carter, "How 'Roots' and 'Black.White' Broke Racial TV Ground," *Television Quarterly* 37, no. 1(2006): 55–60.
9. Malinda S. Smith, "Racism and Motivated Ignorance," *The Ardent Review* 1, no.1 (April 2008): iv.
10. Ibid., vii.
11. Ibid.
12. Schiappa, *Beyond Representational Correctness.*
13. Kathleen Battles and Wendy Hilton-Morrow, "Gay Characters in Conventional Spaces: Will and Grace and the Situational Comedy Genre," *Critical Studies in Mass Communication* 19, no. 1 (2002): 87–105.
14. Schiappa, *Beyond Representational Correctness*, ch. 3.
15. See discussions of parasocial contact in David Giles, "Parasocial Interaction: A Review of the Literature and a Model for Future Research," *Media Psychology* 4, (2002): 279–305; see discussion of literature and results of a new study regarding the ways television figures address viewers in Tilo Hartmann and Charlotte Gold-hoorn, "Horton and Wohl Revisited: Exploring Viewers' Experience of Parasocial Interaction," *Journal of Communication* 61, (2011): 1104–1121; also see results of experimental studies of *Will & Grace* and attitudes regarding homosexuality in Schiappa, *Beyond Representational Correctness.*
16. Schiappa, *Beyond Representational Correctness*, 97.
17. Travis Dixon and Cristina Azocar, "Priming Crime and Activating Blackness: Understanding the Psychological Impact of Overrepresentation of Blacks as Lawbreakers on Television News," *Journal of Communication* 57, no. 2(2007): 229–53.
18. Jerry Kang, "Trojan Horses of Race," *Harvard Law Review* 118 (2004): 1489–1593; Michael K. Brown, et al., *Whitewashing Race: The Myth of a Color-Blind Society* (Berkeley: University of California Press, 2004).
19. Robert Entman and Andrew Rojecki, *The Black Image in the White Mind*; Dixon and Azocar, "Priming Crime and Activating Blackness"; Martin Gilens. *Why Americans Hate Welfare: Race, Media and the Politics of Antipoverty Policy* (Chicago: University of Chicago Press, 1999). Mary Beth Oliver and Dana Fonash, "Race and Crime in the News: Whites' Identification and Misidentification of

Violent and Nonviolent Criminal Suspects," *Media Psychology* 4, (2002): 137–56; Mendelberg, *The Race Card*.

20. See review in Squires, "African Americans and the Media," 233–40.

21. Although a great number of studies in social cognition use experimental methods, some early studies of media and parasocial interaction utilized focus groups as well as experimental studies and surveys. See Giles, "Parasocial Interaction," for a review of these studies. While audience and fan studies from the critical cultural studies approach don't use terms like "parasocial interaction" to describe fans' feelings toward media figures, the thick descriptions of fan discourse resonate with the language used in survey instruments in experimental studies. For example, participants in both types of studies (through survey questions or interview prompts) are asked to characterize whether and how they compare themselves to media figures, how much time they spend with their favorite media, and how close or real they feel the media figures are to their lives.

22. Kang, "Trojan Horses of Race," 1489.

23. Ibid., 1513–16.

24. Incidents of online racist, homophobic, and sexist speech and harassment via social media get significant media attention. In the past few years, several young people's suicides have been attributed to social media harassment; anti-racist organizations, journalists, and scholars have catalogued significant numbers of hate websites and chat rooms. See, for example, the Southern Poverty Law Center's information about hate sites at http://www.splcenter.org/what-we-do/hate-and-extremism; James Clementi, "Letters to My Brother," *Out Magazine*, http://www.out.com/news-commentary/2012/02/01/tyler-clementi-james-letters-my-brother; Jeff Sonderman, "Women Journalists Confront Harassment, Sexism, When Using Social Media," http://www.poynter.org/latest-news/media-lab/social-media/153944/women-journalists-confront-harassment-sexism-when-using-social-media/; Lisa Nakamura and Peter A. Chow White, eds. *Race After the Internet*. (New York: Routledge 2012). See discussions of gender, sexuality, and hate speech online in essays such as: Cory L. Armstrong and Mindy McAdams, "Believing Blogs: Does a Blogger's Gender Influence Credibility?", Ryan Rogers, "Video Game Design and Acceptance of Hate Speech in Online Gaming," and Cynthia A. Cooper, "Anti-Gay Speech on the Internet and the Movement to Counteract Cyber-Hate," all in Rebecca Ann Lind, ed. *Race/Gender/Class/Media: Considering Media Diversity Across Audiences, Content and Producers*, third edition (Saddle River, NJ: Prentice Hall, 2012).

25. Smith, "Racism and Motivated Ignorance," vii.

26. I used cues from photos as well as explicit statements about discussants' racial identity to make this determination. In all excerpts, I substitute first or first and second letters of discussants' names.

27. Kathleen Hall Jamieson, *Beyond the Double Bind: Women and Leadership* (New York: Oxford University Press, 1995); Deidre Johnson and Debra Swanson,

"Undermining Mothers: A Content Analysis of the Representation of Mothers in Magazines," *Mass Communication & Society* 6, no. 3 (2003): 243–65.

28. Hill Collins, *Black Sexual Politics*; Susan Douglas and Meredith Michaels, *The Mommy Myth: The Idealization of Motherhood and How It Has Undermined All Women* (New York: Free Press, 2004).

NOTES TO CHAPTER 5

1. Robert Asen, "A Discourse Theory of Citizenship," *Quarterly Journal of Speech* 90, no. 2 (2004), 191.
2. Ibid., 199.
3. *Racialicious* was originally founded by multiracial activist Jen Chau of Swirl, a multiracial activist organization, and Carmen Sognovini.
4. HighJive, "Culturally Clueless FAQs Number 3," Racialicious.com, March 4, 2009.
5. Channing Kennedy, "Latino Grandfather, Pregnant Woman Tasered at Baptism— But Don't Call the Cops Racist," ColorLines.com, August 3, 2009.
6. Jamilah King, "Jeff Chang: It's Bigger than Politics, the Real Shift is Cultural,"ColorLines.com, November 4, 2010.
7. Andrew Grant-Thomas, "Obama's Speech Addressed Several Categories of People and Communities except Race and Ethnicity," Racialicious.com, February 1, 2010.
8. Thea Lim, "*Racialicious* Responds to 'The End of White America,'" March 17, 2009.
9. Ninoy Brown, "Blanco: In Solidarity with 1.3% of UCSD, " Racialicious.com, February 23, 2010.
10. Ibid.
11. Ibid.
12. Daisy Hernandez, "Prop. 8 Update: America's Post-Gay and Post-Racial," Color-Lines.com, January 26, 2010.
13. Naima Ramos Chapman, "Melissa Harris Lacewell Speaks at Facing Race," Color-Lines.com, September 25, 2010.
14. HighJive, "Culturally Clueless FAQs Number 4," Racialicious.com, March 5, 2009.
15. Kai Wright, "Queer Blogger Roundtable," Colorlines.com, June 29, 2010.
16. Julianne Hing, "Meet the Delegates: David Ochoa." ColorLines.com, August 27, 2008.
17. "Scholar Henry Louis Gates Arrested, for Nothing, at His Own House," BlackS-nob.com, July 21, 2009.
18. Fiqah, "Past-Time Paradise: Down-Home Racism in 'Post-Racial' America," Racialicious.com, June 25, 2010.
19. Ibid.
20. Smith, "Motivated Ignorance."
21. Ope Bukola, "Dr. Laura, Interracial Relationships, and the Challenge of Anti-Racist Responses," Racialicious.com, August 19, 2010.
22. Terry Keleher, "Four Tips for Interracial Parenting," ColorLines.com, December 22, 2010.

NOTES TO THE CONCLUSION

1. Nugent's remarks were roundly criticized on the Left. See Meredith Bennett-Smith, "Ted Nugent: Gun Owners' Next Rosa Parks, Will Sit Down on Front Seat of the Bus." Huffington Post, January 10, 2013, http://www.huffington-post.com/2013/01/10/ted-nugent-gun-owners-nex . . . osa-parks-front-seat-bus_n_2448750.html?view=print&comm_ref=false.

2. Julie Dermansky, "When Martin Luther King Day and Gun Appreciation Day Come Together," Atlantic, January 2013, http://www.theatlantic.com/national/archive/2013/01/when-martin-luther-king-day-and-gun- appreciation-day-come-together/267400/.

3. David A. Love, "Does Slavery Have Any Place in the Gun Control Debate?" The Griot.com, January 23, 2013.

4. Melanie Hunter, "Gun Rights Advocate," CNS News, January 11, 2013. http://cnsnews.com/news/article/gun-rights-advocate-if-blacks-had-gun-rights-day-one-slavery-might-not-have-happened.

5. In a blog post, the Anti-Defamation League listed multiple instances, from the Drudge Report blog to Fox News to former Major League Baseball pitcher John Rocker, using the Hitler and gun control argument. "Holocaust Imagery Taints Gun Control Debate," ADL Blogs, January 24, 2012, http://blog.adl.org/civil-rights/holocaust-gun-control-debate.

6. Evan McMorris-Santoro, "Gun Appreciation Day Leader," Talking Points Memo, January 11, 2013. Comment from reader with screen name Shak-ezula, first comment, http://livewire.talkingpointsmemo.com/entry/gun-appreciation-day-leader-if-blacks-had-guns.

7. Michael Tesler, "TheReturn of Old-Fashioned Racism to White Americans' Partisan Preferences in the Early Obama Era," Journal of Politics 75, no. 1 (2013): 110–23.

8. Gary Segura and Ali A. Valenzuela, "Hope, Tropes and Dopes: Hispanic and White Racial Animus in the 2008 Election," Presidential Studies Quarterly, 40, no. 3 (2010): 494–514.

9. Cindy D. Kam and Donald R. Kinder, "Ethnocentrism as a Short-Term Force in the 2008 American Presidential Election," American Journal of Political Science 56, no. 2 (2012): 326–40.

10. For a very accessible discussion of a handful of studies on race and recent elections, see Thomas B. Edsall, "The Persistence of Racial Resentment," New York Times, February 6, 2013. See also Darrel Enck-Wanzer's commentary on the Tea Party's emergence and rhetoric in "Barack Obama, the Tea Party, and the Threat of Race: On Racial Neoliberalism and Born Again Racism." Communication, Culture & Critique 4 (2011): 23–30.

11. Tim Wise, "We Twisted King's Dream, So We Live with His Nightmare," Color-lines.com, January 17, 2011.

12. See discussion of these sentiments—articulated by commentators of various racial backgrounds—in Wornie L. Reed and Bertin M. Louis, "'No More Excuses':

Problematic Responses to Barack Obama's Election," *Journal of African American Studies*, 13, no. 2 (2009): 97–109.

13. Most infamously Bill O'Reilly said on his eponymous Fox News show that the demographic shift was endangering the power of the "white establishment," *The O'Reilly Report*, Fox News, November 11, 2012, http://nation.foxnews.com/bill-oreilly/2012/11/07/bill-o-reilly-white-establishment-now-minority.

14. Mark Hanrahan, "White Student Union," Huffington Post, October 12, 2012, http://www.huffingtonpost.com/2012/10/11/white-student-union-towson-university_n_1958868.html.

15. Kenneth J. Bindas, "Re-Remembering a Segregated Past: Race in American Memory," *History and Memory* 22, no. 1 (spring/summer 2010): 113–34.

16. Darrel Enck-Wanzer, "Decolonizing Imaginaries: Rethinking 'the People' in the Young Lords' Church Offensive," *Quarterly Journal of Speech* 98, no. 1 (2012): 1–23.

17. Ibid., 5.

18. Robert Wuthnow, "Democratic Renewal and Cultural Inertia: Why Our Best Efforts Fall Short," *Sociological Forum* 20, no. 3 (2005): 343–67.

19. Ibid., paraphrasing Jean Elshtain, 348.

20. Ibid., 345.

21. Ibid, 346.

22. Ibid., 352

23. Ibid., 353.

24. See studies by Michael Dawson, Lawrence Bobo, and colleagues at http://www.michaeldawson.net/data/. In the summary of the studies, the authors note, "The one consistent theme that can be gleaned from analysis of the data across all studies is the continuing, profoundly deep and bitter chasm between black and white opinion across a wide range of political issues and evaluations of individuals, organizations, and American society."

25. Paul Shackel, "Public Memory and the Search for Power in American Historical Archaeology," *American Anthropologist* 103, no. 3 (2001): 655–70.

26. Ibid., 656.

27. Ibid.

28. The Southern Poverty Law Center keeps an extensive record of white supremacist group activity. Also see recent work on white supremacist organizations in Ghassan Hage, *White Nation: Fantasies of White Supremacy in a Multicultural Society* (New York: Routledge, 2000); and Jesse Daniels, *Cyber Racism: White Supremacy Online and the New Attack on Civil Rights* (Lanham, MD: Rowman & Littlefield, 2009).

29. Renee Romano and Leigh Raiford, eds., *The Civil Rights Movement in American Memory* (Athens: University of Georgia Press, 2006); Kelly Madison, "Legitimation Crisis and Containment: The 'Anti-Racist-White-Hero' Film," *Critical Studies in Media Communication* 16 (1999): 399–417; Jennifer Hyland Wang, ""A Struggle of Contending Stories': Race, Gender and Political Memory in 'Forrest Gump,'" *Cinema Journal* 39, no. 3 (2000): 92–115.

30. Ed Gurerro, *Framing Blackness: The African American Image in Film* (Philadelphia: Temple University Press, 1993).

31. Kirk Savage, *Standing Soldiers, Kneeling Slaves: Race, War and Monument in Nineteenth- Century America* (Princeton: Princeton University Press, 1999).

32. Marlon Riggs, "Color Adjustment" (San Francisco: California Newsreel, 1991).

33. Madison, "Anti-Racist White Hero"; Kristen Hoerl, "Burning Mississippi into Memory? Cinematic Amnesia as a Resource for Remembering Civil Rights," *Critical Studies in Media Communication* 26, no. 1 (2009): 54–79.

34. Bindas, 121–22.

35. See, for example, Brown et al, *Whitewashing Race*. For a defense of the idea that whites really are victimized by affirmative action, even if racial resentment is misguided, see Nicholas Laham, *The Reagan Presidency and the Politics of Race: In Pursuit of Colorblind Justice and Limited Government* (Westport, CT: Praeger, 1998). For arguments that affirmative action harms people of color because it gins up white racial resentment, see Shelby Steele, *The Content of Our Character: A New Vision of Race in America* (New York: Harper Collins, 1990). Often overlooked in criticisms of Steele's work is that he does argue that conservative claims to colorblindness rest on a desire to remain "innocent" of racism. While he doesn't play out this argument in ways similar to critical race theorists, he maintains that "racial innocence and guiltlessness [are] preconditions for entitlement and power" (9) which facilitated Reagan-era attacks on affirmative action and welfare programs.

36. Jennifer Seibel Trainor, "'My Ancestors Didn't Own Slaves': Understanding White Talk about Race," *Research in the Teaching of English* 40, no. 2 (2005): 140–67. David Roediger, "White Workers, New Democrats, and Affirmative Action, " in *The House That Race Built*, ed. Wahneema Lubiano, (New York: Vintage, 1998); Thomas Nakayama and Judith N. Martin, eds., *Whiteness: The Communication of a Social Identity* (Thousand Oaks, CA: Sage, 1998).

37. Judge Richard Ceibull apologized with this caveat: "This is a private thing that was, to say the least, very poor judgment on my part. . . . I did not forward it because of the racist nature of it. Although it is racist, I'm not that way, never have been." Associated Press, "Montana Judge Apologizes for Racist Email about Obama's Mother," *Christian Science Monitor*, March 1, 2012, http://www.csmonitor.com/USA/Latest-News-Wires/2012/0301/Montana-judge-apologizes-for-racist-email-about-Obama-s-mother.

38. Bindas, 122–23; Jacqueline Dowd Hall, "The Long Civil Rights Movement and the Political Uses of the Past," *Journal of American History* 91, no. 4 (2005): 1233–63; Christopher Metress, "Making Civil Rights Harder: Literature, Memory and the Black Freedom Struggle," *Southern Literary Journal* 40, no. 2 (2008): 138–50.

39. Cathy J. Cohen, *Democracy Remixed: Black Youth and the Future of American Politics* (New York: Oxford University Press, 2010).

40. One of the few news pieces I could find that actually contained interviews with poor and working-class white voters who were voting for Obama was

Margot Roosevelt, "Southern Whites Troubled by Romney's Wealth, Religion," Reuters.com, September 11, 2012, http://www.reuters.com/article/2012/09/11/us-usa-election-poll-bible-belt-idUSBRE88A05H20120911.

41. Christopher Federico, Howard Lavine, and Christopher Johnston, "The Unexpected Impact of Coded Appeals," Campaign Stops blog, New York Times.com, September 10, 2012, http://campaignstops.blogs.nytimes.com/2012/09/10/the-unexpected-impact-of-coded-appeals/. Most recently, people expressed surprise that Oberlin College, widely known as a liberal school, was the site of another outbreak of racist graffiti and costumes. Richard Perez-Pena, "Racist Incidents Stun Campus and Halt Classes at Oberlin," *New York Times*, March 4, 2013.

abortion: and anti-choice rhetoric, 3, 34; and Black communities, 71, 76, 78, 82
advertising: and post-racial representations, 7, 8, 97, 105, 133, 201
affirmative action: and class, 9; and college admissions, 29, 36–37; opposition to, 24, 45, 78, 201; and post-racial news frames, 165, 190
African American churches: and faith-based initiatives, 73–75, 77; and GLBT rights, 70, 180; and political activism, 67–69; theological diversity of, 70
anti-racism, 11, 51, 64, 73, 130, 165–168, 170

Battlestar Galactica, 104, 130
The Black Snob, 169–170, 182
Booker, Cory, 25–30, 32, 34, 39, 46
Bryant, Joy, 151, 160, 162
Bush, George W., 33, 63, 66, 68. *See also* compassionate conservatism

Census, 4, 23–24
civil rights movement: and Hollywood representations, 200–202; and public memory, 75, 79–81, 170, 187
Clinton, Bill, 23, 193
Clinton, Hillary, 193–194
colorblind: discourse, 11, 18, 21, 24, 101, 183; public policy, 36, 52, 167
ColorLines, 169, 172–173, 178, 189
compassionate conservatism: and faith-based initiatives, 74–75; and voters of color, 73. *See also* Bush, George W.
The Cosby Show, 3, 98; and comparisons to Obama family, 54, 98

Democratic Party: and post-racial strategies, 26, 51; and voters of color, 82; and white voters, 31–32
Douglass, Frederick, 72, 80

The Feminine Mystique, 15
feminist, 119–120, 143, 163

Gates, Henry Louis, Jr., 47, 51–54, 182
GLBT: activism, 70, 171, 178; coalitions with people of color, 185; discrimination against, 34, 130; gay marriage, 68, 70–71, 75, 82–83, 178, 189

homophobia, 70, 180

interracial: conflict, 7–8, 104, 135; families, 42, 97–104, 108–109, 113, 119, 121, 129–131. *See also* post-racial: aesthetics
intersectional analysis, 12, 167, 170, 176, 180

Jackson, Jesse, Jr., 24, 26, 32, 34, 45
Joshua Generation, 17, 25, 26, 30–31, 34, 44
Justice Sunday III: audience reactions to/ media distribution/purpose of, 75–76; speakers, 78; sponsors, 66–67; Supreme Court nominees, 76

Katims, Jason, 107, 120, 127, 144, 159–161
King, Alveda, 78, 83, 85, 92–95
King, Martin Luther, Jr.: conservative appropriation of, 31, 61, 71–72, 80–81, 187, 189–190; holiday and Obama inauguration, 44

Lusk, Herbert, 76–79; 81–83, 92–95, 180

model minorities, 3, 104, 168
Millennial Generation, 14, 40
multiculturalism, critiques of, 5, 8, 65–66

NAACP, 24, 58–60, 98, 135, 176
neoliberalism, 6–7, 24, 100

Obama, Barack: and 2008 election, 4, 18, 37–41; and white voters, 43–47. *See also* post-racial: politicians

parasocial interaction, 98, 138, 163–164
Parenthood: audience responses to, 144–184; depictions of black women, 114, 121, 123, 164; depictions of interracial couple, 109–114, 120–128; movie version, 106–107; television version, 107–110
post-feminism: definition of, 100; discourses in media, 105, 114, 124. *See also* post-racial
post-racial: aesthetics, 100–105; and celebrities of color, 3, 20–21, 41, 49, 55, 149; comedy, 9–11, 56; cultural consumption, 54–55, 165; discourses of national identity, 8–9; emergence of, 3, 5; and multiculturalism, 8; and neoliberalism, 6–7; politicians, 17–18, 22–26, 30–33, 41, 44

race: as biological, 11, 16, 27, 143, 148, 166; and religion, 67–69; as social construction, 5, 11, 101, 167. *See also* intersectional analysis; racism
racial: discrimination, 9, 68, 72, 99; inequality, 59–60, 171; profiling, 4, 8, 9, 47, 51, 53, 172, 198; stereotypes, 21, 43–44, 55, 104, 106, 123, 138, 143–144, 159, 162–164,175–176, 193
Racialicious, 168–169, 171, 173, 175, 183–184
racism: individualized, 6, 10, 12, 49, 52, 64, 133; institutionalized, 6, 11, 17, 49, 52–54, 57, 64, 136, 166, 171–173; and public opinion, 198; and violence, 1, 47, 49, 60, 63, 135, 166, 170, 182–183, 188, 200, 203; and white privilege, 7, 10, 167, 178, 183–184, 190
Reagan, Ronald, 9, 31, 34, 80
Reed, Ralph, 68, 72
Republican Party: and Black candidates, 34–35; and post-racial discourses, 23–25, 32–36, 48–52, 56–57; and voters of color, 68–74
Romney, Mitt, 99, 204

Santorum, Rick, 70, 85–87, 90–94
Sharpton, Al, 26, 32, 46
Sherrod, Shirley, and Andrew Breitbart, 57–61, 173, 178
Sotomayor, Sonia, 50–51, 54, 173

Tea Party: racial opinions of, 188; racist communications of, 48, 53, 59, 101, 195; and reverse-racism, 56–58; and whiteness, 101, 188–189

Washington, Harold, 29–30
Wright, Jeremiah, 41

zombies: and racism, 101; and racial stereotypes,114, 118, 129, 131

Catherine R. Squires is Associate Professor of Communication Studies at the University of Minnesota. After receiving her Ph.D. from Northwestern University in 1999, Dr. Squires was Assistant Professor in Afro-American and African Studies and Communication Studies at the University of Michigan, Ann Arbor. From 2007 to 2013, she held the inaugural Cowles Chair for Journalism, Diversity, and Equality at the University of Minnesota. Dr. Squires's first book, *Dispatches from the Color Line: The Press and Multiracial America*, examined discourses of race mixing in twentieth-century U.S. news.